GOOD HOUSEKEEPING

COMPLETE BOOK OF CAKES AND PASTRIES

GOOD HOUSEKEEPING

COMPLETE BOOK OF CAKES AND PASTRIES

by
Good Housekeeping
Institute

Published in collaboration with
Tate & Lyle Refineries

EBURY PRESS
LONDON

Published by Ebury Press
National Magazine House
72 Broadwick Street
London W1V 2BP

First impression 1981
Second impression 1982

ISBN 0 85223 189 X

House Editor Helen Southall
Designer Derek Morrison
Home economist Susanna Tee

Line drawings by Karen Daws and Kate Simunek
Colour photography by Paul Kemp, pages 17, 27, 30, 39, 76,
93, 94, 111, 121, 124, 150, 167 and 168; Philip Dowell, pages
18, 57, 75, 122 and 123; Melvin Grey, pages 28, 40 and 112;
Bryce Atwell, page 29; Barry Bullough, page 58; Philip Pace,
page 149.

Jacket photograph shows
Black Forest gâteau (page 42)

The publishers would like to thank Selfridges Ltd for their help
in providing props for photography.

Typeset by Advanced Filmsetters (Glasgow) Limited
Printed and bound by New Interlitho s.p.a., Milan

CONTENTS

HANDY CHARTS

CONVERSION TO METRIC MEASUREMENTS

The metric measures in this book are based on a 25-g unit instead of the ounce (28.35 g). Slight adjustments to this basic conversion standard were necessary in some recipes to achieve satisfactory cooking results.

If you want to convert your own recipes from imperial to metric, we suggest you use the same 25-g unit, and use 600 ml in place of 1 pint, with the British Standard 5-ml and 15-ml spoons replacing the old variable teaspoons and tablespoons. These adaptations will sometimes give a slightly smaller recipe quantity and may require a shorter cooking time.

Note Sets of British Standard metric measuring spoons are available in the following sizes—
2.5 ml, 5 ml, 10 ml and 15 ml.

When measuring milk it is more convenient to use the exact conversion of 568 ml (1 pint).

For more general reference, the following tables will be helpful.

METRIC CONVERSION SCALE

	LIQUID			SOLID	
Imperial	*Exact conversion*	*Recommended ml*	*Imperial*	*Exact conversion*	*Recommended g*
$\frac{1}{4}$ pint	142 ml	150 ml	1 oz	28.35 g	25 g
$\frac{1}{2}$ pint	284 ml	300 ml	2 oz	56.7 g	50 g
1 pint	568 ml	600 ml	4 oz	113.4 g	100 g
$1\frac{1}{2}$ pints	851 ml	900 ml	8 oz	226.8 g	225 g
$1\frac{3}{4}$ pints	992 ml	1 litre	12 oz	340.2 g	350 g
			14 oz	397.0 g	400 g
For quantities of $1\frac{3}{4}$ pints and over, litres and fractions of a litre have been used.			16 oz (1 lb)	453.6 g	450 g
			1 kilogram (kg) equals 2.2 lb.		

Note Follow either the metric or imperial measures for the recipes in this book as they are not interchangeable.

OVEN TEMPERATURE CHART

°C	°F	Gas mark	°C	°F	Gas mark
110	225	$\frac{1}{4}$	190	375	5
130	250	$\frac{1}{2}$	200	400	6
140	275	1	220	425	7
150	300	2	230	450	8
170	325	3	240	475	9
180	350	4			

EGGS

Size 4 eggs should be used when making the cakes in this book, except where otherwise stated.

FOREWORD

This book is more than a collection of delicious recipes; it is also a complete guide to the ingredients, equipment and techniques used for baking all types of cakes and gâteaux.

In the introductory section, which gives basic information about cake making, including the preparation of tins, how to tell when a cake is cooked and useful tips on storing and freezing, you will find a number of helpful 'Tricks of the trade' and a 'What went wrong?' chart. The recipes which follow are grouped according to the method by which they are made. A short introduction to each section is followed by a 'master' recipe with step-by-step drawings which clearly illustrate the technique used. Once you have mastered a technique, you will be able to make any of the cakes or pastries included in that section, and it is easy to refer back to the step-by-step drawings if necessary.

Basic icing recipes are given in the final chapter as well as lots of ideas for simple cake decoration. These, together with the information on piping equipment and techniques, will ensure that your finished cakes look as good as they taste.

CAKE-MAKING KNOW-HOW

Cake-making ingredients

Once you have decided on the cake you want to make, read right through the recipe and assemble all the ingredients *before* you begin mixing the cake. Both metric and imperial measures are indicated in these recipes. Use one set only – metric figures are adjusted conversions and not exact equivalents. It is important to weigh and measure quantities accurately to achieve the correct balance of ingredients.

Flour

There are two main types of flour available: strong flour which is made from hard wheat and has a high gluten content of 10–15 per cent; and soft flour which is milled from soft wheat and has a lower gluten content of 7–10 per cent. The gluten content of the flour used affects the raising quality of a mixture.

Strong flour (often referred to as bread flour) has high raising, good water-absorbing qualities. It is used for most yeasted cakes and certain pastries (such as puff pastry) where a large volume and light, open texture is required. Soft flour, being more starchy, absorbs fat well. It is best for most cakes and pastries where a smaller rise and softer, finer texture is required.

Soft flour can be plain or self raising. Self raising flour is popular because it eliminates errors as the raising agents are already evenly blended. Self raising flour is perfect for most rubbed in and creamed mixtures, but it contains too much raising agent for some rich cakes. In this case, a mixture of plain and self raising flour is best. Alternatively, plain flour can be used with the required amount of raising agent. (The quantity needed is stated in the recipe.)

If a recipe calls for self raising flour and you have none, substitute plain flour with the addition of 12.5 ml (2½ level tsp) baking powder to each 225 g (8 oz) flour used. Sift the flour and baking powder together two or three times before use to ensure even blending.

Other flours can be used for variety. Wholemeal flours are made from 100 per cent of the cleaned wheat; wheatmeals contain 85–90 per cent of the cleaned grain, all of the germ and some of the bran. Both plain and self raising wheatmeal flours are available. Self raising wholemeals exist, but are extremely difficult to find.

Wholemeal and wheatmeal flours absorb more liquid than white, so more liquid is required to bring the mixture to the right consistency. Since they give a substantial, dense texture, these flours are not suitable for very light, delicate cakes. Wheatmeal flour is perfectly acceptable in rubbed in and creamed mixtures and for cakes made by the melting method. Wholemeal flour works well in enriched yeast doughs and for other mixtures it can be combined with white flour to improve rise and texture.

Flour that has been sifted (even when there are no other dry ingredients in the recipe) is easier to incorporate. When sifting wheatmeal flour, tip the residue of bran left in the sieve back into the bowl and stir lightly to mix. Wholemeal flour is not usually sifted.

Flour should be stored in a cool, dry place. Wholemeal flours do not store well and should be bought in small quantities.

Fat

The fats most commonly used in cake making are butter and margarine; but others, such as lard and dripping, are sometimes called for. Butter and block margarine are interchangeable, though butter gives a richer flavour and cakes made with butter keep well. Butter is best for Genoese mixtures – margarine gives less volume and a denser texture. Soft tub margarines are suited to special all-in-one recipes. Oil too can be used, but specially proportioned recipes are needed.

As a rule, butter and block margarine should not be used direct from the refrigerator or cold larder. If the fat intended for a creamed mixture is firm, beat it alone until softened, then add the sugar and cream them together. If melted fat is required, heat the fat very gently as it quickly turns brown.

Sugar

Sugar is not just an important sweetener; it also helps produce a soft, spongy texture and improves a cake's keeping qualities.

Caster sugar is the best white sugar to use in cake recipes as it dissolves easily and quickly. It is the ideal choice for creamed mixtures and whisked sponge mixtures.

Icing sugar is very fine and powdery. It is seldom used as an ingredient for basic cake mixtures as the volume produced is poor and the crust hard. It is, however, favoured for some biscuit and meringue recipes and is ideal for decorating cakes and for making icing mixtures.

Granulated sugar is coarser than caster sugar, and therefore less suitable for the majority of cake recipes, although it is perfectly acceptable for rubbed in mixtures. It will do, at a pinch, for creamed mixtures but produces a slightly reduced volume and a speckled crust. Also, the texture of the cake may be a little gritty.

Brown soft sugar, whether dark or light, produces a rich flavour which suits fruit cakes and gingerbreads. These sugars cream well and, when used in place of caster sugar in creamed mixtures, give an equally good volume.

Demerara sugar has a golden colour with a distinctive syrup flavour and is coarser than brown soft sugars. It is best suited to making cakes by the melting method, such as gingerbread, where heat and moisture help to dissolve it. It is not so good for creamed mixtures because its large crystals do not break down during the mixing, but it is ideal for crunchy toppings.

Other sweeteners used in cake recipes

These give the moist, slightly sticky texture associated with cakes made by the melting method (*see page 87*).

Golden syrup can be used to replace part of the sugar content in a recipe. It gives a special flavour which is particularly acceptable combined with spices.

Black treacle is not as sweet as golden syrup. A little added to a rich fruit cake gives a good dark colour and distinctive flavour. Treacle is also a traditional ingredient of gingerbreads.

Honey absorbs and retains moisture, and this helps prevent cakes drying out and going stale. Only part of the sugar content should be replaced by honey – generally not more than half.

Raising agents

The rising or raising process in cakes is achieved by introducing carbon dioxide, air or steam into the mixture and trapping it there. This is done by hand (during the creaming process in some cakes, for example, and by folding and rolling flaky or puff pastry) and by incorporating one or more of the following raising agents into the mixture.

Baking powder is the most commonly used chemical raising agent. Ready-prepared baking powder consists of bicarbonate of soda and an acid-reacting chemical such as cream of tartar, with the addition of flour to preserve the mixture. On contact with moisture and heat these chemicals react together to produce the gas carbon dioxide. When wet, the gluten in the flour is capable of holding bubbles of gas made by the raising agent. These bubbles expand during baking and thus the cake rises. The heat of the oven dries and sets the gluten and so the bubbles are held, giving the cake its characteristic texture. However, cake mixtures are capable of holding only a certain amount of gas. If too much raising agent is used the cake rises very well at first, but then collapses and a heavy, close texture is the final result.

A combination of bicarbonate of soda and cream of tartar is sometimes used to replace baking powder. The usual proportions are one part bicarbonate of soda to two parts cream of tartar.

Yeast is a living plant which requires food and gentle warmth to grow. Food is supplied by carbohydrates in the flour; warmth is provided by having the other ingredients at room temperature and leaving the yeast batter or dough to rise in a warm, humid atmosphere. Given the right conditions, yeast grows rapidly and in the process the gas carbon dioxide is formed.

The bubbles of this gas raise the dough. Whether you choose fresh or dried yeast is a matter of preference and convenience.

Fresh yeast does not keep well and should be bought in small quantities. It should be putty coloured, moist and easy to break. If the yeast appears discoloured and dry, it is probably stale and should be discarded. Using sugar to cream the yeast is not recommended – a high concentration of sugar will kill some of the yeast cells and inhibit fermentation.

Dried yeast is sold in granular form in packets or tins. It is convenient because it will keep in an airtight container for up to six months. Take care to buy bakers' yeast and not tonic or brewers' yeast which are not suitable for baking. Dried yeast is more concentrated than fresh yeast and equivalents are stated on the packet or tin. As a guide, **15 ml (1 level tbsp) dried yeast is equivalent to 25 g (1 oz) fresh yeast.** Most dried yeast must be reconstituted in liquid before use, according to the maker's directions. A new 'easy blend' brand, only recently available, is not dissolved in liquid; instead, it is mixed directly with the measured flour.

For simplicity, the yeast recipes in this book have been written using fresh yeast, but the appropriate equivalent of dried yeast works equally successfully.

Eggs included in a whisked or creamed cake mixture make use of air as a raising agent. If an extra light mixture is required, the egg whites are whisked separately before being added.

In cakes made by the rubbed in method, where beaten egg is added together with the liquid, the egg helps to bind the mixture but does not act as the main raising agent.

For baking purposes, eggs should be used at room temperature. A size 4 egg, weighing roughly 50 g (2 oz), is a suitable size for most recipes and size 4 eggs should be used for the recipes in this book except where otherwise stated.

Liquid is required when the raising process depends on the evolution of steam. Generally the liquid in a mixture is milk or water, but coffee, cider and fruit juice are included in some recipes.

Flavourings

Whenever practical, natural flavourings like lemon or orange are the most pleasant to use. Remember, when using the rind of any citrus fruit, to grate it only lightly as the white pith imparts a bitter flavour. If only a few drops of lemon juice are needed, pierce the fruit with a fork and squeeze out the juice.

Spices and essences Ground spices are handy for general flavouring, but for special recipes, and for your own pleasure too, it's good to have certain whole spices, such as cinnamon, mace and nutmeg, to grind yourself and use on their own or blended with others.

Many of the common cake flavourings are obtainable in the form of essences. These are usually highly concentrated, and should therefore be used sparingly. Caramel is also a concentrated product and just a dash is normally sufficient.

Dried fruit, nuts and peel Choose good quality dried fruits. Should dried fruit, such as sultanas, become hard, leave them to plump up in hot water, then drain and dry them off. Dried fruits can be bought ready-washed, but it's wise to give them a good looking over. Unwashed fruits are cheaper, though, so if you buy them, wash and drain them well, then leave them to dry spread out over muslin or absorbent kitchen paper on a wire rack. Don't put them to dry over direct heat as this tends to make them hard. Remember that seedless raisins are small and similar in size to sultanas, but ready-prepared seeded or stoned raisins are large and juicy, with an excellent flavour, since the seeds are removed after the fruit has been dried. These also need a quick check before use as now and again a stone does get left in. Wash any excess syrup from glacé fruits, dry thoroughly, then dust them lightly with flour before use.

When using nuts such as almonds, walnuts or hazelnuts, in a recipe, check first to see whether they are to be blanched or unblanched, whole, split, flaked, chopped or ground. This may seem a small point, but it saves last-minute irritation. Ready-chopped (or nibbed) almonds are handy, but they may need an extra chopping to make them finer.

Candied orange or lemon peel can be bought separately, then mixed to definite proportions after shredding, grating, mincing or chopping. Ready-mixed chopped peel is no doubt easier and quicker, but there's extra aroma and flavour to be gained by preparing peel yourself. Ready-cut peel may need further chopping to make it finer.

Cake tins

Choose good strong cake tins and include one or two shallow ones for sandwich and layer cakes. Some cake tins have a loose bottom or a device for loosening the cake from the tin to make removing the cake easier. Certain kinds of sandwich tins have sloping sides, while others have a fluted edge. Patty tins can be straight sided (deep or shallow) or with a rounded bottom.

Non-stick tins

Non-stick (silicone-finished) tins *do* clean

easily; even if the residual crumbs have been allowed to stay on for some time and become hard, a wipe with a damp cloth will suffice to remove them. The benefits of easy-clean surfaces are probably more marked with small, awkwardly shaped tins, such as straight-sided patty tins. Non-stick bakeware may need some preparation; a light greasing is recommended by some manufacturers, and advisable for sticky mixtures like gingerbread and cakes with little or no fat content. In some instances, lining a tin with greaseproof paper gives quite a different appearance to the finished crust: a gingerbread baked in an unlined non-stick tin has a very shiny, somewhat heavy, appearance where it has been in direct contact with the tin's surface. On the other hand, you get a good crisp finish to a sponge with a non-stick sandwich tin which has been greased and then coated with a half-and-half mixture of flour and caster sugar sifted together.

Foil and paper baking cases
These may be used in place of tins for small cakes and sponge cakes. These cases need no preparation.

The right tin for the job
Use the size of tin specified in the recipe; cakes baked in the correct-sized tin will have a good shape. Those baked in too large a tin tend to be pale, flat and shrunken, while cakes baked in too small or shallow a tin will bulge over and lose their contours. Use straight-sided tins for layer cakes and the texture as well as the shape will be better. For even browning, choose shiny tins as these distribute the heat evenly and so ensure a delicate golden brown crust.

If you do not have the tin specified in a recipe, a slightly larger tin can be used instead. Because the mixture will be less deep, it will take less time to cook so test

the cake about 5–10 minutes before the end of the recommended cooking time.

Standard cake tins A very large selection of round, square or oblong tins of assorted sizes is available with or without loose bottoms. For day-to-day baking, the 15-cm (6-inch), 18-cm (7-inch) and 20.5-cm (8-inch) tins are adequate but you will need a larger range of sizes for wedding and other celebration cakes.

Sandwich cake tins These are shallow cake tins which are useful for making sandwich and layer cakes and special gâteaux. They are available with straight or fluted sides and in sizes 18–25.5 cm (7–10 inches). A moule-à-manqué tin resembles a deep sandwich tin but has slightly sloping sides. It is principally for cakes which are to be iced as the sloping sides allow the icing to run down easily.

Shallow cake tins Shallow tins of about 18-cm (7-inches) square are useful for bar cakes and cookies, and large shallow oblong or Swiss roll tins suit slab cake mixtures.

Loaf tins These tins are used for cakes as well as for bread and a selection of tins is available. The fluted concertina-shaped loaf tin is known as a Balmoral.

Tube or ring cake tins Any cakes baked in this sort of tin are very easy to cut. Plain and fluted 23-cm (9-inch) ring moulds are ideal for gâteaux. The kugelhupf mould has its own traditional recipe but adapts to many others. Angel cake tins are flat-based with plain or fluted sides. A funnel cake tin with an indented base produces an attractive cake and a wide-fluted ring mould is excellent for a savarin.

Flan rings These ring tins are available with plain or fluted sides and are extremely versatile. Fluted French pastry rings with loose bottoms are excellent for mixtures which are difficult to handle. They are available in sizes ranging from 10 cm (4 inches) to 30.5 cm (12 inches). A sponge flan tin with a raised base is also very useful.

Small cake tins and moulds These are available in various shapes and sizes for making buns, éclairs, sponge fingers, petits fours, pastry tarts, madeleines, etc. They are usually made in sheets of six, nine or twelve but others, such as dariole moulds and boat-shaped patty tins, are available as individual tins.

Spring-release cake tins The most versatile cake tin to have in your cupboard is a spring-release tin with a loose bottom and tubular fitting.

Preparing cake tins

Collect the bakeware needed and prepare it before you begin to mix the cake.

Greasing

Lightly grease the base and sides of all cake tins with fat (preferably unsalted), or brush with oil. Tins may also be dredged with flour as an additional safeguard against the cake sticking. Sprinkle in a little flour, then tilt and shake the tin until the inside is coated. Shake out any surplus flour. Use a half-and-half mixture of flour and caster sugar for whisked sponges to produce a crisper crust.

Lining

For most cakes, it is necessary to line the tin. Greaseproof paper should be greased before the mixture is put in. Non-stick (silicone treated) vegetable parchment does not require greasing.

Non-stick parchment is suitable for most types of cake, but it cannot be used for lifting a cake out of a tin because it is slippery. When removed from the baked cake it leaves a smooth, shiny finish and not the characteristic rough surface. If cleaned carefully, non-stick parchment can be used several times.

Lining should be done carefully: any creases or bumps will mark the surface of the cake. Usually it is sufficient to line only the base of shallow tins, but both the sides and the base of deep cake tins should be lined as described below.

To line a deep cake tin Cut a piece of greaseproof paper long enough to reach round the tin and wide enough to extend about 5 cm (2 inches) above the top edge. Cut another piece to fit the bottom of the tin. Fold up one long edge of the long strip about 2.5 cm (1 inch), creasing it firmly, then snip this folded portion at 1-cm ($\frac{1}{2}$-inch) intervals with a pair of scissors; this enables the paper band to fit a square or round tin neatly. Grease the tin and place the strip of paper in position first. The bottom piece keeps the snipped edge of the band in position and makes a neat lining. Grease the paper.

To line a sandwich tin Cut a round of

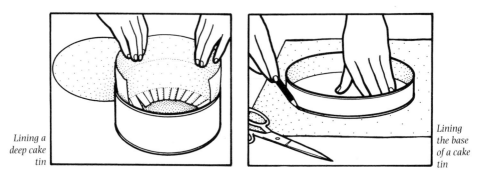

Lining a deep cake tin

Lining the base of a cake tin

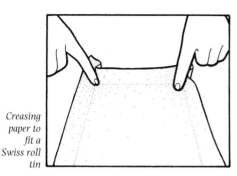

Creasing paper to fit a Swiss roll tin

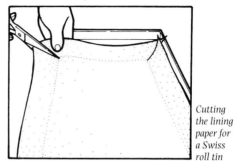

Cutting the lining paper for a Swiss roll tin

greaseproof paper to fit the bottom of the greased tin exactly. Grease the lining. To give a straight-sided shallow tin extra depth, line the sides also (as for a deep cake tin), letting the side strip project 2.5 cm (1 inch) above the rim.

To line a Swiss roll tin Cut a piece of paper about 5 cm (2 inches) larger all round than the tin. Place it on the tin, creasing it to fit the tin, and in each corner make a cut from the corner of the paper as far as the corner of the crease. Grease both paper and tin and put in the paper so that it fits closely, overlapping at the corners.

To line a sponge flan tin After greasing the inside well, place a round of greased greaseproof paper over only the raised part of the tin.

Fluted moulds and ring tins Because of their shape, these tins are seldom lined. They should be greased very carefully: if the cake sticks, its appearance will be spoilt. A tin intended for an Angel cake is an exception: it must not be greased. Instead, it should be washed and dried thoroughly or the mixture will not rise.

Extra protection for fruit mixtures Line the sides and base of the tin with a double thickness of greaseproof paper and grease the lining paper. Wrap a double thickness of brown paper round the outside and secure it with string. Place the tin on a double thickness of brown paper or news-

paper in the oven. This prevents the outside of the cake over-browning and drying out during the long, slow cooking.

Making cakes in tins of unusual shape
To make an unconventionally shaped fruit or sponge cake, such as a numeral or a heart shape, the amount of cake mixture needed can be worked out from the capacity of the tin. Fill the tin with water and for every 600 ml (1 pint) the tin will hold use fruit or Victoria sandwich mixture made with the ingredients listed below. Multiply the quantities as required. When filling the tin with water, remember only to fill it as deep as you want the finished cake to be – not necessarily to the top.

Fruit cake

150 g (5 oz) currants
50 g (2 oz) sultanas
50 g (2 oz) seedless raisins
12 glacé cherries, halved
45 ml (3 level tbsp) chopped mixed peel
100 g (4 oz) plain flour
1.25 ml ($\frac{1}{4}$ level tsp) ground mixed spice
75 g (3 oz) butter or margarine
75 g (3 oz) brown soft sugar
1$\frac{1}{2}$ eggs, beaten

Victoria sandwich

50 g (2 oz) butter or margarine
50 g (2 oz) caster sugar
1 egg, beaten
50 g (2 oz) self raising flour

Grease well and, if necessary, line the tin you wish to use. If making the fruit cake, make up the mixture as described on page 72, turn it into the prepared tin and bake in the oven at 150°C (300°F) mark 2 until a fine skewer inserted in the centre comes out clean. Leave the cake to cool completely in the tin before turning out.

Directions for making up the Victoria sandwich mixture are given on page 54. Turn the mixture into the greased and lined tin and bake in the oven at 180°C (350°F) mark 4 until well risen, golden brown and firm but springy to the touch. Leave the cake in the tin for about 5 minutes, then turn out and leave to cool on a wire rack.

It is difficult to give an accurate guide to cooking times for cakes baked in odd-shaped containers because the more contact the heat has with the tin sides, the faster it cooks.

Sandwich cakes made into horseshoes and small shallow heart shapes will take about 25–30 minutes. Sandwich cakes 5 cm (2 inches) deep, cooked in larger and more solid shapes such as hexagons, quatrefoils and large heart shapes, take 40–45 minutes. Check the cake after 30 minutes as the top may brown before the cake is cooked through. If it does, cover with greaseproof paper.

It is not really feasible to cook a sandwich cake in a tin larger than 25 cm (10 inches) across as the edges will overcook long before the middle is done. However, fruit cake mixtures adapt well to large tins. A heart, numeral or horseshoe-shaped fruit cake takes $2-2\frac{1}{2}$ hours to cook (again cover if it starts to brown on top).

Baking the cake

Before starting to mix the cake, turn the oven on at the recommended baking temperature so it will have reached the correct temperature by the time it is required. Use the oven positions recommended by the manufacturer.

Testing whether a cake is cooked
Small cakes should be well risen, golden brown in colour and just firm to the touch. They should begin to shrink from the sides of the tin on being taken out of the oven.

Larger cakes present more difficulty, especially for beginners. The oven heat and time of cooking give a reasonable indication, but the following tests are helpful:
1. For light mixtures, press the centre top of the cake very lightly with the fingertips. The cake should be spongy and should give only very slightly to pressure. When the fingertip is removed, the surface should rise again immediately, retaining no impression.

2. If you are baking a fruit cake, lift it gently from the oven and listen to it, putting it close to your ear. A continued sizzling sound indicates that the cake is not cooked through.
3. Insert a fine skewer or metal knitting needle (never a cold knife) in the centre of the cake. It should come out perfectly clean. If any mixture is sticking to it, the cake requires more cooking.

Cooling the cake
Allow the cake to cool for a few minutes or more, as instructed, before turning it out of the tin; during this time it will shrink away from the sides and become more easy to remove. If necessary, ease the cake from the sides of the tin with a palette knife. Turn the cake out very gently and remove any lining paper. Cool the cake, right side up, on a wire rack. Leave the cake until cold before icing or storing.

Mixing Luxury fruit cake (*page 74*)

Tricks of the trade

To clean dried fruit
For quick cleaning, rub the fruit on a wire sieve or in a tea towel with a little flour, then pick over to remove any stalks. Discard surplus flour.

To stone raisins
Work raisins between the fingertips to remove stones, occasionally dipping the fingers in water.

To shred caps of peel
Remove the sugar and cut the peel into fine shreds or chop it with a very sharp knife. If the peel is very hard, soak it for a minute or two in boiling water, then dry and cut it up.

To blanch almonds
Put the nuts in a pan with cold water to cover, bring just to the boil, strain and run cold water over them. Then rub between finger and thumb to remove the skins, which will slip off quite easily.

To sliver almonds
First blanch the nuts, then split each in half with a small, sharp-pointed knife. Place flat on a chopping board and, while the nuts are still damp, cut into long, thin strips.

You can buy ready-chopped blanched almonds which are known as 'nibbed' almonds.

To toast nuts
Spread whole, chopped or slivered nuts in a shallow pan and brown lightly under a medium grill, turning them occasionally; or bake in the oven at 180°C (350°F) mark 4 for 10–12 minutes, watching them carefully.

To skin hazelnuts
Heat them through in the oven or under a low grill, shaking them occasionally to turn. Then place them in a clean cloth or polythene bag and rub until the papery skins crumble off.

To separate an egg
Give the egg a sharp knock against the side of a basin or cup and break the shell in half. Tapping it lightly two or three times is liable to crush the shell instead of breaking it cleanly and may cause the yolk to mix with the white. Having broken the shell, pass the yolk back and forth from one half of the shell to the other, letting the white drop into the basin. Put the yolk into another basin.

If you are separating more than one egg, use a third basin for cracking the eggs (so that if any of the yolk should break, only the one white will be spoilt).

To melt chocolate
Break the chocolate into pieces, put it into a bowl and stand this over hot (*not* boiling) water. See that no water gets into the bowl and that the temperature of the chocolate does not become too high – chocolate melts at about 40°C (104°F).

To whip cream
Use double or whipping cream and chill it beforehand. Place the cream in a chilled, deep bowl and whisk with a cold rotary or balloon whisk until fluffy and just holds its shape. Do not over-beat.

To layer a cake
Measure the depth of the layers up the side of the cake and insert some toothpicks or cocktail sticks at intervals as a cutting guide. Use a sharp-bladed knife – if possible, long enough to give a clean sweep – and rest the knife above and against the toothpicks or cocktail sticks while cutting.

Clockwise from top right: Fluted caraway buns (*page 70*), Ginger whirls (*page 59*), Mincemeat yo-yos (*page 69*), Walnut and sultana rockies (*page 34*)

Storing and freezing cakes

Storing

When the cake is completely cold put it in a tin with a tightly fitting lid.

Most types of cake are best eaten quite fresh, but rich fruit cakes and gingerbreads improve with keeping and should be stored for at least 24 hours before being cut – even longer if they are really rich. Fruit cakes which are to be kept for several months should be wrapped in greaseproof paper then foil before being put in the tin.

Un-iced cakes can be stored by wrapping them first in greaseproof paper and then in foil or cling film. This is especially useful for awkward-sized cakes. Iced cakes are best stored in a tin, but can be very loosely 'capped' with foil, so that the icing is not disturbed. Cream filled or decorated cakes should be stored in the refrigerator.

After a celebration cake has been decorated it should be lightly covered with paper and allowed to dry overnight. It should then be completely covered with cling film, sealed to exclude all dust, and left covered until required. White cakes show every mark and there is no way of removing dust from icing. As royal icing tends to become hard when kept, a cake should not be decorated too long before it is required.

Meringues and biscuits should also be stored in a tightly closed tin or container. Each variety should be stored separately. Never store cakes and biscuits in the same tin as the biscuits will absorb moisture from the cakes and lose their crispness. Most iced biscuits are best if eaten when they are very fresh.

Basic cake freezing know-how

Storage time	Preparation	Freezing	Thawing and serving
CAKES *cooked* including sponge flans, Swiss rolls and layer cakes: 6 months *Iced cakes:* 2 months	Bake in usual way. Leave until cold on a wire rack. Swiss rolls are best rolled up in cornflour, not sugar, if they are to be frozen without a filling. Do not spread or layer cakes with jam before freezing. Keep essences to a minimum and go lightly on the spices.	Wrap plain cake layers separately, or together with waxed paper between layers. Open freeze iced cakes (whole or cut) until icing has set, then wrap, seal and pack in boxes to protect the icing.	Iced cakes: unwrap before thawing, so the wrapping will not stick to the icing. Cream cakes: may be sliced while frozen for a better shape and quick thawing. Plain cakes: leave in package and thaw at room temperature. Un-iced large cakes thaw in about 3–4 hours at room temperature, layer cakes take about 1–2 hours and small cakes about 30 minutes: iced layer cakes take up to 4 hours.
CAKE MIXTURES *uncooked* 2 months	Whisked sponge mixtures do not freeze well uncooked. Put rich creamed mixtures into containers, or line the tin to be used later with greased foil and add the cake mixture.	Freeze uncovered. When frozen, remove from tin, package in foil and overwrap. Return to freezer.	To thaw, leave at room temperature for 2–3 hours, then fill tins to bake. Pre-formed cake mixtures can be returned to the original tin, without wrapping but still in foil lining. Place frozen in pre-heated oven and bake in usual way, but allow longer cooking time.

Storage time	Preparation	Freezing	Thawing and serving
PASTRY* *uncooked* *Short pastries:* 3 months *Flaky pastries:* 3–4 months	Roll out to size required. Open freeze pie shells until hard, to avoid damage. Rounds of pastry can be stacked with wax paper between for pie bases or tops.	Stack pastry shapes with two pieces of waxed paper between layers: if needed, one piece of pastry can be removed without thawing the whole batch. Place the stack on a piece of cardboard, wrap and seal.	Thaw flat rounds at room temperature, fit into pie plate and proceed with recipe. Unbaked pie shells or flat cases should be returned to their original container before cooking: they can go into the oven from the freezer (ovenproof glass should first stand for 10 minutes at room temperature); add about 5 minutes to normal baking time.
PASTRY *cooked* *Pastry cases:* 6 months	Prepare as usual. Empty cases freeze satisfactorily, but with some change in texture.	Wrap carefully – very fragile.	Flan cases should be thawed at room temperature for about 1 hour. Refresh if wished, by heating, uncovered, in the oven at 170°C (325°F) mark 3 for 10 minutes.
CREAM *Whipped:* 3 months *Commercially frozen:* up to 1 year	Use only pasteurised cream, with a butter-fat content of 40% or more (i.e. double cream). For best results, half-whip cream with 5 ml (1 level tsp) caster sugar to each 150 ml (¼ pint). Whipped cream may be piped into rosettes on waxed paper.	Transfer cream to suitable container, e.g. waxed carton, leaving head space for expansion. Open freeze rosettes; when firm, pack in a single layer in foil.	Thaw in refrigerator, allowing 24 hours, or 12 hours at room temperature. Put rosettes in position as decoration before thawing, as they cannot be handled once thawed. Rosettes take less time to thaw.

*Note there is little advantage in bulk-freezing uncooked shortcrust pastry, as it takes about 3 hours to thaw before it can be rolled out. For bulk-freezing flaky pastries – prepare up to the last rolling; pack in freezer bags or foil and overwrap. To use, leave for 3–4 hours at room temperature, or overnight in the refrigerator.

Freezing

Most undecorated cakes – sponge, creamed Victoria, Madeira, light fruit cakes and small buns – will freeze well. Wrap them in freezer wrapping and seal, excluding as much air as possible. Frosted and iced cakes are only suitable for short-term storage. It is a good idea to freeze the parts for a filled cake separately, putting together, for example, the sandwich layers, cream rosettes and strawberries while they are still frozen and allowing the cake to thaw out before serving. It is not worth using up valuable freezer space for rich fruit cakes as these keep so well anyway.

When freezing a glacé-iced or butter-cream frosted gâteau, put it in the freezer without wrapping and open freeze until firm, then wrap. To prevent crushing, the cake may be placed in a heavy cardboard box. Pack cup cakes in a single layer in a rigid cardboard box, then overwrap with foil and freeze.

Cakes made with pastry can also be frozen. Choux pastries can be frozen, unfilled, packed in a rigid container or polythene bag. To serve, place the frozen choux in the oven at 190°C (375°F) mark 5 for about 5 minutes, then cool. This will help to make the pastry crisp.

What went wrong?

Too close a texture?
This may be caused by:
1 Too much liquid.
2 Too little raising agent.
3 Insufficient creaming of the fat and sugar – air should be well incorporated at this stage.
4 Curdling of the creamed mixture when the eggs are added (a curdled mixture holds less air than one of the correct consistency).
5 Over-stirring or beating the flour into a creamed mixture when little or no raising agent is present.

Uneven texture with holes?
This may be caused by:
1 Over-stirring or uneven mixing in of the flour.
2 Putting the mixture into the cake tin in small amounts – pockets of air trapped in the mixture.

Dry and crumbly texture?
This may be caused by:
1 Too much raising agent.
2 Too long a cooking time in too cool an oven.

'Peaking' and 'cracking'?
This may be caused by:
1 Too hot an oven.
2 The cake being placed too near top of the oven.
3 Too stiff a mixture.
4 Too small a cake tin.

Fruit sinking to the bottom of the cake?
This may be caused by:
1 Damp fruit.
2 Sticky glacé cherries.
3 Too soft a mixture: a rich fruit cake mixture should be fairly stiff, so that it can support the weight of the fruit.
4 Opening or banging the oven door while the cake is rising.
5 Using self raising flour where the recipe requires plain, or using too much baking powder – the cake over-rises and cannot carry the fruit with it.

Fruit cakes dry and crumbly?
This may be caused by:
1 Cooking at too high a temperature.
2 Too stiff a mixture.
3 Not lining the tin thoroughly – for a large cake, double greaseproof paper should be used.

Close, heavy-textured whisked sponge?
This may be caused by:
1 The eggs and sugar being insufficiently beaten, so that not enough air is enclosed.
2 The flour being stirred in too heavily or for too long – very light folding movements are required and a metal spoon should be used.

Cakes sinking in the middle?
This may be caused by:
1 Too soft a mixture.
2 Too much raising agent.
3 Too cool an oven, which means that the centre of the cake does not rise.
4 Too hot an oven, which makes the cake appear to be done on the outside before it is cooked through, so that it is taken from the oven too soon.
5 Insufficient baking.

Burnt fruit on the outside of a fruit cake?
This may be caused by:
1 Too high a temperature.
2 Lack of protection: as soon as the cake begins to colour, a piece of brown paper or a double thickness of greaseproof paper should be placed over the top for the remainder of the cooking time to prevent further browning.

A heavy layer at the base of a Genoese sponge?
This may be caused by:
1 The melted fat being too hot – it should be only lukewarm and just flowing.
2 Uneven or insufficient folding in of fat or flour.
3 Pouring the fat into the centre of the mixture instead of round the edge.

FAMILY FARE

Served very fresh, plain cakes have a soft, light texture. Easy to make and economical too, these wholesome cakes can be deliciously varied.

The term 'plain cake' is apt to puzzle beginners: it simply refers to the ratio of fat to flour and not to the presence or absence of fruit or other flavourings. For plain cakes, the proportion of fat to flour is half or less and the rubbing in method of cake-making is used. (It is not practicable to rub in a higher proportion of fat as the mixture quickly becomes sticky and difficult to manage.)

'Rubbing in' is a literal description of the method: the fat is lightly 'worked' into the flour between the fingers and thumbs until the mixture resembles fine breadcrumbs. Some air is incorporated during this process, which helps to make the cake light, but the main raising agents are chemical.

Adding the liquid is a crucial stage in the making of a plain cake. Too much liquid can cause a heavy, doughy texture and insufficient liquid results in a dry cake. Add the liquid cautiously, using just enough to bring the mixture to the right consistency. For large cakes, the mixture should have a soft dropping consistency. That is, it should drop easily from the spoon when the spoon handle is gently tapped against the side of the bowl. For small cakes and buns that are baked on a flat baking sheet, the mixture should be stiff enough to hold its shape without spreading too much during baking. A stiff consistency describes a mixture which will cling to the spoon.

Because they are low in fat, most plain cakes are best served as fresh as possible, preferably on the day they are made.

Rock buns

These plain buns are shaped in small heaps for baking. The mixture must not be too wet or they will spread and lose their rocky shape.

225 g (8 oz) plain flour
pinch of salt
10 ml (2 level tsp) baking powder
50 g (2 oz) butter
50 g (2 oz) lard
75 g (3 oz) demerara sugar
75 g (3 oz) mixed dried fruit
grated rind of $\frac{1}{2}$ a lemon
1 egg, beaten
a little milk

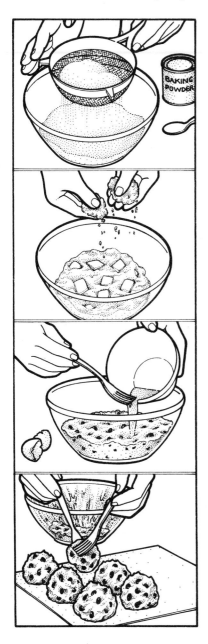

Lightly grease two baking sheets. Sift together the flour, salt and baking powder into a mixing bowl. Cut the butter and lard into small pieces and add it to the flour.

Rub the fat lightly into the flour between thumb and fingertips, holding the hands high above the bowl to keep the mixture cool and light. Shake the bowl occasionally to bring any large lumps to the surface. Rub in thoroughly until the mixture resembles fine breadcrumbs.

Add the sugar, fruit and lemon rind to the mixture and mix in thoroughly. Make a well in the centre, gradually pour in the beaten egg and mix with a fork. Add just enough milk to mix to a moist but stiff dough.

Using two forks, shape small quantities of mixture into rocky heaps on the prepared baking sheets. Bake in the oven at 200°C (400°F) mark 6 for about 20 minutes until golden brown. Leave to cool on a wire rack and serve while still fresh.

Makes 12

Cherry cake

Illustrated in colour on page 30

225 g (8 oz) self raising flour
pinch of salt
100 g (4 oz) butter or block margarine
100 g (4 oz) caster sugar
175 g (6 oz) glacé cherries, washed,
    dried and quartered
1 egg, beaten
2.5 ml ($\frac{1}{2}$ tsp) vanilla essence
about 75 ml (5 tbsp) milk

Grease and line the base of a 1.4-litre ($2\frac{1}{2}$-pint) loaf tin measuring 19×11 cm ($7\frac{1}{2} \times 4\frac{1}{2}$ inches) across the top. Sift together the flour and salt into a bowl. Rub in the fat until the mixture resembles fine breadcrumbs. Stir in the sugar and cherries. Make a well in the centre and pour in the egg, essence and some of the milk. Gradually work in the dry ingredients, adding more milk if necessary to give a dropping consistency. Turn the mixture into the prepared tin and level the surface. Bake in the oven at 180°C (350°F) mark 4 for about $1\frac{1}{4}$ hours until well risen, golden brown and firm to the touch. Turn out and leave to cool on a wire rack.

Vinegar cake

225 g (8 oz) plain flour
pinch of salt
100 g (4 oz) butter or block margarine
75 g (3 oz) brown soft sugar
50 g (2 oz) currants
50 g (2 oz) sultanas
45 ml (3 tbsp) chopped mixed peel
5 ml (1 level tsp) bicarbonate of soda
about 45 ml (3 tbsp) milk
15 ml (1 tbsp) vinegar

Grease and line an 18-cm (7-inch) cake tin. Sift together the flour and salt into a bowl. Rub in fat until the mixture resembles fine breadcrumbs. Stir in the sugar, dried fruit and mixed peel and make a well in the centre. Dissolve the bicarbonate of soda in a little of the milk and pour into the well. Add the vinegar and more milk and gradually work in the dry ingredients, adding extra milk if necessary to give a dropping consistency. Turn the mixture into the prepared tin and level the surface. Bake in the oven at 190°C (375°F) mark 5 for 15 minutes, then reduce to 180°C (350°F) mark 4 and bake for a further hour. Turn out and leave to cool on a wire rack.

Banana teabread

200 g (7 oz) self raising flour
1.25 ml ($\frac{1}{4}$ level tsp) bicarbonate of soda
2.5 ml ($\frac{1}{2}$ level tsp) salt
75 g (3 oz) butter or block margarine
175 g (6 oz) caster sugar
2 eggs, beaten
450 g (1 lb) bananas, peeled and mashed
100 g (4 oz) nuts, coarsely chopped

Grease and line a 1.4-litre ($2\frac{1}{2}$-pint) loaf tin measuring 19×11 cm ($7\frac{1}{2} \times 4\frac{1}{2}$ inches) across the top. Sift together the flour, bicarbonate of soda and salt into a bowl. Rub the fat into the flour until the mixture resembles fine breadcrumbs. Stir in the sugar. Beat the eggs and banana together and then stir into the mixture. Stir in the nuts. Turn into the prepared tin and bake in the oven at 180°C (350°F) mark 4 for about $1\frac{1}{4}$ hours until well risen and just firm. Turn out and leave to cool on a wire rack. Keep for 24 hours before serving sliced and buttered.

VARIATION

Honey and banana teabread Reduce the amount of sugar used to 100 g (4 oz) and the bananas to 225 g (8 oz). Beat 30 ml (2 level tbsp) honey into the banana mixture and add 225 g (8 oz) mixed dried fruit before putting the mixture into the prepared loaf tin.

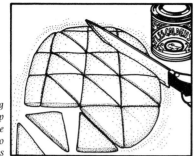

Cutting Syrup oat scone dough into triangles

Syrup oat scones

350 g (12 oz) self raising flour
15 ml (3 level tsp) baking powder
5 ml (1 level tsp) ground ginger
75 g (3 oz) butter or block margarine
50 g (2 oz) porridge oats
60 ml (4 level tbsp) golden syrup
about 200 ml (7 fl oz) milk, at room temperature

Grease and preheat two baking sheets in the oven. Sift together the flour, baking powder and ground ginger into a bowl. Rub in the fat until the mixture resembles fine breadcrumbs. Stir in the oats. Warm the syrup gently and add to the milk. Mix the dry ingredients to a soft dough with the syrup and milk, adding more milk if necessary. Roll out 1 cm ($\frac{1}{2}$ inch) thick on a floured working surface and cut into 5-cm (2-inch) triangles, kneading and re-rolling the dough. Place the scones on the prepared baking sheets. Brush with milk and bake in the oven at 230°C (450°F) mark 8 for 10–12 minutes.
Makes about 20

Scones

225 g (8 oz) self raising flour
2.5 ml ($\frac{1}{2}$ level tsp) salt
5 ml (1 level tsp) baking powder
25–50 g (1–2 oz) butter or block margarine
150 ml ($\frac{1}{4}$ pint) milk
beaten egg or milk to glaze (optional)

Preheat a baking sheet in the oven. Sift together the flour, salt and baking powder into a bowl. Rub in the fat until the mixture resembles fine breadcrumbs. Make a well in the centre and stir in enough milk to give a fairly soft dough. Turn it on to a floured working surface, knead very lightly if necessary to remove any cracks, then roll out lightly to about 2 cm ($\frac{3}{4}$ inch) thick, or pat it out with the hand. Cut into 10–12 rounds with a 5-cm (2-inch) cutter dipped in flour, or cut into triangles with a sharp knife. Place on the baking sheet, brush if you wish with beaten egg or milk and bake in the hottest part of the oven at 230°C (450°F) mark 8 for 8–10 minutes until well risen and brown. Cool on a wire rack. Serve split and buttered.

Alternative raising agents
If plain flour and baking powder are used instead of self raising flour, allow 15 ml (3 level tsp) baking powder to 225 g (8 oz) flour and sift them together twice before using. If you use cream of tartar and bicarbonate of soda in place of baking powder, allow 5 ml (1 level tsp) cream of tartar and 2.5 ml ($\frac{1}{2}$ level tsp) bicarbonate of soda to 225 g (8 oz) plain flour with ordinary milk, or 2.5 ml ($\frac{1}{2}$ level tsp) bicarbonate of soda and 2.5 ml ($\frac{1}{2}$ level tsp) cream of tartar with soured milk.

VARIATIONS

Everyday fruit scones Add 50 g (2 oz) currants, sultanas, seedless raisins or chopped dates (or a mixture of fruit) to the dry ingredients in the basic recipe.
Illustrated in colour opposite

Rich afternoon tea scones Follow the basic recipe, adding 15–30 ml (1–2 level tbsp) caster sugar to the dry ingredients and using 1 beaten egg with 75 ml (5 tbsp) water or milk in place of 150 ml ($\frac{1}{4}$ pint) milk; 50 g (2 oz) dried fruit may also be included, if liked.

Everyday fruit scones (*above*), Strawberry shortcakes (*page 117*)

Page 28: Tutti frutti lemon layer cake (*page 65*)

Page 29: Brandy cornets (*page 90*), Coffee cream éclairs (*page 133*), Chocolate and coffee gâteau (*page 46*)

Wholemeal scone round

15 ml (3 level tsp) baking powder
pinch of salt
50 g (2 oz) plain flour
50 g (2 oz) caster sugar
175 g (6 oz) plain wholemeal flour
50 g (2 oz) butter or block margarine
about 150 ml ($\frac{1}{4}$ pint) milk

Preheat a baking sheet in the oven. Sift together the baking powder, salt and plain flour into a bowl. Add the sugar and wholemeal flour. Rub in the fat until the mixture resembles fine breadcrumbs. Make a well in the centre and pour in the milk. Mix to a soft but manageable dough. Knead lightly on a floured working surface. Shape into a flat 15-cm (6-inch) round and mark with the back of a floured knife into six triangles. Place on the baking sheet and bake in the. oven at 230°C (450°F) mark 8 for about 15 minutes. Leave to cool slightly, then serve, split and buttered, while still warm.

Note If you wish to use self raising wholemeal flour, reduce the amount of baking powder in the recipe to 5 ml (1 level tsp).

Date scone bars

225 g (8 oz) plain flour
2.5 ml ($\frac{1}{2}$ level tsp) bicarbonate of soda
5 ml (1 level tsp) cream of tartar
pinch of salt
50 g (2 oz) butter or block margarine
25 g (1 oz) caster sugar
75 g (3 oz) stoned dates
about 150 ml ($\frac{1}{4}$ pint) milk

Preheat a baking sheet in the oven. Sift together the flour, bicarbonate of soda, cream of tartar and salt into a bowl. Rub in the fat until the mixture resembles fine breadcrumbs. Add the sugar. Using kitchen scissors, snip the dates into small pieces and add to the mixture. Mix to a light dough with the milk. Roll out into a 30.5 × 10-cm (12 × 14-inch) oblong. Brush with milk and place on the baking sheet. Mark into eight bars with the back of a knife. Bake in the oven at 230°C (450°F) mark 8 for about 15 minutes. Break apart and leave to cool on a wire rack. Serve split and buttered.
Makes 8

Farmhouse sultana cake

Illustrated in colour opposite

225 g (8 oz) plain flour
10 ml (2 level tsp) mixed spice
5 ml (1 level tsp) bicarbonate of soda
225 g (8 oz) plain wholemeal flour
175 g (6 oz) butter or block margarine
225 g (8 oz) dark brown soft sugar
225 g (8 oz) sultanas
1 egg, beaten
about 300 ml ($\frac{1}{2}$ pint) milk
10 sugar cubes

Grease and line a 20.5-cm (8-inch) square, loose bottomed cake tin. Sift the plain flour, spice and bicarbonate of soda into a large bowl and stir in the wholemeal flour. Rub in the fat until the mixture resembles fine breadcrumbs and stir in the sugar and sultanas. Make a well in the centre and gradually pour in the egg and milk. Beat gently until well mixed and of a soft dropping consistency, adding more milk if necessary.

Turn the mixture into the prepared tin and level the surface. Roughly crush the sugar cubes with the end of a rolling pin and scatter over the cake. Bake in the oven at 170°C (325°F) mark 3 for about 1 hour 40 minutes or until a fine, warmed skewer inserted into the centre comes out clean. Remove the cake from the tin and leave to cool on a wire rack.

Clockwise from top right: Cherry cake (*page 25*), Marmalade mace teabread (*page 34*), Farmhouse sultana cake (*above*)

Griddle scones

If you do not possess a 'griddle' or 'girdle', use a thick-bottomed frying pan or the solid hot-plate of an electric cooker. To prepare a cast iron griddle, heat it well, rub with salt and absorbent kitchen paper, remove salt and reheat it slowly and thoroughly for 15 minutes. Before cooking the scones, lightly grease the griddle with a little lard or cooking oil. A griddle with a non-stick surface is ideal and requires no special treatment.

225 g (8 oz) plain flour
5 ml (1 level tsp) bicarbonate of soda
10 ml (2 level tsp) cream of tartar
5 ml (1 level tsp) salt
small knob of lard or margarine
25 g (1 oz) caster sugar
about 150 ml ($\frac{1}{4}$ pint) milk

Heat then grease a griddle, hot-plate or heavy frying pan. Sift together the flour, bicarbonate of soda, cream of tartar and salt into a bowl. Rub in the fat until the mixture resembles fine breadcrumbs and add the sugar. Make a well in the centre and pour in the milk. Mix to a soft but manageable dough. Divide the dough into two portions. Lightly knead and roll into two flat rounds about 0.5 cm ($\frac{1}{4}$ inch) thick. Cut each round into six even triangles and cook on the griddle until evenly brown on one side; turn them and cook on the second side. Allow 5 minutes on each side. Leave to cool on a wire rack.
Makes 12

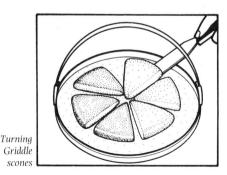

Turning Griddle scones

Buttermilk cherry loaf cake

225 g (8 oz) self raising flour
7.5 ml (1$\frac{1}{2}$ level tsp) baking powder
1.25 ml ($\frac{1}{4}$ level tsp) mixed spice
1.25 ml ($\frac{1}{4}$ level tsp) ground ginger
100 g (4 oz) butter or block margarine
100 g (4 oz) dark brown soft sugar
175 g (6 oz) glacé cherries, halved
7.5 ml (1$\frac{1}{2}$ tsp) black treacle
1 egg, beaten
150 ml ($\frac{1}{4}$ pint) buttermilk

Grease and line a 1.4-litre (2$\frac{1}{2}$-pint) loaf tin measuring 19 × 11 cm (7$\frac{1}{2}$ × 4$\frac{1}{2}$ inches) across the top. Sift together the flour, baking powder and spices into a bowl. Rub in the fat until the mixture resembles fine breadcrumbs. Stir in the sugar and cherries. Make a well in the centre. Mix together the treacle, egg and buttermilk and stir into the dry ingredients. Turn the mixture into the tin and level the surface. Bake in the oven at 180°C (350°F) mark 4 for 1–1$\frac{1}{4}$ hours. Turn out and leave to cool on a wire rack.

Lemon cake

225 g (8 oz) self raising flour
pinch of salt
100 g (4 oz) butter or block margarine
100 g (4 oz) caster sugar
grated rind and juice of 1 small lemon
1 egg, beaten
about 90–120 ml (6–8 tbsp) milk

Grease a 15-cm (6-inch) cake tin. Sift together the flour and salt into a bowl. Rub in the fat until the mixture resembles fine breadcrumbs. Stir in the sugar and lemon rind. Make a well in the centre and pour in the egg, lemon juice and some of the milk. Gradually work in the dry ingredients, adding more milk if necessary to give a dropping consistency. Turn the mixture into the prepared tin and level the surface. Bake in the oven at 180°C (350°F) mark 4 for about 1¼ hours until golden and firm to the touch. Turn out and leave to cool on a wire rack.

Treacle scones

225 g (8 oz) self raising flour
5 ml (1 level tsp) baking powder
5 ml (1 level tsp) mixed spice
pinch of salt
50 g (2 oz) butter or block margarine
25 g (1 oz) caster sugar
15 ml (1 level tbsp) black treacle
about 150 ml (¼ pint) milk

Preheat a baking sheet in the oven. Sift together the flour, baking powder, spice and salt into a bowl. Rub in the fat until the mixture resembles fine breadcrumbs. Add the sugar. Warm the treacle gently and add to the milk. Mix the dry ingredients to a soft dough with the treacle and milk. Roll out to about 2 cm (¾ inch) thick and stamp out into 6.5-cm (2½-inch) rounds. Brush with milk, place on the baking sheet and bake in the oven at 230°C (450°F) mark 8 for 10–15 minutes. Serve split and buttered.
Makes about 10

Eggless cake

450 g (1 lb) plain flour
10 ml (2 level tsp) ground ginger
225 g (8 oz) lard
175 g (6 oz) caster sugar
175 g (6 oz) sultanas
175 g (6 oz) currants
10 ml (2 level tsp) bicarbonate of soda
300 ml (½ pint) milk
30 ml (2 tbsp) vinegar

Grease and line a 2-litre (3½-pint) loaf tin measuring 24 × 13.5 cm (9½ × 5½ inches) across the top. Sift together the flour and ginger into a bowl. Rub in the lard until the mixture resembles fine breadcrumbs. Add the sugar and dried fruit. Make a well

in the centre. Dissolve the bicarbonate of soda in the milk, add the vinegar and mix quickly into the dry ingredients. Turn the mixture into the prepared tin and make a hollow in the top. Bake in the oven at 190°C (375°F) mark 5 for about 2 hours. Turn out and leave to cool on a wire rack.

Date and pineapple loaf

350 g (12 oz) self raising flour
175 g (6 oz) butter or block margarine
175 g (6 oz) caster sugar
100 g (4 oz) stoned dates, chopped
100 g (4 oz) glacé pineapple, finely
  chopped
2 eggs
45 ml (3 tbsp) milk
5 ml (1 tsp) pineapple essence
12 cubes of sugar, crushed

Grease and line a 2-litre (3½-pint) loaf tin measuring 24 × 13.5 cm (9½ × 5½ inches) across the top. Sift the flour into a bowl. Rub in the fat until the mixture resembles fine breadcrumbs and add the sugar, dates and pineapple. Make a well in the centre. Beat the eggs, milk and essence together. Pour on to the dry ingredients and mix to a soft consistency. Turn the mixture into the prepared tin, level the surface and sprinkle the sugar over. Bake in the oven at 180°C (350°F) mark 4 for about 1¼ hours. Turn out and leave to cool on a wire rack. Store in an airtight tin for 1–2 days before cutting.

Sprinkling Date and pineapple loaf with sugar

Marmalade mace teabread

Illustrated in colour on page 30

225 g (8 oz) self raising flour
pinch of salt
2.5 ml ($\frac{1}{2}$ level tsp) ground mace
100 g (4 oz) butter or block margarine
100 g (4 oz) demerara sugar
1 egg, beaten
90 ml (6 level tbsp) chunky marmalade
60 ml (4 tbsp) milk
3 crystallised orange slices (optional)

Grease and line a 2-litre (3$\frac{1}{2}$-pint) loaf tin measuring 24 × 13.5 cm (9$\frac{1}{2}$ × 5$\frac{1}{2}$ inches) across the top. Sift together the flour, salt and mace into a bowl. Rub in the fat until the mixture resembles fine breadcrumbs. Add the demerara sugar. Make a well in the centre and pour in the egg, 60 ml (4 level tbsp) marmalade and milk. Turn the mixture into the prepared tin, level the surface and top with the halved slices of orange. Bake in the oven at 180°C (350°F) mark 4 for about 1 hour. Turn out and leave to cool on a wire rack. Whilst still warm, brush the surface of the cake with the remaining warmed marmalade. Cool.

Note If wrapped in foil, this teabread stores well for up to a week.

Walnut and sultana rockies

Illustrated in colour on page 18

225 g (8 oz) plain flour
pinch of salt
2.5 ml ($\frac{1}{2}$ level tsp) mixed spice
50 g (2 oz) butter
50 g (2 oz) lard
100 g (4 oz) demerara sugar
50 g (2 oz) walnut halves, chopped
50 g (2 oz) sultanas
25 g (1 oz) chopped mixed peel
1 egg, beaten
a little milk

Grease two baking sheets. Sift together the flour, salt and spice into a bowl. Rub in the fats until the mixture resembles fine breadcrumbs. Add the sugar, walnuts, sultanas and mixed peel. Using a fork, bind them together with egg and a little milk, if necessary, to give a very stiff dough. Continue using a fork to make small rough heaps on the greased baking sheets. Bake in the oven at 200°C (400°F) mark 6 for 15–20 minutes. Leave to cool for a short time before transferring to a wire rack to cool completely.
Makes about 12

Walnut coffee rock cakes

Illustrated in colour on page 76

225 g (8 oz) self raising flour
100 g (4 oz) butter or block margarine
50 g (2 oz) walnuts, chopped
75 g (3 oz) demerara sugar
1 egg
30 ml (2 tbsp) coffee essence
about 45 ml (3 tbsp) milk
75 g (3 oz) icing sugar

Lightly grease two baking sheets. Sift the flour into a bowl and rub in half the fat. Mix in the chopped walnuts and demerara sugar. Beat the egg with 15 ml (1 tbsp) coffee essence and the milk. Add to the dry ingredients and mix to a firm dough, adding more milk only if really necessary. Spoon the mixture into twelve heaps on the baking sheets, allowing them room to spread. Bake in the oven at 200°C (400°F) mark 6 for 15–20 minutes. Leave to cool on wire racks.

Soften the remaining butter and beat in the sifted icing sugar and 15 ml (1 tbsp) coffee essence. Cut a small cap off each cake and sandwich back with the butter cream. Dust with sifted icing sugar.
Makes about 12

LIGHT AS SPONGE

A light, delicate sponge cake, filled simply with cream and fruit, is always a welcome treat. The classic sponge cake, which is fatless, is made by first whisking together eggs and caster sugar, then folding in the flour. The rise and lightness of the cake depend on the air which is incorporated during whisking.

In some recipes, the egg whites are whisked separately and folded into the egg and sugar mixture to give an especially light, but slightly firmer result. Sometimes, a little melted butter is added to give a moister cake with better keeping qualities: this type of sponge is known as 'Genoese'.

To achieve a good sponge, the eggs and sugar must be whisked until really thick and creamy: the mixture should be thick enough to leave a trail when the whisk is lifted from the surface. The process is speeded up by placing the mixing bowl over a pan of hot (not boiling) water.

Adding the flour in the right way is equally important. Sprinkle the flour – which must be sifted – over the mixture, a little at a time, and gently fold it in with a large metal spoon. The flour must be thoroughly blended, but agitate the mixture as little as possible to avoid breaking down the air bubbles. If adding melted butter, make sure it is just liquid and not too hot by leaving it to stand for a few minutes before use. Pour in the butter, around the sides of the bowl, and fold it in very lightly. Overworking at this final stage can ruin the whole mixture.

Bake all whisked sponge mixtures as soon as possible after mixing as they tend to lose volume if left to stand.

Whisked sponge cake

The whisking method produces the lightest of all cakes. It is used for many gâteaux, fruit cakes and layer cakes.

3 eggs, size 2
100 g (4 oz) caster sugar
75 g (3 oz) plain flour

Grease and line two 18-cm (7-inch) sandwich tins and dust with a little flour or, if liked, a mixture of a little plain flour and caster sugar. Put the eggs and sugar in a large deep bowl and stand this over a pan of hot water. The bowl should fit snugly in the pan and the bottom of the bowl should not touch the bottom of the pan.

Whisk the eggs and sugar together until doubled in volume and thick enough to leave a trail on the surface when the whisk is lifted. If whisking by hand, this will take 15–20 minutes. If a hand-held electric mixer is used, the whisking will take only half as long. Remove the bowl from the heat and continue whisking for a further 5 minutes until the mixture is cooler and creamy looking.

Sift half the flour over the mixture and fold it in very lightly, using a large metal spoon. Sift and fold in the remaining flour in the same way.

Pour the mixture into the prepared tins, tilting the tins to spread the mixture evenly. Do not use a palette knife or spatula to smooth the mixture as this will crush out the air bubbles. Bake the cakes in the oven at 190°C (375°F) mark 5 for 20–25 minutes until firm but springy to the touch. If necessary, run a knife round the edge of the tins to loosen the cakes, then turn out and leave to cool on a wire rack.

Swiss roll

3 eggs
100 g (4 oz) caster sugar
100 g (4 oz) plain flour
15 ml (1 tbsp) hot water
caster sugar to dredge
100 g (4 oz) jam, warmed

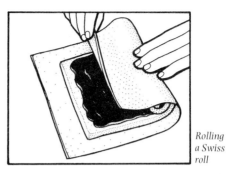

Rolling a Swiss roll

Grease and line a 33×23-cm (13×9-inch) Swiss roll tin. Put the eggs and sugar in a large bowl, stand this over a pan of hot water and whisk until thick, creamy and pale in colour. The mixture should be stiff enough to leave a trail on the surface when the whisk is lifted. Remove the bowl from the heat and whisk until cool. Sift half the flour over the mixture and fold in very lightly with a metal spoon. Sift and fold in the remaining flour, then lightly stir in the hot water.

Pour the mixture into the prepared tin, and tilt the tin backwards and forwards to spread the mixture in an even layer. Bake in the oven at 220°C (425°F) mark 7 for 7–9 minutes until golden brown, well risen and firm to the touch. Meanwhile, place a sheet of greaseproof paper over a tea towel lightly wrung out in hot water. Dredge the paper thickly with caster sugar.

Quickly turn out the cake on to the paper, trim off the crusty edges with a sharp knife and spread the surface with warmed jam. Roll up the cake with the aid of the paper. Make the first turn firmly so that the whole cake will roll evenly and have a good shape when finished, but roll more lightly after this turn. Place seam-side down on a wire rack and dredge with sugar. Leave to cool.

VARIATION
Chocolate Swiss roll Replace 15 ml (1 level tbsp) flour with 15 ml (1 level tbsp) cocoa powder. Turn out the cooked sponge and trim as above, then cover with a sheet of greaseproof paper and roll with the paper inside. When the cake is cold, unroll and remove the paper. Spread with whipped cream or butter cream (*see page 170*) and re-roll. Dust with icing sugar.

Gâteau cardinal

This is a speciality of Boulogne-sur-mer.

1 quantity crème au beurre (*see page 170*)
50 g (2 oz) glacé cherries, finely chopped
30 ml (2 tbsp) kirsch or rum
Genoese sponge baked in two 20.5-cm
    (8-inch) sandwich tins (*see page 38*)
50 g (2 oz) walnuts, finely chopped
30 ml (2 level tbsp) crushed meringue or
    crushed macaroons
175 g (6 oz) redcurrant jelly

Reserve 60 ml (4 tbsp) of the crème au beurre for piping and divide the rest in half. Mix one half with the cherries and kirsch or rum. Sandwich the sponges together with the cherry filling. Spread the remaining crème au beurre around the sides and roll in the nuts and meringue.

Melt the jelly with 15 ml (1 tbsp) water and allow to cool slightly. Coat the top of the cake thickly with the jelly and leave to cool and set in the refrigerator. Using the reserved crème au beurre and a piping bag fitted with a small star nozzle, pipe the word 'Cardinal' over the jelly on top of the cake and pipe a small shell border around the top edge.

Genoese sponge

A Genoese sponge forms the ideal base for many gâteaux. It is lighter than a Victoria sandwich, cuts well and has a pleasant buttery taste.

For a sponge baked in two 18-cm (7-inch) sandwich tins or one 18-cm (7-inch) cake tin

40 g (1½ oz) butter
65 g (2½ oz) plain flour
15 ml (1 level tbsp) cornflour
3 eggs, size 2
75 g (3 oz) caster sugar

For a sponge baked in two 20.5-cm (8-inch) sandwich tins or one 20.5-cm (8-inch) cake tin

50 g (2 oz) butter
90 g (3½ oz) plain flour
15 ml (1 level tbsp) cornflour
4 eggs, size 2
100 g (4 oz) caster sugar

Grease and line the appropriate cake tin(s). Put the butter into a saucepan and heat gently until melted, then remove from the heat and leave to stand for a few minutes to cool slightly and to allow the salt and any sediment to settle. Sift the flours together into a bowl.

Put the eggs and sugar in a bowl, stand this over a pan of hot water and whisk until thick, creamy and pale in colour. The mixture should be stiff enough to leave a trail on the surface when the whisk is lifted. Remove from the heat and continue whisking until cool.

Fold half the flour into the egg mixture with a metal spoon and pour half the cooled butter round the edge of the mixture. Gradually fold in the remaining butter and flour alternately. Be sure to fold in very lightly or the fat will sink to the bottom and cause a heavy cake.

Pour the mixture into the prepared tin(s). Bake sandwich cakes in the oven at 180°C (350°F) mark 4 for 25–30 minutes, or a deep cake for 35–40 minutes, until golden brown and firm to the touch. Turn out and leave to cool on a wire rack.

VARIATION
Chocolate Genoese For either cake size, replace 15 g (½ oz) plain flour with 15 g (½ oz) cocoa powder.

Dobos torte

4 eggs
275 g (10 oz) caster sugar
150 g (5 oz) plain flour
crushed biscuits or chopped nuts to
  decorate

For the chocolate filling
100 g (4 oz) plain chocolate
3 egg whites
175 g (6 oz) icing sugar
225 g (8 oz) butter

Line two baking sheets with non-stick (silicone) paper. Put the eggs in a bowl with 175 g (6 oz) caster sugar. Stand the bowl over a pan of hot water and whisk until the mixture is very thick and fluffy, then remove from the heat. Sift half the flour over the mixture and fold in lightly with a metal spoon. Add the remaining flour in the same way.

Gently spread some of the mixture out on the baking sheets in large rounds measuring about 20.5 cm (8 inches) in diameter. Bake in the oven at 190°C (375°F) mark 5 for 7–10 minutes until golden brown. Loosen from the baking sheets and trim each round to a neat shape with a sharp knife, using a saucepan lid as a guide. Re-line the baking sheets, spread on some more mixture and bake as above. There will be enough mixture to make six or seven rounds. Trim all the rounds in the same way and lift them on to wire racks to cool. Take the round with the best surface and lay it on an oiled baking sheet.

Make some caramel by putting the re-

Gâteau Bigarreau (*page 49*)

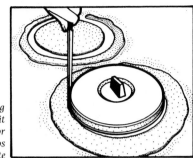

Trimming a biscuit round for Dobos torte

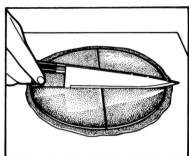

Marking sections on caramel topping for Dobos torte

maining caster sugar in a small heavy-based saucepan, placing it over a gentle heat, allowing the sugar to dissolve without stirring and boiling it steadily to a rich brown. Pour it over the selected biscuit round, spreading it with a knife that has been brushed over with oil. Mark into eight sections and trim round the edge.

To make the chocolate filling, break up the chocolate, put it in a small bowl over a pan of hot water and heat gently, stirring, until the chocolate has melted. Remove from the heat and leave to cool slightly. Put the egg whites and icing sugar in a bowl and stand this over a pan of hot water. Whisk until very thick, then remove from the heat. Cream the butter until pale and beat the egg and sugar mixture into it gradually, then stir in the melted chocolate. Sandwich the remaining biscuit rounds together in one stack with some of the filling and put the caramel-covered one on top. Spread the sides of the torte with some more filling and press the crushed biscuit crumbs or chopped nuts round the sides. Pipe the remaining filling round the top edge to make a decorative border.

Note For a simpler filling, melt 50 g (2 oz) plain chocolate as above and leave to cool slightly. Cream 150 g (5 oz) butter and gradually beat in 225 g (8 oz) sifted icing sugar. Beat in the melted chocolate while it is still soft.

Angel cake

The true American Angel cake is made of very fine flour not normally obtainable in Britain, but this recipe makes a very similar cake. Sift the flour three or four times through a fine sieve. The method is slightly unusual as the egg yolks are not used. The texture of the finished cake is so fine that it is sometimes difficult to cut with a knife. Use two forks to serve the cake instead.

65 g (2½ oz) plain flour
165 g (5½ oz) caster sugar
5 egg whites
pinch of salt
5 ml (1 level tsp) cream of tartar
a few drops of almond essence

Have ready a clean, dry and ungreased 23-cm (9-inch), 1.7-litre (3-pint) angel cake tin. Sift the flour with 50 g (2 oz) sugar. Whisk the egg whites with the salt, cream of tartar and almond essence until stiff. Whisk in the remaining sugar. Lightly but evenly fold in the sifted flour and sugar. Pour the cake mixture into the prepared tin and quickly draw the blade of a knife through the mixture to release any large air bubbles.

Bake in the oven at 190°C (375°F) mark 5 for 30–35 minutes until golden brown and firm to the touch. Invert the tin on to a wire rack and leave for about 1 hour. When the cake is cold, loosen the edges with a palette knife and gently shake the cake out of the tin.

Clockwise from top left: Rich fruit and nut cake *(page 77),* Fluted gingerbread loaf *(page 90),* Cream filled cinnamon roll *(page 50)*

Genoese gâteau

$\frac{1}{2}$ **a lemon**
50 g (2 oz) caster sugar
Genoese sponge baked in two 18-cm
   (7-inch) sandwich tins (*see page 38*)
double quantity lemon crème au beurre
   (*see page 171*)
75 g (3 oz) almonds, chopped and toasted

First, prepare the glazed lemon slices. Cut the lemon half into four slices about 0.5 cm ($\frac{1}{4}$ inch) thick. Place in a small frying pan, cover with water and poach gently until the skin is tender. Remove the slices, drain off nearly all the water from the pan and add the sugar. Heat gently to dissolve the sugar, return the lemon slices to the pan and boil to reduce to a glaze. Turn the slices to coat, then leave to cool.

Sandwich the sponges together with some of the crème au beurre. Place on a piece of greaseproof paper or on a thin silver board, then on an up-turned pudding basin. Reserve half the remaining crème au beurre and use the rest to coat the top and sides of the cake. With a palette knife, swirl the top in sweeping lines, leaving the sides smooth, then press the toasted almonds lightly into position around the edge of the cake. Transfer the gâteau to a serving plate and mark the crème au beurre on top into eight portions.

Place the reserved crème au beurre in a piping bag fitted with a large star nozzle.

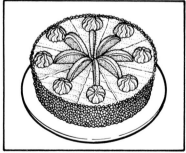

*Genoese
gâteau*

Pipe large rosette whirls in the centre of each marked portion about 2.5 cm (1 inch) from the outer edge. Cut the lemon slices in half and press one end of each into a rosette, with the other ends meeting in the centre of the gâteau. Leave the gâteau in a cool place, to firm up the crème au beurre, before serving.

Black Forest gâteau (Schwarzwälder Kirschtorte)

Illustrated on the jacket

This is a magnificent gâteau traditionally served in Germany with afternoon coffee. Served chilled, it also makes a splendid dessert.

100 g (4 oz) butter
6 eggs
225 g (8 oz) caster sugar
75 g (3 oz) plain flour
50 g (2 oz) cocoa powder
2.5 ml ($\frac{1}{2}$ tsp) vanilla essence
two 425-g (15-oz) cans stoned black
   cherries
60 ml (4 tbsp) kirsch
400 ml ($\frac{3}{4}$ pint) whipping cream
chocolate curls (*see page 164*) **to decorate**

Grease and line a 23-cm (9-inch) round cake tin. Place the butter in a bowl, stand this over a pan of warm water and cream until really soft but not melted.

Put the eggs and sugar together in a large bowl, stand this over a pan of hot water and whisk until very thick and pale. The mixture should be thick enough to leave a trail on the surface when the whisk is lifted. Remove from the heat, sift the flour and cocoa into the bowl and lightly fold it into the mixture with a metal spoon, followed by the vanilla essence and softened butter. Turn the mixture into the prepared tin, tilt the tin to spread the mixture evenly, and bake in the oven at 180°C (350°F) mark 4 for about 40 minutes until risen and firm to the touch. Turn the cake out of the tin and leave to cool on a wire rack covered with grease-proof paper.

Strain the syrup from the cans of cherries, reserving the cherries and 75 ml (5 tbsp) syrup separately. Add the kirsch to the syrup.

Split the cake into three layers. Place a layer on a flat plate and spoon over 45 ml (3 tbsp) of the cherry syrup. Whisk the cream until stiff and spread some thinly over the sponge layer. Reserve a few cherries for decoration and scatter half the remainder over the cream. Repeat the layers of sponge, syrup, cream and cherries, finishing with the third cake round. Spoon over the remaining syrup.

Fill a piping bag, fitted with a large star nozzle, with the remaining whipped cream and pipe whirls of cream around the edge of the cake. Decorate with the reserved cherries and fill the centre of the gâteau with chocolate curls.

Baked cherry cheesecake

50 g (2 oz) digestive biscuits
15 g ($\frac{1}{2}$ oz) butter
4 eggs, size 2, separated
225 g (8 oz) caster sugar
450 g (1 lb) cream cheese
40 g ($1\frac{1}{2}$ oz) plain flour, sifted
30 ml (2 tbsp) lemon juice
300 ml ($\frac{1}{2}$ pint) soured cream
425-g (15-oz) can stoned black cherries
20 ml (4 level tsp) arrowroot

Lightly grease a 19-cm ($7\frac{1}{2}$-inch) round loose-bottomed cake tin. Put the biscuits in a strong polythene bag and crush them with a rolling pin. Melt the butter and stir in the biscuit crumbs. Sprinkle over the base of the prepared tin.

Whisk the egg yolks with the sugar until thick and creamy. Beat the cream cheese lightly. Add the whisked mixture to the cheese and mix until smooth. Stir in the flour, lemon juice and soured cream. Whisk the egg whites until stiff and fold into the mixture. Pour into the tin. Bake in the oven at 130°C (250°F) mark $\frac{1}{2}$ for $1\frac{1}{2}$ hours. Turn off the heat and leave in the oven for 2 hours without opening the door. Remove from the oven and leave to cool in the tin. Carefully remove the cheesecake from the tin.

Drain the cherries, reserving 150 ml ($\frac{1}{4}$ pint) syrup and arrange over the top of the cheesecake. Blend the arrowroot with a little of the syrup. Bring the remaining syrup to the boil. Add the arrowroot and, stirring all the time, cook for a few minutes until thickened. Leave to cool slightly, then spoon the syrup over the cherries on top of the cheesecake.

ALTERNATIVE TOPPINGS FOR BAKED CHEESECAKE

1 150 ml ($\frac{1}{4}$ pint) soured cream and 25 g (1 oz) toasted flaked almonds sprinkled on top.

2 225 g (8 oz) fresh strawberries, hulled, and 150 ml ($\frac{1}{4}$ pint) whipped cream, piped in rosettes.

3 175 g (6 oz) black grapes, 312-g (11-oz) can of mandarin oranges, the juice used for the glaze.

4 60 ml (4 level tbsp) honey, grated rind and juice of $\frac{1}{2}$ a lemon, 25 g (1 oz) chopped nuts, 15 g ($\frac{1}{2}$ oz) sultanas, a lemon twist for decoration.

5 50 g (2 oz) chocolate, melted and piped over the top in a lattice design. Make small chocolate curls (*see page 164*) to scatter around the edge.

6 411-g (14½-oz) can apricots with 50 g (2 oz) white or black grapes. For the glaze, use 75 ml (5 tbsp) apricot juice glaze (*see below*) with 15 ml (1 tbsp) brandy and 5 ml (1 level tsp) caster sugar added.

To make 75 ml (5 tbsp) glaze use 75 ml (5 tbsp) liquid and thicken with 10 ml (2 level tsp) arrowroot. Flavour as liked.

Bûche de Noël (Yule log)

Bûche de Noël is the traditional cake eaten in France at Christmas time. The tradition of serving both this and also the English Yule log dates back to when a huge log used to be burnt on Christmas Eve.

3 eggs
100 g (4 oz) caster sugar
100 g (4 oz) plain flour
15 ml (1 tbsp) hot water
caster sugar
1 quantity chocolate crème au beurre (*see page 171*)
icing sugar to decorate

Grease and line a 30.5 × 20.5-cm (12 × 8-inch) Swiss roll tin. Put the eggs and sugar in a large bowl, stand this over a pan of hot water and whisk until thick and creamy in colour. The mixture should be stiff enough to leave a trail on the surface when the whisk is lifted. Remove from the heat and whisk until cool. Sift half the flour over the mixture and fold in very lightly with a metal spoon. Sift and fold in the remaining flour, then lightly stir in the hot water.

Pour the mixture into the prepared tin. Bake in the oven at 220°C (425°F) mark 7 for 8–12 minutes until golden brown, well risen and firm to the touch. Meanwhile, place a sheet of greaseproof paper over a tea towel wrung out in hot water. Dredge the paper with caster sugar.

Quickly turn out the cake on to the paper, trim off the crusty edges with a sharp knife and roll up with the paper inside. Leave to cool on a wire rack. When cold, unroll the cake carefully, removing the paper. Spread a third of the crème au beurre over the surface and re-roll. Leave until firm. Coat with the remaining crème au beurre and mark lines with a fork to resemble tree bark. Chill before serving. Dust lightly with icing sugar and decorate with a sprig of real or artificial holly.

VARIATION

For a Marron Bûche, replace the crème au beurre filling with a 440-g (15½-oz) can of sweetened chestnut purée.

Reine de Saba (Gâteau au chocolat)

This chocolate gâteau is baked so that the centre remains slightly undercooked and deliciously moist.

10 ml (2 level tsp) instant coffee
100 g (4 oz) plain chocolate
100 g (4 oz) butter
100 g (4 oz) caster sugar
3 eggs, separated
75 g (3 oz) ground almonds
whipped cream to serve

For the icing and decoration
5 ml (1 level tsp) instant coffee
100 g (4 oz) plain chocolate
50 g (2 oz) butter
blanched almond halves, toasted

Grease and line a 23-cm (9-inch) diameter round cake tin. Dissolve the coffee in 30 ml (2 tbsp) hot water. Break up the chocolate and put it in a bowl with the coffee liquid and butter and place the bowl over a pan of hot water. Heat gently, stirring, until smooth, then remove from the heat.

Put the sugar and egg yolks in a bowl, stand this over a pan of hot water, and whisk until pale and thick. The mixture should be thick enough to leave a trail on the surface when the whisk is lifted. Stir the egg and sugar mixture into the melted chocolate, then lightly fold in the ground almonds with a metal spoon. Whisk the egg whites until stiff and carefully fold them into the mixture. Turn the mixture into the prepared tin and bake in the oven at 180°C (350°F) mark 4 for about 40 minutes until the outside is firm and the centre of the cake is still slightly creamy when tested with a skewer. Allow the cake to cool in the tin before turning out on to a wire rack.

When the cake is cool, prepare the icing. Dissolve the coffee in 15 ml (1 tbsp) hot water. Break up the chocolate and add it to the coffee liquid, stand the bowl over a pan of hot water and heat gently, stirring, until smooth. Remove from the heat and beat in the butter. Spread evenly on top of the cake. Leave in a cool place to set. Decorate with almonds and serve each slice with a spoonful of whipped cream.

Chocolate carnival cake

chocolate Genoese sponge baked in two 18-cm (7-inch) sandwich tins (*see page 38*)
100 g (4 oz) plain chocolate to make chocolate 'fins' (*see opposite*)
icing sugar to decorate

For the rich butter filling
100 g (4 oz) caster sugar
3 egg yolks
150 ml ($\frac{1}{4}$ pint) milk
225 g (8 oz) butter
50 g (2 oz) plain chocolate

For the filling, cream the sugar and egg yolks until thick and pale. Gently heat the milk, then add to the mixture. Return the mixture to the pan or to a double saucepan and cook over a low heat, stirring, until thick enough to coat the back of a wooden spoon, but do not boil. Leave to cool. Cream the butter until soft and gradually beat it into the cooled mixture. Break up the plain chocolate and put in a small bowl with 15 ml (1 tbsp) water. Stand the bowl over a pan of hot water and heat gently, stirring, until the chocolate has melted. Remove from the heat and leave to cool, then beat into the butter filling.

Sandwich the sponges together with some of the filling. Cover completely with more filling, then draw a serrated icing comb around the sides and fix the 'fins' in position (on their sides pointing to the centre) on top of the cake. Dredge with icing sugar.

Chocolate fins
Break up the plain chocolate and put it in a small bowl over a pan of hot water. Heat gently, stirring, until the chocolate has melted. Draw a 21.5-cm (8½-inch) circle on non-stick paper, spoon the chocolate into the centre and spread thinly just to cover the circle. When it is beginning to set, use a knife and an 18-cm (7-inch) cake tin to mark a circle. Trim the edges and mark the chocolate into twelve portions for 'fins'. Allow the chocolate to set completely before removing the 'fins' from the paper.

Making chocolate fins

Russian tipsy cake

25 g (1 oz) plain chocolate
3 eggs
115 g (4½ oz) caster sugar
75 g (3 oz) plain flour
pinch of salt

For the sugar syrup
30–45 ml (2–3 level tbsp) granulated
sugar
45 ml (3 tbsp) sherry

For the filling and decoration
300 ml (½ pint) double cream
a few drops of vanilla essence
chocolate triangles (*see page 164*)

Grease and line two 20.5-cm (8-inch) sandwich tins. Break the chocolate into pieces and put it in a bowl with 45 ml (3 tbsp) water. Stand the bowl over a pan of hot water and heat gently, stirring, until the chocolate has melted. Remove the bowl from the heat and leave the chocolate to cool.

Put the eggs and sugar together into a bowl, stand this over a pan of hot water and whisk until pale and thick. The mixture should be thick enough to leave a trail when the whisk is lifted from the surface. Remove the bowl from the heat and continue whisking until cool. Sift the flour and salt into the bowl and fold in carefully with a metal spoon. Spoon half the mixture into another bowl and stir in the melted chocolate.

Using a large spoon, put alternate spoonfuls of the two mixtures into the prepared tins. Swirl a knife through the mixture in each tin to give a marbled effect and bake in the oven at 190°C (375°F) mark 5 for 25–30 minutes or until risen and firm to the touch. Turn out and leave to cool on a wire rack.

To make the sugar syrup, put the sugar in a pan with 60 ml (4 tbsp) water and heat gently to dissolve the sugar. Bring to the boil and boil for 2–3 minutes. Remove from the heat, stir in the sherry and leave to cool. Split both cooled cakes in two and spoon the syrup over the layers. Whisk the cream until stiff and whisk in a little vanilla essence. Sandwich the sponge layers together with two thirds of the cream and spoon the remainder into a piping bag fitted with a large star nozzle. Pipe rosettes of cream round the top of the cake and finish with chocolate triangles.

Chocolate and coffee gâteau

Illustrated in colour on page 29

6 eggs
175 g (6 oz) caster sugar
15 ml (1 tbsp) coffee essence
25 g (1 oz) cocoa powder
100 g (4 oz) plain flour
25 g (1 oz) cornflour
25 g (1 oz) ground almonds
75 g (3 oz) butter

For the filling and decoration
treble quantity coffee butter cream (*see*
page 170)
75 g (3 oz) walnuts, chopped
50 g (2 oz) plain chocolate to make
'cobwebs'
sugar coffee beans

Grease and line two 24-cm (9½-inch) diameter sandwich tins. Put the eggs and sugar in a bowl, stand this over a pan of hot water and whisk until thick and creamy. The mixture should be thick enough to leave a trail on the surface when the whisk is lifted. Whisk in the coffee essence. Remove the bowl from the heat and continue whisking until cool.

Sift together the cocoa, flour, cornflour and almonds and carefully fold half into the egg and sugar mixture, using a metal spoon. Put the butter in a saucepan and heat gently until just melted, but not oily, and add to the mixture, pouring it round the side and folding it in alternately with the remaining dry ingredients. Spoon the mixture into the prepared tins, tilting the tins to level the surface, and bake in the oven at 190°C (375°F) mark 5 for about 30 minutes until risen and firm to the touch. Turn out and leave to cool on a wire rack.

Use some of the coffee butter cream to sandwich the cakes together and spread some on the sides of the cake. Spread the chopped walnuts on a piece of greaseproof paper, lift the cake and roll the sides in the nuts to coat the butter cream. Top the cake with more butter cream and spoon the remainder into a piping bag. Decorate the cake with piped butter cream, chocolate 'cobwebs' (*see below*) and sugar coffee beans. Keep the cake in a cool place until the icing is firm.
Serves 8–10

Chocolate 'cobwebs'

To make the chocolate 'cobwebs', break up the chocolate and put it in a bowl standing over a pan of hot water. Heat gently, stirring, until the chocolate has melted. Pour the chocolate into a grease-proof paper piping bag (*see page 165*) fitted with a small plain nozzle. On non-stick paper, trace in pencil round a medium, 9.5-cm (3¼-inch), boat-shaped cutter. Pipe chocolate round the outline and fill in with a wiggly, continuous trellis-work to make

a cobweb design. Continue making 'cobwebs' in this way until all the melted chocolate has been used. Chill until set, then peel away the paper. The cobwebs can be made a few days ahead and stored in an airtight tin in a cool place.

Frosted walnut cake

25 g (1 oz) butter
3 eggs
75 g (3 oz) caster sugar
50 g (2 oz) self raising flour
25 g (1 oz) cornflour
40 g (1½ oz) walnuts, chopped
2.5 ml (½ tsp) vanilla essence
double quantity seven-minute frosting (*see page 172*)
walnut halves to decorate

Grease and line an 18-cm (7-inch) round cake tin. Melt the butter and leave to stand for a few minutes. Put the eggs and sugar in a large bowl, stand this over a saucepan of hot water and whisk until pale and creamy. Remove the egg mixture from the heat and whisk again until cool. Sift the flour and cornflour into the bowl and fold into the mixture alternately with the melted butter, using a metal spoon. Add the nuts and vanilla essence. Pour into the prepared tin and level the surface. Bake in the oven at 180°C (350°F) mark 4 for about 45 minutes until golden brown and springy to the touch. Turn out and leave to cool on a wire rack.

When the cake is cool, split it in half. Make the seven-minute frosting and, working quickly, spread a little on one half of the cake and sandwich the two halves together. Stand the cake on a wire rack with a plate beneath it and pour the remaining icing over the cake. Using a palette knife, quickly smooth it evenly over the cake in a 'whirled' pattern. Decorate the top of the cake with walnut halves before the icing sets.

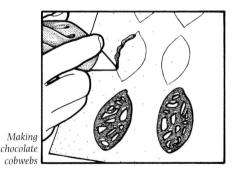

Making chocolate cobwebs

Nusstorte

This is made in a similar way to a whisked sponge but fine breadcrumbs and nuts are used instead of flour. A mixture of nuts can be used, as in this recipe.

7 eggs, separated
150 g (5 oz) caster sugar
a few drops of vanilla essence
50 g (2 oz) fine dry white breadcrumbs
75 g (3 oz) mixed walnuts and toasted
**   almonds, finely chopped**
walnut halves to decorate

For the chocolate icing
50 g (2 oz) plain chocolate
3 eggs, beaten
175 g (6 oz) caster sugar
a few drops of vanilla essence

Grease and line three 20.5-cm (8-inch) sandwich tins. Put the egg yolks with the sugar in a bowl, stand this over a pan of hot water, and whisk until thick and creamy. The mixture should be thick enough to leave a trail when the whisk is lifted. Remove from the heat.

Whisk the egg whites stiffly. Add the vanilla essence to the egg yolks and sugar. Mix together the breadcrumbs and chopped nuts and fold carefully into the egg yolk mixture with a metal spoon, followed by the egg whites. Turn the mixture into the prepared tins. Bake in the oven at 180°C (350°F) mark 4 for about 25 minutes until firm and lightly browned. Allow the cakes to cool in the tins before carefully turning them out.

For the icing, break up the chocolate and put it in a small bowl over a pan of hot water. Heat gently, stirring, until the chocolate has melted, then remove from the heat and leave until cool but still soft. Put the eggs and sugar into a double saucepan and heat, stirring, until the mixture thickens, taking great care not to overheat or it will curdle. Remove the pan from the heat and stir in the melted chocolate and vanilla essence. Beat until thick, then allow to cool. Use the icing to sandwich the three cakes together, reserving some to spread on top. Decorate with walnut halves.

Mocha roulade

15 ml (1 level tbsp) instant coffee powder
100 g (4 oz) plain chocolate
4 eggs, size 2, separated
100 g (4 oz) caster sugar
300 ml ($\frac{1}{2}$ pint) double cream
175 g (6 oz) white grapes, halved and
**   seeded**

Put the coffee in a small bowl with 15 ml (1 tbsp) water and blend to a smooth paste. Break up the chocolate, add to the coffee, stand the bowl over a pan of hot water and heat gently, stirring, until the chocolate has melted. Remove the bowl from the heat and leave to cool slightly.

Cut a 30.5-cm (12-inch) square of non-stick (silicone) paper and fold up 2.5 cm (1 inch) all round the edge. Snip into the corners and secure with paperclips to form a free-standing paper case. Place on a baking sheet.

Put the egg yolks and sugar in a bowl, stand the bowl over a pan of hot water and whisk together until pale and thick. Remove from the heat and stir in the coffee and chocolate. Whisk the egg whites until stiff and fold carefully into the mixture with a metal spoon. Pour the mixture into the paper case and tilt the baking sheet to spread it evenly. Bake in the oven at 180°C (350°F) mark 4 for about 15 minutes until firm. Cover with a damp tea towel, to prevent a sugary crust forming, and leave overnight.

Remove the towel and flip the roulade over on to a sheet of sugared greaseproof paper. Whisk the cream until stiff and mix half with two thirds of the grapes, reserving the remainder for decoration.

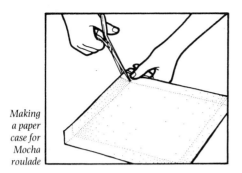

Making a paper case for Mocha roulade

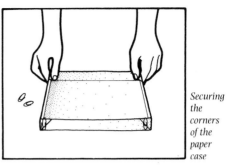

Securing the corners of the paper case

Spread the cream and grape mixture over the roulade and roll it up with the help of the greaseproof paper. Spoon the remaining cream into a piping bag fitted with a large star nozzle and pipe whirls of cream down the centre of the roulade. Arrange the grape halves on top.

Gâteau caraque

100 g (4 oz) caster sugar
4 eggs, size 2
100 g (4 oz) plain flour

For the filling and decoration
apricot glaze (*see page 176*)
A quantity chocolate crème au beurre (*see page 171*)
grated chocolate
chocolate caraque (*see page 164*)
icing sugar

Grease and line two 30.5×11-cm (12 × 4½-inch) shallow oblong tins. Put the sugar and eggs in a large bowl, stand this over a pan of hot water and whisk until really thick and creamy. The whisk should leave a trail when lifted from the mixture. Remove from the heat, sift the flour over the mixture and fold in carefully with a metal spoon. Divide between the two prepared tins, tilting the tins to spread the mixture evenly. Bake in the oven at 220°C (425°F) mark 7 for about 25 minutes until well risen and golden brown. Turn out and leave to cool on a wire rack.

Sandwich the sponges together with

apricot glaze. Spread the chocolate crème au beurre round the sides and roll in coarsely grated chocolate. Brush the top of the cake with apricot glaze.

Arrange the chocolate caraque pieces side by side over the apricot glaze on top of the cake and dredge with icing sugar.

Gâteau Bigarreau

Illustrated in colour on page 39

45 ml (3 level tbsp) apricot jam
45 ml (3 level tbsp) redcurrant jelly
300 ml (½ pint) double cream
1 quantity praline (*see page 176*)
1 whisked sponge cake (*see page 36*)
450 g (1 lb) fresh cherries, washed

Strain the jam and jelly into a pan and add 15–30 ml (1–2 tbsp) water. Simmer gently until smooth, then leave to cool. Whip the cream until stiff. Spoon half the whipped cream into a piping bag fitted with a large star nozzle. Into the remaining cream, fold 30 ml (2 tbsp) of the praline. Sprinkle the remaining praline on to a sheet of greaseproof paper. Brush the sides of the two cake halves with some of the jam and jelly glaze and then roll the sides in the praline. Sandwich the cakes together with the praline cream and brush the top with glaze. Stone the cherries, if liked, then arrange them on top of the cake to cover completely. Brush the cherries with the remaining glaze, and pipe the reserved cream around the top edge of the gâteau to decorate.

Mandarin gâteau

312-g (11-oz) can mandarins, drained
grated rind of $\frac{1}{2}$ an orange
10 ml (2 tsp) kirsch or curaçau
1 quantity continental butter cream
   (*see page 171*)
Genoese sponge baked in two 20.5-cm
   (8-inch) sandwich tins (*see page 38*)
50 g (2 oz) nibbed almonds, toasted
icing sugar to decorate

Reserve eight mandarin oranges for decoration and roughly chop the remainder. Add the orange rind and liqueur to the butter cream and mix well. Stir the chopped mandarins into half the butter cream and use to sandwich the sponges. Spread a quarter of the remaining butter cream around the sides of the cake. Press the nuts around the sides. Spread another quarter of the butter cream on top of the cake. Dust the top with icing sugar. With a piping bag fitted with a star nozzle, pipe eight rosettes, using the remaining butter cream, on top. Arrange the reserved mandarins on top of the rosettes.

Coffee almond layer

Illustrated in colour on page 123

5 eggs, size 2
30 ml (2 tbsp) coffee essence
150 g (5 oz) caster sugar
100 g (4 oz) plain flour
25 g (1 oz) cornflour

For the butter cream
225 g (8 oz) unsalted butter
30 ml (2 tbsp) dark rum
275 g (10 oz) icing sugar

For the decoration
100 g (4 oz) flaked almonds, toasted
icing sugar
instant coffee powder

Grease and line two 21.5-cm (8½-inch) sandwich tins. Put the eggs, coffee essence and sugar in a deep bowl, stand this over a pan of hot, but not boiling, water and whisk until pale and really thick. Remove from the heat and cool. Sift the flours together and then re-sift into the egg mixture. Using a metal spoon, fold the flour in carefully. Spoon the mixture equally into the prepared tins and level the surface. Bake in the oven at 190°C (375°F) mark 5 for about 25 minutes until risen, golden and firm to the touch. Leave in the tins for about 5 minutes, then turn out the sponges and leave them to cool on a wire rack.

To make the butter cream, cream the butter and gradually beat in the rum and sifted icing sugar. Sandwich the coffee sponges together with some of the butter cream and use the rest to coat the cake completely.

To decorate, press toasted almonds into the butter cream and dredge with icing sugar. Cover the top with a piece of paper with a 7.5-cm (3-inch) circle cut from the centre. Sift instant coffee over the hole and carefully remove the paper.
Serves 12

Cream filled cinnamon roll

Illustrated in colour on page 40

3 eggs
100 g (4 oz) caster sugar
100 g (4 oz) plain flour
5 ml (1 level tsp) ground cinnamon
15 ml (1 tbsp) hot water
150 ml ($\frac{1}{4}$ pint) double cream
icing sugar

Grease and line a 33.5 × 23-cm ($13\frac{1}{4}$ × $9\frac{1}{4}$-inch) Swiss roll tin. Put the eggs and sugar in a large bowl, stand this over a pan of hot water and whisk until thick and creamy in colour. The mixture should be stiff enough to leave a trail on the surface when the whisk is lifted. Remove from the heat and whisk until cool. Sift half the flour and cinnamon over the mixture and fold in very lightly using a metal spoon. Sift and fold in the remaining flour, then lightly stir in the hot water. Pour the mixture into the prepared tin. Bake in the oven at 220°C (425°F) mark 7 for 7–9 minutes until golden brown and firm to the touch.

Meanwhile, place a sheet of greaseproof paper over a tea towel lightly wrung out in hot water. Dredge the paper thickly with caster sugar. Quickly turn out the cake and trim the crusty edges with a sharp knife. Roll up with the aid of the greaseproof paper. Leave to cool.

Whisk the cream until it just holds its shape. Gently unroll the cinnamon roll and spread the cream over and up to the edges. Roll up again.

Liberally dust with sifted icing sugar. Mark criss-crosses on the icing sugar with a very hot skewer. This cinnamon roll should be eaten the day it is made.

Redcurrant griestorte

3 eggs, size 2, separated
100 g (4 oz) caster sugar
grated rind and juice of $\frac{1}{2}$ a lemon
50 g (2 oz) fine semolina
15 ml (1 level tbsp) ground almonds
150 ml ($\frac{1}{4}$ pint) double cream
15 ml (1 tbsp) milk
100 g (4 oz) redcurrants
sifted icing sugar to decorate

Grease and line a 20.5×30.5-cm (8× 12-inch) Swiss roll tin with non-stick paper to extend above the sides. Grease the paper and sprinkle with a little caster sugar and a dusting of flour.

Put the egg yolks and sugar together in a bowl standing over a pan of hot water, and whisk until thick and pale, then remove from the heat. Whisk in the lemon juice and stir in the rind, semolina and almonds. Whisk the egg whites until stiff and fold into the mixture with a metal spoon. Turn the mixture into the prepared tin and level the surface. Bake in the oven at 180°C (350°F) mark 4 for about 30 minutes until risen and golden brown.

Turn the griestorte carefully on to a sheet of non-stick paper dusted with caster sugar. Trim the edges, roll up loosely with the sugared non-stick paper inside and leave to cool on a wire rack.

Whisk the cream and milk together until it just holds its shape. Unroll the griestorte, remove the paper, and spread over the cream leaving a gap around the edges. String the redcurrants, reserving a few on the stem for decoration, and sprinkle over the cream. Roll up, pressing gently into shape. Sprinkle with icing sugar and decorate with the reserved redcurrants. Eat on the day of making.

Gâteau Cendrillon

1 large quantity Genoese sponge mixture
 (*see page 38*)
15 ml (1 tbsp) coffee essence
1 quantity coffee crème au beurre (*see page 171*)
$\frac{1}{2}$ quantity apricot glaze (*see page 176*)
1 quantity coffee fondant icing (*see page 173*)
a few flaked almonds, toasted, to decorate

To the basic recipe for Genoese sponge, add the coffee essence at the whisking stage. Bake in the usual way, split the sponge when cold and sandwich with two thirds of the coffee crème au beurre. Brush with apricot glaze, coat the whole cake with fondant icing and leave to set.

Spoon the remaining crème au beurre into a piping bag fitted with a large star nozzle and decorate the top of the cake with whirls of crème au beurre, topped with flaked almonds.

Mocha refrigerator cake

Illustrated in colour on page 167

**chocolate Genoese sponge baked in one
    18-cm (7-inch) cake tin (*see page 38*)
15 ml (1 level tbsp) instant coffee
240 ml (8½ fl oz) boiling water
60 ml (4 tbsp) coffee flavoured liqueur
50 g (2 oz) butter
75 g (3 oz) icing sugar
50 g (2 oz) ground almonds
25 g (1 oz) cocoa powder
300 ml (½ pint) double cream
50 g (2 oz) flaked almonds, toasted
chocolate circles to decorate (*see page 164*)**

Cut the cake into three layers. Place a circle of greaseproof paper in the bottom of an 18-cm (7-inch) cake tin and put a layer of cake on top. Dissolve the coffee in the boiling water. Reserve 30 ml (2 tbsp) coffee and 15 ml (1 tbsp) coffee liqueur and mix together the remaining coffee and liqueur. Pour one third of this mixture over the sponge layer in the tin.

Cream together the butter, icing sugar, ground almonds, cocoa and the reserved coffee and liqueur. Spread half the chocolate filling over the sponge and cover with the second layer of sponge. Pour over another third of the coffee mixture and spread with the remaining chocolate filling. Top with the final sponge layer and pour over the remaining coffee mixture. Cover with greaseproof paper and a plate with a weight on top and chill for at least 2 hours in the refrigerator before turning out the cake.

Whisk the cream until stiff and spread it over the sides and top of the cake in a thin layer, reserving a little for decoration. Press the flaked almonds around the sides. Fill a piping bag fitted with a large star nozzle with the remaining cream and pipe whirls on the top of the cake. Decorate with chocolate circles.

Glazed pineapple gâteau

**1 large quantity Genoese sponge mixture
    (*see page 38*)**

For the filling
**300 ml (½ pint) double cream
175 g (6 oz) apricot glaze (*see page 176*)**

For the decoration
**226-g (8-oz) can pineapple slices
30 ml (2 level tbsp) caster sugar
6 glacé cherries
flaked almonds
50 g (2 oz) icing sugar, sifted
lemon juice**

Grease and line two 30.5 × 11.5-cm (12 × 4½-inch) shallow oblong tins. Make up the sponge mixture and divide it between the prepared tins. Bake in the oven at 190°C (375°F) mark 5 for about 20 minutes. Turn out and leave to cool on a wire rack.

To decorate, whip the cream until stiff and sandwich the sponges together with a little apricot glaze and the cream. Brush the sides and top with more apricot glaze. Drain the pineapple slices. In a pan, dissolve the sugar in the pineapple juice without boiling, then bring to the boil. Add the pineapple slices and slowly simmer for 20–25 minutes, until the fruit is clear and the juice almost completely reduced. Leave until cold. Arrange the pineapple slices on top of the cake, with a cherry in the centre of each, and sprinkle with flaked almonds. Coat the top of the cake with a thin lemon glacé icing made by beating the sifted icing sugar with a little lemon juice. The icing should be thick enough to just coat the back of a spoon.

BUTTER-RICH CAKES

Cakes which contain half or more fat in proportion to flour are especially rich-tasting and moist. They are firm enough to be cut into fancy shapes and take well to icing, so are ideal for children's party cakes and small iced cakes.

Rich cakes are made by the creaming method. The fat and sugar are beaten together until as pale and fluffy as whipped cream, the eggs are beaten in and the flour is then folded in. In some recipes the egg whites are whisked separately and folded in with the flour.

You need a mixing bowl large enough to accommodate vigorous beating without any danger of the ingredients overflowing. If beating by hand, use a wooden spoon and warm the bowl first to make the process easier. Scrape the mixture down from the sides of the bowl from time to time to ensure no sugar crystals are left. An electric mixer is a time and labour-saving alternative to creaming by hand, but remember it cannot be used for incorporating the flour.

Use eggs at room temperature and beat thoroughly after each addition to reduce the risk of the mixture curdling. (A mixture that curdles holds less air and produces a heavy, dense cake.) As an extra precaution against the mixture curdling, add a spoonful of the sifted flour with the second and every following addition of egg and beat thoroughly. To keep the mixture light, fold in the remaining flour gradually, using a metal spoon.

Victoria sandwich

100 g (4 oz) butter or margarine
100 g (4 oz) caster sugar
2 eggs, beaten
100 g (4 oz) self raising flour
caster sugar to dredge

For the filling
60 ml (4 tbsp) jam *or*
150 ml ($\frac{1}{4}$ pint) double cream, whipped *or*
$\frac{1}{2}$ quantity butter cream (*see page 170*)

Grease two 18-cm (7-inch) sandwich tins and line the base of each with greased greaseproof paper. Put the fat and sugar into a warmed mixing bowl and cream together with a wooden spoon until pale and fluffy. Scrape the mixture down from the sides of the bowl during creaming from time to time to ensure that no sugar crystals are left.

Add the egg a little at a time, beating well after each addition. Gradually sift the flour on to the mixture and fold it in as quickly and lightly as possible using a metal spoon.

Place half the mixture in each of the prepared sandwich tins.

Lightly smooth the surface of the mixture in the tins with a palette knife to ensure an even surface when cooked. Bake both cakes on the same shelf in the oven at 190°C (375°F) mark 5 for about 20 minutes until they are well risen, golden, firm to the touch and beginning to shrink away from the sides of the tins.

Turn out and leave the sponges to cool on a wire rack, then sandwich them together with jam, whipped cream or butter cream and sprinkle the top with caster sugar.

Chocolate sandwich Replace 45 ml (3 level tbsp) flour with 45 ml (3 level tbsp) cocoa powder. For a more moist cake, blend the cocoa with a little water to give a thick paste and beat it into the creamed ingredients with the egg. Use vanilla or chocolate butter cream (*see page 170*) as filling.

Coffee sandwich Dissolve 10 ml (2 level tsp) instant coffee in a little water and add it to the creamed mixture with the egg, or use 10 ml (2 tsp) coffee essence. Use coffee butter cream (*see page 170*) as filling.

Orange or lemon sandwich Add the finely grated rind of one orange or one lemon to the mixture and use orange or lemon curd or orange or lemon butter cream (*see page 170*) as filling. Use some of the juice from the orange or lemon to make glacé icing (*see page 171*).

Cup cakes Divide the mixture between 18 paper cases and bake as above. If liked, fold 50 g (2 oz) chocolate polka dots, sultanas, raisins, chopped walnuts or glacé cherries into the mixture with the flour. When cold, top each cup cake with a little glacé icing made with 350 g (12 oz) icing sugar (*see page 171*).

Madeira cake

100 g (4 oz) plain flour
100 g (4 oz) self raising flour
175 g (6 oz) butter
175 g (6 oz) caster sugar
5 ml (1 tsp) vanilla essence
3 eggs, beaten
15–30 ml (1–2 tbsp) milk
2–3 thin slices citron peel

Grease and line an 18-cm (7-inch) round cake tin. Sift the flours together. Cream the butter and sugar together until pale and fluffy, then beat in the vanilla essence. Add the egg a little at a time, beating well after each addition. Fold in the sifted flour with a metal spoon, adding a little milk if necessary to give a dropping consistency.

Turn the mixture into the prepared tin and bake in the oven at 180°C (350°F) mark 4 for 20 minutes. Lay the citron peel on top of the cake, return it to the oven and bake for a further 40 minutes until firm to the touch. Turn out and leave to cool on a wire rack.

VARIATIONS

For an orange madeira cake, beat in the grated rind of 2 oranges before adding the eggs.

For a more unusual shaped cake, turn the mixture into a well greased 1.7-litre (3-pint) fancy kugelhupf mould and bake as above.

Apple cake

350 g (12 oz) self raising flour
2.5 ml ($\frac{1}{2}$ level tsp) salt
5 ml (1 level tsp) ground cinnamon
2.5 ml ($\frac{1}{2}$ level tsp) ground nutmeg
2.5 ml ($\frac{1}{2}$ level tsp) ground cloves
5 ml (1 level tsp) bicarbonate of soda
400 ml ($\frac{3}{4}$ pint) apple purée
100 g (4 oz) butter or margarine
175 g (6 oz) light brown soft sugar
1 egg, separated
100 g (4 oz) seedless raisins

Grease and line a 20.5-cm (8-inch) round cake tin. Sift together the flour, salt and spices. Add the bicarbonate of soda to the apple purée and stir until dissolved. Cream the fat and sugar together until pale and fluffy, then beat in the egg yolk. Fold in the flour and apple purée alternately, then stir in the raisins. Whisk the egg white until stiff, and fold in with a metal spoon. Turn the mixture into the prepared tin. Bake in the oven at 180°C (350°F) mark 4 for about 1–1$\frac{1}{2}$ hours until firm to the touch. Turn out and leave to cool on a wire rack.

Marble cake

175 g (6 oz) butter or margarine
175 g (6 oz) caster sugar
2 eggs, size 2, beaten
175 g (6 oz) self raising flour
milk to mix
25 g (1 oz) cocoa powder
$\frac{1}{2}$ quantity chocolate butter cream (*see page 170*)

Grease and line a 20.5-cm (8-inch) round cake tin. Cream the fat and sugar together until pale and fluffy. Add the egg a little at a time, beating well after each addition. Gradually sift the flour over the mixture and fold in lightly with a metal spoon, adding a little milk to give a soft dropping consistency. Place half the mixture in a separate bowl and sift and fold in the cocoa powder.

Put large spoonfuls of plain and chocolate mixture alternately into the prepared tin. Lightly swirl through the mixture with a knife to give a marbled effect and level the surface. Bake in the oven at 180°C (350°F) mark 4 for 1–1$\frac{1}{4}$ hours until well risen and firm to the touch. Turn out and leave to cool on a wire rack. To finish, spread the chocolate butter cream over the top of the cake.

Clock birthday cake

Marble cake baked in one 20.5-cm (8-inch) tin (*see above*)
$\frac{1}{2}$ quantity chocolate butter cream (*see page 170*)
double quantity glacé icing (*see page 171*)
20 ml (4 level tsp) cocoa powder
225 g (8 oz) almond paste (*see page 175*)
edible flower decorations
candles

Slice the cake in half and sandwich together with the butter cream. Place on a wire rack over a plate, coat completely with glacé icing and leave to set.

Clock birthday cake

Knead the cocoa powder into the almond paste to make chocolate coloured paste. Roll out the almond paste and, using animal cutters, cut out shapes to represent rabbits or other animals as liked. Arrange the shapes around the side of the cake. Between them, put the edible flower decorations. Knead and roll out the almond paste trimmings and cut out the numerals and place them round the top edge of the cake to make the clock face. Cut out almond paste clock hands and set them to show the child's age. Place the correct number of candles round the appropriate numeral on the clock face or round the top edge of the cake.

Battenberg cake

175 g (6 oz) butter or margarine
175 g (6 oz) caster sugar
a few drops of vanilla essence
3 eggs, beaten
175 g (6 oz) self raising flour
30 ml (2 level tbsp) cocoa powder
a little milk to mix, if necessary
225 g (8 oz) almond paste (*see page 175*)
caster sugar to dredge
225 g (8 oz) apricot jam, melted

Grease and line a 30×20.5-cm (12×8-inch) Swiss roll tin and divide it lengthways with a 'wall' of greaseproof paper. Cream the fat and sugar together until pale and fluffy, then beat in the vanilla essence. Add the egg a little at a time,

Coffee flavoured Battenberg cake (*above and page 59*)

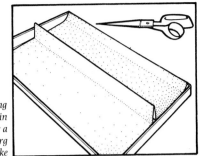

Preparing the tin for a Battenberg cake

Covering a Battenberg cake with almond paste

beating well after each addition. Gradually sift the flour over the mixture and fold it in lightly with a metal spoon.

Turn half the mixture into one side of the tin and level the surface. Sift the cocoa over the other half and fold in with a metal spoon, adding a little milk if necessary to give a dropping consistency. Turn the chocolate mixture into the tin and level the surface. Bake in the oven at 190°C (375°F) mark 5 for 40–45 minutes until well risen and firm to the touch. Turn out and leave to cool on a wire rack.

When the cakes are cold, trim them to an equal size and cut each in half length-ways. On a working surface sprinkled with caster sugar, roll out the almond paste to a 30-cm (12-inch) square. Place one strip of cake on the almond paste so that it lies up against the edge of the paste. Place an alternate coloured strip of cake next to it. Brush the top and sides of the cake with melted jam and layer up with alternate coloured strips. Press well together. Coat the top and sides of the cake with jam.

Bring the almond paste up and over the cake to cover it. Press the paste firmly on to the cake, then seal and trim the join. Place the cake seam-side down and trim both ends with a sharp knife. Crimp the top edges of the paste with the thumb and forefinger and mark the top in a criss-cross pattern with a knife. To finish, dredge lightly with caster sugar.

VARIATION

Illustrated in colour on page 57

For a coffee flavoured battenberg, use 20 ml (4 tbsp) coffee essence and 15 ml (1 tbsp) milk instead of cocoa. Replace the apricot jam with ginger marmalade and decorate the cake with pieces of crystallised ginger.

Ginger whirls

Illustrated in colour on page 18

225 g (8 oz) butter or margarine
75 g (3 oz) icing sugar
200 g (7 oz) plain flour
25 g (1 oz) cornflour
10 ml (2 level tsp) ground ginger
30 ml (2 tbsp) ginger marmalade
stem ginger (optional)

Arrange twelve paper cases in patty tins. Cream the fat until soft, then sift in the icing sugar and cream together until pale and fluffy. Sift together the flour, cornflour and ground ginger and fold into the mixture. Spoon the mixture into a piping bag fitted with a large star nozzle and pipe a whirl into each paper case. Bake in the oven at 190°C (375°F) mark 5 for 15–20 minutes until golden brown. Leave to cool on a wire rack. Fill the centre of each whirl with a little ginger marmalade and top with a sliver of stem ginger (if used).
Makes 12

Clockwise from top right: Raisin streusel cake (*page 67*), Caraway cobbler ring cake (*page 63*), Poppy seed yeast cake (*page 142*), Swedish cardamom cake (*page 92*)

Chocolate fudge cake

225 g (8 oz) plain flour
30 ml (2 level tbsp) cocoa powder
5 ml (1 level tsp) baking powder
2.5 ml ($\frac{1}{2}$ level tsp) bicarbonate of soda
large pinch of salt
50 g (2 oz) plain chocolate
100 g (4 oz) butter or margarine
175 g (6 oz) light brown soft sugar
1 egg, size 2
150 ml ($\frac{1}{4}$ pint) natural yogurt
2.5 ml ($\frac{1}{2}$ tsp) vanilla essence
$\frac{1}{2}$ quantity chocolate butter cream (*see
    page 170*)
25 g (1 oz) walnuts, chopped, to decorate

For the chocolate frosting
75 g (3 oz) butter, softened
150 g (5 oz) icing sugar
30 ml (2 level tbsp) cocoa powder
50 g (2 oz) plain chocolate

Grease and line a 28 × 18-cm (11 × 7-inch) tin, leaving 2.5 cm (1 inch) paper above the edge of the tin. Sift together the flour, cocoa, baking powder, bicarbonate of soda and salt. Break up the chocolate and put it in a bowl with 30 ml (2 tbsp) water. Place over a saucepan of hot water and heat gently, stirring, until the chocolate has melted. Leave to cool.

Cream the fat and sugar together until light and fluffy. Beat in the egg, then fold in the chocolate, the dry ingredients, the yogurt and vanilla essence. Turn the mixture into the prepared tin and level the surface. Bake in the oven at 190°C (375°F) mark 5 for 1 hour until risen and firm to the touch. Turn out and leave to cool on a wire rack.

When cold, split the cake in two and sandwich together with the chocolate butter cream.

To make the chocolate frosting, cream the butter, sift in the icing sugar and cocoa powder and cream again. Melt the chocolate in a small bowl over a pan of hot water, leave to cool, then beat into the creamed mixture. Smooth the frosting over the top of the cake and decorate with chopped walnuts.

Orange seed cake

100 g (4 oz) butter or margarine
100 g (4 oz) caster sugar
grated rind and juice of 1 orange
2 eggs, separated
175 g (6 oz) self raising flour
5 ml (1 level tsp) caraway seeds

Grease and line an 18-cm (7-inch) straight sided sandwich tin. Cream the fat, sugar and finely grated orange rind until pale and fluffy. Beat in the egg yolks, one at a time, keeping the mixture stiff. Stir in the flour with the caraway seeds and 60 ml (4 tbsp) orange juice. Lastly, stiffly whisk the egg whites and fold into the mixture. Turn into the prepared tin. Bake in the oven at 190°C (375°F) mark 5 for about 30 minutes or until golden brown and firm to the touch. This cake should rise slightly in the centre. Turn out and leave to cool on a wire rack.

Tipsy hedgehog cake

This is an eighteenth-century recipe which, although it looks fun, is rather sophisticated.

175 g (6 oz) butter or margarine
250 g (9 oz) caster sugar
3 eggs, beaten
175 g (6 oz) self raising flour
apricot jam
150 ml ($\frac{1}{4}$ pint) sweet sherry, marsala or
    madeira
600 ml (1 pint) double cream
juice of 2 oranges
175 g (6 oz) blanched almonds
a few seedless raisins

Grease and line a 20.5-cm (8-inch) round cake tin. Cream the fat and 175 g (6 oz) sugar together until pale and fluffy. Add

Cut a curved portion from the sponge

Cut the portion into three sections

Arrange the cake pieces on a plate

Tipsy hedgehog cake

the egg, a little at a time, beating well after each addition. Sift the flour over the mixture and fold in lightly with a metal spoon. Turn the mixture into the prepared tin and bake in the oven at 190°C (375°F) mark 5 for about 40 minutes until well risen, golden and firm to the touch. Turn out and leave to cool on a wire rack.

Place the cold cake on a wooden board or level working surface and cut as shown in the drawings. Arrange the pieces on a serving plate as shown and stick them together with apricot jam. Pour over the sherry and leave to soak for about 2 hours.

Whisk the cream and remaining sugar together until thick, then whisk in the orange juice. Pile on to the cake and spread over the cake to cover it completely, mounding the cream to emphasise the 'hedgehog' shape. Cut the almonds into slivers and toast under a hot grill until golden brown. Allow to cool, then stick into the cream to represent spines. Use raisins to make the eyes, nose and feet.

Madeleines

1 quantity Victoria sandwich mixture (*see page 54*)
30 ml (2 level tbsp) red jam, sieved and melted
50 g (2 oz) desiccated coconut
5 glacé cherries, halved
angelica

Grease ten dariole moulds. Divide the cake mixture between the moulds filling them three-quarters full. Bake in the oven at 180°C (350°F) mark 4 for about 20 minutes until well risen and firm to the touch. Turn out and leave to cool on a wire rack.

When the cakes are almost cold, trim the bases so they stand firmly and are the same height. Spear each one on a skewer, brush with melted jam, then roll them in desiccated coconut to coat. Top each madeleine with half a glacé cherry and small pieces of angelica.
Makes 10

Rüeblitorte (Carrot cake)

Many cantons in Switzerland have their own favourite cakes, this one is the speciality of Aargu.

225 g (8 oz) butter
225 g (8 oz) caster sugar
4 eggs, beaten
225 g (8 oz) self raising flour
grated rind and juice of 1 lemon
15 ml (1 tbsp) kirsch
225 g (8 oz) carrots, peeled and grated
100 g (4 oz) ground almonds

For the decoration
225 g (8 oz) icing sugar
75 g (3 oz) almond paste (*see page 175*)
orange food colouring
angelica

Grease and line a 20.5-cm (8-inch) round cake tin. Cream the butter and caster sugar together until pale and fluffy. Add the egg a little at a time, beating well after each addition. Sift the flour over the mixture and fold it in with the lemon rind and juice, reserving 10 ml (2 tsp) juice. Stir in the kirsch, grated carrot and ground almonds. Spoon the mixture into the prepared tin and level the surface. Bake in the oven at 180°C (350°F) mark 4 for $1\frac{1}{2}$ hours until well risen and golden brown. After $1\frac{1}{4}$ hours, cover with foil to prevent over-browning. The cake is cooked when a skewer, inserted in the centre, comes out clean. Turn out and leave to cool on a wire rack. Preferably, keep the cake until the following day before icing and serving.

Sift the icing sugar into a bowl and add the reserved lemon juice and about 15 ml (1 tbsp) warm water. The icing should be thick enough to coat the back of a spoon. Spread on top of the cake. Colour the almond paste orange and shape into small carrots, make angelica 'carrot tops' and arrange on top of the cake.

Butterfly cakes

Illustrated in colour on page 168

100 g (4 oz) butter or margarine
100 g (4 oz) caster sugar
2 eggs, beaten
175 g (6 oz) self raising flour
icing sugar to decorate

For the filling
100 g (4 oz) butter or margarine
175 g (6 oz) icing sugar
a few drops of almond essence

Arrange twelve paper cases in patty tins. Cream the fat and sugar together until pale and fluffy. Add the egg a little at a time, beating well after each addition. Sift the flour over the mixture and fold in lightly with a metal spoon. The mixture should have a stiff dropping consistency. Divide the mixture equally between the paper cases and bake in the oven at 190°C (375°F) mark 5 for 15–20 minutes until well risen and firm to the touch. Leave to cool on a wire rack.

To make the filling, cream the fat until soft, then gradually sift and beat in the icing sugar. Beat in the almond essence. Cut a slice from the top of each cold cake and pipe or fork a generous amount of filling over the surface. Cut each slice of cake in half, then replace at an angle in the filling to resemble butterflies' wings. Sprinkle with sifted icing sugar.
Makes 12

VARIATIONS

1 For chocolate butterfly cakes, dissolve 15 ml (1 level tbsp) cocoa powder in some hot water and cool. Beat into the mixture before adding the eggs. For the filling, add brown soft sugar to the fat and add 5 ml (1 level tsp) cocoa powder instead of almond essence.

2 For coffee butterfly cakes, beat in 5 ml (1 tsp) coffee essence before adding the eggs. For the filling, add brown soft sugar to the fat and add coffee essence instead of almond essence.

Caraway cobbler ring cake

Illustrated in colour on page 58

For the topping
50 g (2 oz) butter or margarine
50 g (2 oz) blended white vegetable fat
75 g (3 oz) light brown soft sugar
grated rind of $\frac{1}{2}$ a lemon
1 egg, beaten
200 g (7 oz) self raising flour
25 g (1 oz) cornflakes, crushed
5 ml (1 level tsp) caraway seeds

For the sponge base
100 g (4 oz) butter or margarine
100 g (4 oz) caster sugar
grated rind of $\frac{1}{2}$ a lemon
2 eggs, size 2, beaten
100 g (4 oz) self raising flour

Grease a 19-cm (7$\frac{1}{2}$-inch), 1.5-litre (2$\frac{1}{2}$-pint) angel cake tin. To make the topping, cream the fats and sugar together until pale and fluffy, then beat in the lemon rind and egg. Sift the flour over the mixture and fold in lightly with a metal spoon, then stir in half the cornflakes. Combine the remaining cornflakes with the caraway seeds. With lightly floured hands, shape the dough into small balls. Toss in the cornflakes and caraway mixture to coat and chill until firm.

Meanwhile, make the sponge base. Cream the fat and sugar together until pale and fluffy and beat in the lemon rind. Add the egg, a little at a time, beating well after each addition. Sift the flour over the mixture and fold in with a metal spoon. Turn the mixture into the prepared tin and level the surface. Bake in the oven at 180°C (350°F) mark 4 for 20 minutes. Remove the tin from the oven and quickly

place the cornflake-coated balls over the sponge base. Return to the oven and bake for a further 15 minutes until golden. Leave in the tin for 15 minutes, then loosen the edges with a palette knife, transfer to a wire rack and leave to cool.

Chocolate layer gâteau

225 g (8 oz) butter
225 g (8 oz) caster sugar
4 eggs, size 2, beaten
45 ml (3 level tbsp) cocoa powder
225 g (8 oz) self raising flour
1$\frac{1}{2}$ quantities chocolate crème au beurre
  (*see page 171*)
75 g (3 oz) flaked almonds, toasted
apricot jam, sieved
1 quantity chocolate glacé icing (*see
  page 171*)
sugar coffee beans

Grease and line two 23-cm (9-inch) cake tins.

Cream the butter and sugar together until pale and fluffy. Add the egg a little at a time, beating well after each addition. Blend the cocoa powder with 45 ml (3 tbsp) water and beat gradually into the creamed mixture. Sift the flour over the mixture and fold in lightly with a metal spoon. Divide the mixture between the prepared tins and level the surface. Bake in the oven at 180°C (350°F) mark 4 for 35–40 minutes until just spongy to the touch. Turn the cakes out and leave them to cool on a wire rack.

When cool, split the cakes in half. Sandwich the four layers together with crème au beurre, reserving some for the sides and to decorate. Coat the sides with crème au beurre and cover with toasted almonds. Brush the top with apricot jam and cover with chocolate glacé icing, easing it gently to the edge. Leave to set. Decorate with piped chocolate crème au beurre and sugar coffee 'beans'.

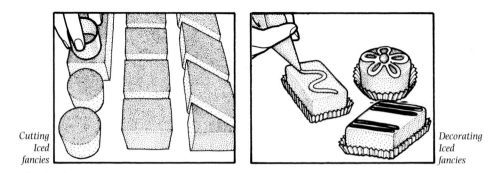

Cutting Iced fancies

Decorating Iced fancies

Iced fancies

1½ quantities Victoria sandwich mixture
  (*see page 54*)
white glacé icing using 350 g (12 oz) icing
  sugar (*see page 171*)
pink and yellow food colouring
cocoa powder

To decorate
mimosa balls
crystallised violets
grated chocolate

Grease and line an 18 × 23.5-cm (7 × 10-inch) rectangular cake tin. Turn the Victoria sandwich mixture into the prepared tin. Bake in the oven at 190°C (375°F) mark 5 for about 25 minutes until well risen and golden brown. Turn out and leave to cool on a wire rack.

Cut the cake into three strips. Cut four circles from one strip, five rectangles from another and four diamonds from the last piece of cake. Place the cakes on a wire rack with a plate or tray underneath to collect surplus icing. Divide the glacé icing into four. Colour one portion pink, one yellow and leave a double portion white.

Using two thirds of the white icing, coat the top and sides of the diamond-shaped cakes. Coat the top and sides of the circular cakes yellow and the rectangular ones pink. Leave until set. Place each cake in a paper case. Divide the remaining white icing and stir sifted cocoa powder into one third. Spoon both the chocolate and white icing into separate greaseproof icing bags (*see page 165*) fitted with small plain nozzles. Pipe a zig-zag line in white icing on the rectangular cakes and an outline of petals on the circular cakes. Pipe straight lines in chocolate icing on the diamond-shaped cakes.

Leave the piped icing until almost set before adding the decorations. Place a mimosa ball in the centre of each flower on the circular cakes. Place a crystallised violet in the centre of each rectangular cake. Carefully sprinkle grated chocolate on to the diamond-shaped cakes between the piped lines, with the aid of a palette knife.
Makes 13

Rich cherry cake

150 g (5 oz) self raising flour
50 g (2 oz) plain flour
45 ml (3 level tbsp) cornflour
45 ml (3 level tbsp) ground almonds
225 g (8 oz) glacé cherries, halved
175 g (6 oz) caster sugar
175 g (6 oz) butter
3 eggs, beaten
6 sugar cubes

Grease and line an 18-cm (7-inch) round, loose bottomed cake tin. Sift together the flours and cornflour into a bowl and stir in the ground almonds and cherries. Cream the butter and sugar together until pale and fluffy. Add the egg a little at a time, beating well after each addition. Fold in the dry ingredients with a metal spoon. Turn the mixture into the prepared tin, making sure the cherries are evenly distributed, and hollow the centre slightly to ensure an even surface when cooked. Roughly crush the sugar cubes with a rolling pin and sprinkle over the top of the mixture. Bake in the oven at 180°C (350°F) mark 4 for 1–1$\frac{1}{2}$ hours until well risen, golden and firm to the touch. Turn out and leave to cool on a wire rack.

Date ripple loaf

Illustrated in colour on page 123

225 g (8 oz) cooking apple, peeled and cored
150 g (5 oz) stoned dates
grated rind and juice of 1 lemon
45 ml (3 tbsp) water
100 g (4 oz) butter
100 g (4 oz) dark brown soft sugar
2 eggs, beaten
100 g (4 oz) self raising flour

Grease and line a rectangular cake tin measuring 26 × 10 cm (10$\frac{1}{2}$ × 4 inches) across the top. Chop the apple and 125 g (4 oz) dates and place in a pan with the lemon rind, juice and water. Cook over a gentle heat until a soft purée. Beat well and cool.

Cream the butter and sugar together until light and fluffy. Add the egg, a little at a time, beating thoroughly after each addition. Sift the flour over the mixture and fold in lightly with a metal spoon. Spoon a third of the cake mixture into the prepared tin and spread it to cover the base. On top of this, spread half the date mixture. Repeat the layering, finishing with cake mixture. Cut the remaining 25 g (1 oz) dates into thin slivers and arrange in

a line down the length of the cake. Bake in the oven at 170°C (325°F) mark 3 for about 1 hour 10 minutes. Cover with foil halfway through the cooking time. Turn out and leave to cool on a wire rack.

Note This mixture will also fit a 1.4-litre (2$\frac{1}{2}$-pint) loaf tin measuring 19 × 11 cm (7$\frac{1}{2}$ × 4$\frac{1}{2}$ inches) across the top.

Tutti frutti lemon layer cake

Illustrated in colour on page 28

175 g (6 oz) butter or margarine
175 g (6 oz) caster sugar
grated rind of 1 lemon
3 eggs, beaten
175 g (6 oz) self raising flour
15 g ($\frac{1}{2}$ oz) angelica, chopped
25 g (1 oz) glacé cherries, chopped
15 g ($\frac{1}{2}$ oz) flaked almonds

For the filling
40 g (1$\frac{1}{2}$ oz) butter
75 g (3 oz) icing sugar
10 ml (2 tsp) lemon juice

Grease and line two 20.5-cm (8-inch) sandwich tins. Cream the fat and sugar together until pale and fluffy, then beat in the lemon rind. Add the egg, a little at a time, beating well after each addition. Sift the flour over the mixture and fold in lightly with a metal spoon. Divide the mixture equally between the tins and level the surfaces. Scatter the angelica, cherries and almonds over the surface of one cake mixture. Bake in the oven at 180°C (350°F) mark 4 for about 25 minutes until well risen, golden and firm to the touch. Turn out and leave to cool on a wire rack.

To make the filling, cream the butter until soft, then gradually sift and beat in the icing sugar. Beat in the lemon juice. Spread the filling over the plain sponge, then sandwich the cakes together.

Light fruit cake

Illustrated in colour on pages 75 and 122

175 g (6 oz) butter
175 g (6 oz) caster sugar
3 eggs, size 2, beaten
100 g (4 oz) plain flour
150 g (5 oz) self raising flour
50 g (2 oz) glacé cherries, halved
225 g (8 oz) mixed dried fruit
grated rind and juice of $\frac{1}{2}$ a lemon
walnut halves
15 ml (1 level tbsp) granulated sugar

Grease and line an 18-cm (7-inch) round cake tin. Cream the butter and sugar together until pale and fluffy. Add the egg, a little at a time, beating well after each addition. Sift the flours together and add the cherries and mixed dried fruit. Fold into the creamed mixture with a metal spoon, alternately with the lemon rind and juice. Turn the mixture into the prepared tin and level the surface. Top with halved walnuts, sprinkle with granulated sugar and bake in the oven at 170°C (325°F) mark 3 for about 1 hour 40 minutes until firm to the touch. Turn out and leave to cool on a wire rack.

Brandy ginger ring

150 g (5 oz) butter
100 g (4 oz) light brown soft sugar
2 eggs, size 2, beaten
15 ml (1 level tbsp) ginger marmalade
15 ml (1 level tbsp) golden syrup
175 g (6 oz) plain flour
5 ml (1 level tsp) bicarbonate of soda
10 ml (2 level tsp) ground ginger
15 ml (1 tbsp) milk

For the filling and decoration
175 g (6 oz) butter
250 g (9 oz) icing sugar
45 ml (3 tbsp) brandy
12–14 brandy cornets (*see page 90*)
stem ginger

Grease a flat-based, sloping-sided 1.4-litre (2½-pint) angel cake ring measuring 19 cm (7½ inches) in diameter. Line the base with greaseproof paper.

Cream the butter and sugar together until pale and fluffy. Add the eggs a little at a time, beating well after each addition. Fold in the marmalade and syrup. Sift together the flour, soda and ginger and fold into the mixture, together with the milk. Turn the mixture into the prepared tin and level the surface. Bake in the oven at 170°C (325°F) mark 3 for about 1 hour until risen, golden and firm to the touch. Turn out and leave to cool on a wire rack.

Split the cake into four layers. For the filling, cream the butter and gradually sift in the icing sugar, beating until light and fluffy, then beat in the brandy. Sandwich the layers together with brandy butter, reserving a little for filling the cornets. Fill a piping bag fitted with a large star nozzle with the remaining brandy butter and pipe whirls into the brandy cornets. Arrange the cornets round the top of the cake and decorate with a piece of stem ginger.

Orange and pineapple cake

Illustrated in colour on page 123

100–175 g (4–6 oz) glacé pineapple cubes
50 g (2 oz) ground almonds
75 g (3 oz) self raising flour
75 g (3 oz) plain flour
grated rind and juice of 1 small orange
175 g (6 oz) butter
175 g (6 oz) caster sugar
3 eggs, beaten
apricot jam, warmed
50 g (2 oz) icing sugar

Grease and line the base of a 1.1-litre (2-pint) moule à manqué tin measuring 20.5 cm (8 inches) across the top. With a wet sharp knife, cut each cube of the 100 g

(4 oz) pineapple into four slices. When using 175 g (6 oz) pineapple, finely chop the extra 50 g (2 oz).

In a bowl, combine the ground almonds, sifted flours, orange rind and finely chopped pineapple, if used. Cream the butter and sugar together until pale and fluffy. Add the egg, a little at a time, beating well after each addition. Fold in the dry ingredients alternately with 30 ml (2 tbsp) of the orange juice. Turn the mixture into the prepared tin and level the surface. Bake in the oven at 180°C (350°F) mark 4 for 45–55 minutes until well risen and spongy to the touch. Turn out and leave to cool on a wire rack with the base uppermost.

Brush the base of the cake with apricot jam. Arrange slices of the glacé pineapple over the jam. Blend the sifted icing sugar with just enough orange juice or water to give a thin coating consistency. Spoon over the pineapple and leave to set.

Raisin streusel cake

Illustrated in colour on page 58

For the topping
100 g (4 oz) caster sugar
100 g (4 oz) plain flour
5 ml (1 level tsp) ground cinnamon
100 g (4 oz) butter

For the cake
225 g (8 oz) self raising flour
2.5 ml ($\frac{1}{2}$ level tsp) ground nutmeg
pinch of ground cloves
1.25 ml ($\frac{1}{4}$ level tsp) salt
100 g (4 oz) butter
100 g (4 oz) caster sugar
3 eggs, beaten
60 ml (4 tbsp) milk
225 g (8 oz) seedless raisins

Grease and line a 24-cm ($9\frac{1}{2}$-inch) round, loose-bottomed cake tin. To make the topping, put the sugar, flour and cinnamon into a bowl, add the butter and rub in between finger and thumb tips until the mixture resembles coarse breadcrumbs.

To make the cake, sift together the flour, nutmeg, cloves and salt. Cream the butter and sugar together until pale and fluffy. Add the egg a little at a time, beating well after each addition. Fold in the flour with a metal spoon, then stir in the milk. and raisins. Turn the mixture into the prepared tin and level the surface. Sprinkle the crumb topping evenly over the cake mixture. Bake in the oven at 190°C (375°F) mark 5 for 40–50 minutes until golden. Remove from the tin and leave to cool on a wire rack.

Cherry madeira ring

175 g (6 oz) plain flour
5 ml (1 level tsp) baking powder
175 g (6 oz) glacé cherries, quartered
100 g (4 oz) butter
100 g (4 oz) caster sugar
grated rind and juice of 1 large lemon
2 eggs, size 2, beaten
100 g (4 oz) icing sugar

Grease a 1.4-litre ($2\frac{1}{2}$-pint) plain ring mould. Sift the flour and baking powder and stir in 100 g (4 oz) cherries. Cream the butter and sugar together until pale and fluffy, then beat in the lemon rind. Add the egg a little at a time, beating well after each addition. Lightly fold in the flour and cherries with 30 ml (2 tbsp) lemon juice.

Turn the mixture into the prepared tin and level the surface. Bake in the oven at 170°C (325°F) mark 3 for about 45 minutes until well risen, golden and firm to the touch. Turn out and leave to cool on a wire rack.

Sift the icing sugar into a bowl and blend with 15–30 ml (1–2 tbsp) lemon juice to give a coating consistency. Drizzle the icing over the top of the cold cake and scatter over the remaining cherries.

Devil's food cake

This cake was first made in the United States, where it is usually eaten as a dessert.

450 g (1 lb) plain flour
15 ml (3 level tsp) bicarbonate of soda
pinch of salt
75 g (3 oz) cocoa powder
345 ml ($\frac{1}{2}$ pint + 3 tbsp) milk
10 ml (2 tsp) vanilla essence
150 g (5 oz) butter
400 g (14 oz) brown soft sugar
4 eggs, beaten

For the American frosting and decoration
700 g (1$\frac{1}{2}$ lb) caster sugar
180 ml ($\frac{1}{4}$ pint + 2 tbsp) water
3 egg whites
25 g (1 oz) plain chocolate (optional)

Grease three 21.5-cm (8$\frac{1}{2}$-inch) straight-sided sandwich tins and line the bases with greased greaseproof paper. Sift together the flour, bicarbonate of soda and salt into a bowl. Mix together the cocoa, milk and vanilla essence until smooth. Cream the butter until pale in colour, then gradually beat in the brown sugar. Add the eggs gradually, beating well after each addition. Lightly fold in the flour and cocoa mixtures alternately until all is added. Divide the mixture between the tins and level the surface. Bake in the oven at 180°C (350°F) mark 4 for about 35 minutes until firm to the touch. Turn out and leave to cool on a wire rack.

Put the sugar for the frosting in a pan with the water, dissolve over a low heat, then boil rapidly to 115°C (240°F) (use a sugar thermometer). Meanwhile, whisk the egg whites in a large bowl until stiff. Allow the bubbles in the syrup to settle, then slowly pour the hot syrup on to the egg whites, beating constantly. Once all the sugar syrup is added, continue beating until the mixture stands in peaks and just starts to become matt round the edges. (The icing sets quickly, so work rapidly.)

Sandwich the three cakes together with a little of the frosting and spread the remaining frosting over the cake with a palette knife. Pull the icing up into peaks all over, then leave the cake on a wire rack for about 30 minutes, to allow the icing to set slightly.

Break up the chocolate, if used, and put it in a small bowl over a pan of hot water. Heat gently, stirring, until the chocolate has melted. Dribble the chocolate over the top of the cake with a teaspoon to make a swirl pattern.

Butterscotch sandwich

225 g (8 oz) self raising flour
pinch of salt
225 g (8 oz) dark brown soft sugar
100 g (4 oz) butter
175 ml (6 fl oz) milk
7.5 ml (1$\frac{1}{2}$ tsp) vanilla essence
2 eggs, beaten
8 walnut halves to decorate

For the butter cream
100 g (4 oz) butter
30 ml (2 level tbsp) golden syrup
10 ml (2 tsp) lemon juice
225 g (8 oz) icing sugar

For the butterscotch topping
50 g (2 oz) butter
90 g (3$\frac{1}{2}$ oz) brown soft sugar
45 ml (3 tbsp) milk
about 75 g (3 oz) icing sugar

Grease a 20.5-cm (8-inch) diameter, 6.5-cm (2$\frac{1}{2}$-inch) deep moule à manqué (sloping-sided) cake tin and line the base with greaseproof paper. Sift together the flour and salt into a bowl and stir in the brown sugar. Cream the butter until soft and slowly add the dry ingredients until crumbly. Continue beating, adding the milk and essence, for 2 minutes. Add the eggs and beat for a further 1–2 minutes. Pour into the prepared tin and level the surface. Bake in the oven at 190°C (375°F) mark 5 for about 1 hour until risen, golden and firm to the touch. Turn out and leave to cool on a wire rack.

Meanwhile, make the butter cream. Cream the butter, syrup and lemon juice together. Sift in the icing sugar and beat it into the mixture. Slice the cake in half and sandwich together with some of the butter cream. Spread the rest round the sides and ridge with a fork.

To make the topping, melt the butter in a pan and stir in the brown sugar. Boil for 1–2 minutes. Stir in the milk, bring to the boil again and then leave to cool until lukewarm. Gradually stir in enough icing sugar to give a coating consistency. Spread over the top of the cake and swirl with a knife. Decorate with the walnut halves.

Dark chocolate swirl cake

175 g (6 oz) butter or margarine
175 g (6 oz) caster sugar
2 eggs, beaten
60 ml (4 level tbsp) cocoa powder
175 ml (6 fl oz) milk
5 ml (1 tsp) vanilla essence
225 g (8 oz) plain flour
7.5 ml (1½ level tsp) bicarbonate of soda
pinch of salt
1 square Bakers' unsweetened chocolate, melted
100 g (4 oz) icing sugar
50 g (2 oz) plain chocolate, melted

Grease and line two 19-cm (7-inch) straight-sided sandwich tins. Cream 100 g (4 oz) of the fat and the sugar together until pale and fluffy. Beat in the egg a little at a time, beating well after each addition. Blend the cocoa with 90 ml (6 tbsp) milk to a smooth paste. Stir in the remaining milk with the essence. Sift the flour with the bicarbonate of soda and salt and fold into the creamed mixture, alternating with the cocoa liquid. Spoon the mixture into the prepared tins. Swirl the unsweetened chocolate around the top of one cake. Bake in the oven at 180°C (350°F) mark 4 for about 30 minutes. Leave to cool in the tins before turning out on to a wire rack.

Beat the remaining butter, sift in the icing sugar and continue to cream well. Work in the melted plain chocolate. Use this butter cream to sandwich the cakes together with the chocolate swirl on top.

Mincemeat yo-yos

Illustrated in colour on page 18

100 g (4 oz) butter
50 g (2 oz) blended white vegetable fat
75 g (3 oz) light brown soft sugar
1 egg, size 2
90 ml (6 level tbsp) mincemeat
200 g (7 oz) plain flour
2.5 ml (½ level tsp) bicarbonate of soda
75 g (3 oz) icing sugar
5 ml (1 tsp) lemon juice

Grease two or three baking sheets. Cream 50 g (2 oz) butter and the white fat until soft. Add the sugar and continue beating until pale and fluffy. Beat in the egg and 45 ml (3 level tbsp) mincemeat. Sift the flour and bicarbonate of soda over the mixture and fold in lightly with a metal spoon. Leave in the refrigerator until firm.

Using the hands, shape the mixture into about 24 walnut-sized balls. Place well apart on the prepared baking sheets. Bake in the oven at 180°C (350°F) mark 4 for about 12 minutes until well risen and puffy. Lift on to a wire rack and leave to cool.

Meanwhile, make the filling. Cream the remaining 50 g (2 oz) butter with the sifted icing sugar, lemon juice and the remaining mincemeat until of a spreading consistency. When cold, sandwich the yo-yos in pairs with the mincemeat filling.
Makes 12–15

Toddy cake

225 g (8 oz) butter or margarine
175 g (6 oz) light brown soft sugar
grated rind and juice of 1 lemon
3 eggs, beaten
175 g (6 oz) self raising flour
60 ml (4 tbsp) whisky
30 ml (2 level tbsp) thick honey
175 g (6 oz) icing sugar, sifted
50 g (2 oz) walnut halves to decorate

Grease and line two 18-cm (7-inch) straight sided sandwich tins. Cream 175 g (6 oz) of the fat with the sugar and grated lemon rind until pale and fluffy. Gradually beat in the egg, keeping the mixture stiff. Sift half the flour over the mixture and fold in lightly with a metal spoon. Fold in the whisky and lastly the remaining flour. Spoon the mixture into the prepared tins. Bake in the oven at 190°C (375°F) mark 5 for about 30 minutes. Turn out and leave to cool on a wire rack.

Beat the remaining butter with the honey and gradually work in the icing sugar with 15 ml (1 tbsp) lemon juice. Sandwich the cake together with half the butter cream and swirl the rest over the top with a palette knife. Decorate with the walnut halves.

Coburg buns

6 blanched almonds
150 g (5 oz) plain flour
5 ml (1 level tsp) bicarbonate of soda
2.5 ml ($\frac{1}{2}$ level tsp) ground allspice
2.5 ml ($\frac{1}{2}$ level tsp) ground ginger
2.5 ml ($\frac{1}{2}$ level tsp) ground cinnamon
50 g (2 oz) butter or margarine
50 g (2 oz) caster sugar
1 egg, beaten
15 ml (1 level tbsp) golden syrup
60 ml (4 tbsp) milk

Grease twelve fluted bun tins and place half an almond in each. Sift together the flour, bicarbonate of soda and spices. Cream the fat and sugar together until pale and fluffy. Add the egg a little at a time, beating well after each addition. Mix the syrup and milk and add alternately with the flour mixture, folding in lightly with a metal spoon. Divide the mixture between the tins and bake in the oven at 180°C (350°F) mark 4 for about 25 minutes until firm to the touch. Turn out and leave to cool on a wire rack.
Makes 12

Fluted caraway buns

Illustrated in colour on page 18

75 g (3 oz) butter or margarine
50 g (2 oz) caster sugar
2 eggs, beaten
30 ml (2 level tbsp) lemon cheese or curd
100 g (4 oz) self raising flour
pinch of salt
2.5 ml ($\frac{1}{2}$ level tsp) caraway seeds
1 quantity glacé icing (*see page 171*)
glacé cherries, halved

Using lard, grease well nine fluted patty tins measuring about 7 cm ($2\frac{3}{4}$ inches) wide and 3 cm ($1\frac{1}{4}$ inches) deep. Cream the fat and sugar together until pale and fluffy. Add the egg, a little at a time, beating well after each addition. Fold in the lemon cheese. Sift in the flour and salt and fold it in followed by the caraway seeds. Divide the mixture between the prepared tins and bake in the oven at 170°C (325°F) mark 3 for about 25 minutes. Turn out and leave to cool bottom sides up on a wire rack. Decorate each with a little blob of stiff glacé icing and half a glacé cherry. Or serve the other way up, simply dusted with sifted icing sugar.
Makes about 9

TRADITIONAL FRUIT CAKES

Packed with sweet juicy fruit, peel and nuts, rich fruit cakes make very good eating. They don't stale easily, even when cut, so are invaluable to keep on hand in the cake tin. A very rich fruit mixture is the usual choice for formal celebration cakes: the baked cake stores well and provides a good firm base for Royal icing.

Some fruit cakes, such as Genoa cake and Family fruit cake, are ready for cutting a day or so after baking. However, very rich mixtures (such as Christmas and Wedding cakes) should be baked two or three months before they are needed to allow the flavour to mellow. Prick the surface of the cake with a fine skewer, then spoon over some brandy or other spirit every few weeks. This helps keep the cake moist and flavoursome during storage.

Like other rich cakes, rich fruit cakes are made by the creaming method. The mixture may be slightly stiffer though, to support the weight of the fruit. Remember that all dried fruit should be thoroughly clean and dry for use; glacé fruit must be rinsed to remove excess syrup, then dried. Unless you are making a celebration cake, it is wise to toss the prepared fruit in a little of the flour. (Celebration mixtures contain so much fruit there is little chance – or room – for it to sink in the cake.)

Making a very rich fruit cake is quite a job – it's useful to know that, once prepared and in the tin, the mixture can be loosely covered with a clean cloth and left overnight in a cool place.

Rich fruit cake

Prepare the ingredients for the size of fruit cake you wish to make according to the chart opposite. Grease and line the appropriate size of cake tin, using a double thickness of greaseproof paper, and tie a double band of brown paper round the outside. Wash and dry all the fruit if necessary, chopping any over-large pieces, and mix well together in a large bowl. Add the flaked almonds. Sift the flour and spices into another bowl with a pinch of salt.

Put the butter, sugar and lemon rind into a warmed mixing bowl and cream together with a wooden spoon until pale and fluffy. Add the beaten eggs, a little at a time, beating well after each addition.

Gradually fold the flour lightly into the mixture with a metal spoon, then fold in the brandy. Finally, fold in the fruit and nuts.

Turn the mixture into the prepared tin, spreading it evenly and making sure there are no air pockets.

Make a hollow in the centre to ensure an even surface when cooked. Stand the tin on a piece of newspaper or brown paper in the oven and bake at 150°C (300°F) mark 2 for the required time (see chart), until a fine skewer inserted in the centre comes out clean. To prevent the cake from over-browning, cover it with greaseproof paper after about 1½ hours.

When cooked, leave the cake to cool in the tin before turning out on to a wire rack. Prick the top of the cake all over with a fine skewer and slowly pour 30–45 ml (2–3 tbsp) brandy over it before storing. Wrap the cake in a double thickness of greaseproof paper and store upside down in an airtight tin.

Quantities and sizes for rich fruit cakes

To make a formal cake for a birthday, wedding or anniversary, the following chart will show you the amount of ingredients required to fill the chosen cake tin or tins, whether round or square.

Square tin size		15 cm (6 inches) square	18 cm (7 inches) square	20.5 cm (8 inches) square
Round tin size	15 cm (6 inches) diameter	18 cm (7 inches) diameter	20.5 cm (8 inches) diameter	23 cm (9 inches) diameter
Currants	225 g (8 oz)	350 g (12 oz)	450 g (1 lb)	625 g (1 lb 6 oz)
Sultanas	100 g (4 oz)	125 g (4½ oz)	200 g (7 oz)	225 g (8 oz)
Raisins	100 g (4 oz)	125 g (4½ oz)	200 g (7 oz)	225 g (8 oz)
Glacé cherries	50 g (2 oz)	75 g (3 oz)	150 g (5 oz)	175 g (6 oz)
Mixed peel	25 g (1 oz)	50 g (2 oz)	75 g (3 oz)	100 g (4 oz)
Flaked almonds	25 g (1 oz)	50 g (2 oz)	75 g (3 oz)	100 g (4 oz)
Lemon rind	a little	a little	a little	¼ lemon
Plain flour	175 g (6 oz)	215 g (7½ oz)	350 g (12 oz)	400 g (14 oz)
Mixed spice	1.25 ml (¼ level tsp)	2.5 ml (½ level tsp)	2.5 ml (½ level tsp)	5 ml (1 level tsp)
Cinnamon	1.25 ml (¼ level tsp)	2.5 ml (½ level tsp)	2.5 ml (½ level tsp)	5 ml (1 level tsp)
Butter	150 g (5 oz)	175 g (6 oz)	275 g (10 oz)	350 g (12 oz)
Sugar	150 g (5 oz)	175 g (6 oz)	275 g (10 oz)	350 g (12 oz)
Eggs, beaten	2½	3	5	6
Brandy	15 ml (1 tbsp)	15 ml (1 tbsp)	15–30 ml (1–2 tbsp)	30 ml (2 tbsp)
Time (approx.)	2½–3 hours	3 hours	3½ hours	4 hours
Weight when cooked	1.1 kg (2½ lb)	1.6 kg (3¼ lb)	2.2 kg (4¾ lb)	2.7 kg (6 lb)

Square tin size	23 cm (9 inches) square	25.5 cm (10 inches) square	28 cm (11 inches) square	30.5 cm (12 inches) square
Round tin size	25.5 cm (10 inches) diameter	28 cm (11 inches) diameter	30.5 cm (12 inches) diameter	
Currants	775 g (1 lb 12 oz)	1.1 kg (2 lb 8 oz)	1.5 kg (3 lb 2 oz)	1.7 kg (3 lb 12 oz)
Sultanas	375 g (13 oz)	400 g (14 oz)	525 g (1 lb 3 oz)	625 g (1 lb 6 oz)
Raisins	375 g (13 oz)	400 g (14 oz)	525 g (1 lb 3 oz)	625 g (1 lb 6 oz)
Glacé cherries	250 g (9 oz)	275 g (10 oz)	350 g (12 oz)	425 g (15 oz)
Mixed peel	150 g (5 oz)	200 g (7 oz)	250 g (9 oz)	275 g (10 oz)
Flaked almonds	150 g (5 oz)	200 g (7 oz)	250 g (9 oz)	275 g (10 oz)
Lemon rind	¼ lemon	½ lemon	½ lemon	1 lemon
Plain flour	600 g (1 lb 5 oz)	700 g (1 lb 8 oz)	825 g (1 lb 13 oz)	1 kg (2 lb 6 oz)
Mixed spice	5 ml (1 level tsp)	10 ml (2 level tsp)	12.5 ml (2½ level tsp)	12.5 ml (2½ level tsp)
Cinnamon	5 ml (1 level tsp)	10 ml (2 level tsp)	12.5 ml (2½ level tsp)	12.5 ml (2½ level tsp)
Butter	500 g (1 lb 2 oz)	600 g (1 lb 5 oz)	800 g (1 lb 12 oz)	950 g (2 lb 2 oz)
Sugar	500 g (1 lb 2 oz)	600 g (1 lb 5 oz)	800 g (1 lb 12 oz)	950 g (2 lb 2 oz)
Eggs, beaten	9	11	14	17
Brandy	30–45 ml (2–3 tbsp)	45 ml (3 tbsp)	60 ml (4 tbsp)	90 ml (6 tbsp)
Time (approx.)	6 hours	7 hours	8 hours	8½ hours
Weight when cooked	4 kg (9 lb)	5.2 kg (11½ lb)	6.7 kg (14¾ lb)	7.7 kg (17 lb)

Family fruit cake

100 g (4 oz) plain flour
100 g (4 oz) self raising flour
2.5 ml ($\frac{1}{2}$ level tsp) ground nutmeg
2.5 ml ($\frac{1}{2}$ level tsp) ground ginger
grated rind of $\frac{1}{2}$ a lemon
50 g (2 oz) ground almonds
175 g (6 oz) butter or margarine
175 g (6 oz) caster sugar
4 eggs, size 2, beaten
350 g (12 oz) mixed dried fruit
100 g (4 oz) glacé cherries, halved
15 ml (1 tbsp) milk
25 g (1 oz) almonds, blanched and slivered

Grease and line a 20.5-cm (8-inch) round cake tin. Sift the flours, nutmeg and ginger into a bowl. Add the lemon rind and almonds. Cream the fat and sugar together until pale and fluffy. Add the egg a little at a time, beating well after each addition. Fold in the flour mixture with a metal spoon and then the fruit and milk. Turn the mixture into the prepared tin and make a slight hollow in the centre. Scatter the almonds over the top. Bake in the oven at 180°C (350°F) mark 4 for 1 hour, then lower the oven temperature to 170°C (325°F) mark 3 and bake for a further 30 minutes. Allow to cool slightly in the tin before removing to a wire rack.

Speedy fruit cake

175 g (6 oz) self raising flour
5 ml (1 level tsp) baking powder
25 g (1 oz) ground almonds
grated rind of 1 orange
175 g (6 oz) butter
175 g (6 oz) caster sugar
3 eggs, beaten
411-g (14$\frac{1}{2}$-oz) jar mincemeat
icing sugar

Grease, flour and line the base of a 20.5-cm (8-inch) angel cake tin. Sift the flour and baking powder into a bowl and add the ground almonds and orange rind. Cream the butter and sugar together until pale and fluffy. Add the egg a little at a time, beating well after each addition. Mix the mincemeat with 45 ml (3 level tbsp) flour. Fold the mincemeat and flour alternately into the creamed mixture. Turn the mixture into the prepared tin and bake in the oven at 170°C (325°F) mark 3 for about 1$\frac{3}{4}$ hours. Turn the cake out of the tin and leave it to cool on a wire rack.

Before serving, dust the top with sifted icing sugar.

Luxury fruit cake

This super Christmas cake recipe cuts down on bake ahead time because the fruit is marinated.

175 g (6 oz) currants
225 g (8 oz) sultanas
225 g (8 oz) seedless raisins
50 g (2 oz) chopped mixed peel
grated rind and juice of 2 oranges
150 ml ($\frac{1}{4}$ pint) sherry or brandy
225 g (8 oz) butter or margarine
225 g (8 oz) dark brown soft sugar
4 eggs, size 2, beaten
250 g (9 oz) plain flour
25 g (1 oz) self raising flour
75 g (3 oz) glacé cherries
50 g (2 oz) walnuts, chopped

Grease and line a 20.5-cm (8-inch) round cake tin and tie a double band of brown paper round the outside. Combine the dried fruits and mixed peel in a large basin. Stir in the orange rind and juice, and the sherry or brandy. Press down well, cover the basin and leave overnight.

Cream the fat and sugar together until pale and fluffy. Add the egg a little at a time with some of the flour, beating well after each addition. Sift the remaining flour over the mixture and fold in lightly with a metal spoon. Stir in the soaked fruit, juices, cherries and walnuts. Turn

Light fruit cake (*page 66*)

Bring
and
Buy

apple
and
walnut
teabread

chocolate
nut
finac.

the mixture into the prepared tin. Level the surface and make a slight hollow in the centre. Stand the tin on a layer of newspaper or brown paper. Bake in the oven at 150°C (300°F) mark 2 for 3½–4 hours. If over-browning after 3 hours cover with a thick layer of greaseproof paper. Leave in the tin until completely cold, then turn out. Wrap the cake in greaseproof paper. Overwrap with foil or put in an airtight tin to store.

at 180°C (350°F) mark 4 for about 2 hours. Allow to cool slightly in the tin before turning out and leaving to cool completely on a wire rack.

For the glaze, combine the jam and syrup. Bring to the boil and heat until it looks glazed. Brush the top of the ring with the glaze. Arrange the walnut halves on top with split almonds between. Trickle any remaining glaze over the nuts.

Rich fruit and nut cake

Illustrated in colour on page 40

225 g (8 oz) butter or margarine
225 g (8 oz) light brown soft sugar
5 eggs, beaten
225 g (8 oz) plain flour
pinch of salt
350 g (12 oz) mixed dried fruit
50 g (2 oz) chopped mixed peel
100 g (4 oz) glacé cherries, halved
75 g (3 oz) nibbed almonds
50 g (2 oz) walnuts, chopped
grated rind of 1 orange
walnut halves and split almonds, to
   decorate

For the glaze:
60 ml (4 level tbsp) apricot jam
30 ml (2 level tbsp) golden syrup

Grease and line a 20.5-cm (8-inch) round tin. To make a hole in the centre, wrap a small opened can or cardboard cylinder, about 4–5 cm (1½–2 inches) in diameter, in foil. Stand in the centre of the cake tin and pack the prepared cake mixture around it.

Cream the fat and sugar together until pale and fluffy. Add egg a little at a time, beating well after each addition. Sift the flour and salt over the mixture and fold in lightly with a metal spoon. Add the dried fruit, mixed peel, cherries, nuts and orange rind. Turn the mixture into the prepared tin and level the surface. Bake in the oven

Dundee cake

100 g (4 oz) currants
100 g (4 oz) seedless raisins
50 g (2 oz) blanched almonds, chopped
100 g (4 oz) chopped mixed peel
275 g (10 oz) plain flour
225 g (8 oz) butter or margarine
225 g (8 oz) light brown soft sugar
grated rind of 1 lemon
4 eggs, beaten
25 g (1 oz) split almonds to decorate

Grease and line a 20.5-cm (8-inch) round cake tin. Combine the fruit, chopped nuts and mixed peel in a bowl. Sift in a little flour and stir until the fruit is evenly coated. Cream the fat and sugar together until pale and fluffy, then beat in the lemon rind. Add the egg, a little at a time, beating well after each addition. Sift the flour over the mixture and fold in lightly with a metal spoon, then fold in the fruit and nut mixture.

Turn the mixture into the prepared tin and hollow the centre slightly. Arrange the split almonds on the top. Bake in the oven at 170°C (325°F) mark 3 for about 2½ hours until a fine warmed skewer inserted in the centre comes out clean. Check the cake near the end of the cooking time and cover the surface with brown paper if it is over browning. Leave the cake in the tin for 15 minutes, then turn out and leave to cool on a wire rack.

Clockwise from top right: Apple and walnut teabread (*page 84*), One-stage small cakes (*page 83*), Walnut coffee rock cakes (*page 34*), Chocolate nut bars (*page 86*)

Simnel cake

Originally this cake was baked for Mothering Sunday, in the days when many girls went into service and Mothering Sunday was the one day in the year they were allowed home. It is now more usual to have Simnel cake at Easter.

550 g (1¼ lb) almond paste *(see page 175)*
350 g (12 oz) currants
100 g (4 oz) sultanas
75 g (3 oz) chopped mixed peel
225 g (8 oz) plain flour
pinch of salt
5 ml (1 level tsp) ground cinnamon
5 ml (1 level tsp) ground nutmeg
175 g (6 oz) butter or margarine
175 g (6 oz) caster sugar
3 eggs, beaten
milk to mix
apricot jam, sieved and warmed or
    beaten egg
glacé icing (optional)

Grease and line an 18-cm (7-inch) cake tin. Divide the almond paste into three; take one portion and roll it out to a round the size of the cake tin. Wash and dry the currants and sultanas if necessary. Mix together the fruit and mixed peel. Sift together the flour, salt and spices into a bowl. Cream the fat and sugar together until pale and fluffy. Add the egg a little at a time, beating well after each addition. Fold in half the flour and fruit with a metal spoon, then fold in the remainder. Add enough milk to make a fairly soft consistency. Put half the mixture into the prepared tin, smooth and cover with the round of almond paste. Put the remaining mixture on top and level the surface. Bake in the oven at 170°C (325°F) mark 3 for about 1 hour, lower the heat to 150°C (300°F) mark 2 and bake for 3 hours until the cake is golden brown and firm to the touch. Allow to cool in the tin.

Take another third of the almond paste and roll out to a round the size of the tin;

make small balls from the remaining third – eleven is the traditional number. Brush the top of the cake with warmed apricot jam or beaten egg, cover with the round of paste and place the small balls round the edge. Brush the paste with any remaining egg or jam and brown under the grill. The top of the cake may then be coated with glacé icing, made by mixing 45 ml (3 level tbsp) sifted icing sugar with a little cold water until it will coat the back of the spoon. Decorate the cake with a tiny model chicken or coloured sugar eggs.

Christmas cake

225 g (8 oz) currants
225 g (8 oz) sultanas
225 g (8 oz) seedless raisins, chopped
100 g (4 oz) chopped mixed peel
100 g (4 oz) glacé cherries, halved
50 g (2 oz) nibbed almonds
225 g (8 oz) plain flour
pinch of salt
2.5 ml (½ level tsp) ground mace
2.5 ml (½ level tsp) ground cinnamon
225 g (8 oz) butter
225 g (8 oz) dark brown soft sugar
grated rind of 1 lemon
4 eggs, size 2, beaten
30 ml (2 tbsp) brandy

Grease and line a 20.5-cm (8-inch) cake tin, using a double thickness of greaseproof paper and tie a double band of brown paper round the outside. Wash and dry all the fruit if necessary. Mix the currants, sultanas, raisins, mixed peel, cherries and nuts. Sift the flour, salt and spices into a bowl. Cream the butter, sugar and lemon rind together until pale and fluffy. Add the eggs, a little at a time, beating well after each addition.

Fold half the sifted flour mixture lightly into the mixture with a metal spoon, then fold in the rest and add the brandy. Finally, fold in the fruit. Turn the mixture into the prepared tin, spreading it evenly, and making sure there are no air pockets. Make a hollow in the centre. Stand the tin on a layer of newspaper or brown paper in the oven and bake at 150°C (300°F) mark 2 for about $3\frac{3}{4}$ hours. To avoid over-browning the top, cover it with several layers of greaseproof paper after $1\frac{1}{2}$ hours. When the cake is cooked, leave to cool in the tin and then turn out on to a wire rack.

To store, wrap the cake in several layers of greaseproof paper, then in foil and put in an airtight tin.

Economical Christmas cake

225 g (8 oz) sultanas
100 g (4 oz) currants
225 g (8 oz) seedless raisins
275 g (10 oz) plain flour
5 ml (1 level tsp) mixed spice
a little grated nutmeg
225 g (8 oz) margarine
225 g (8 oz) caster sugar
a little grated lemon rind
a few drops of vanilla essence
a few drops of almond essence
4 eggs, beaten
15 ml (1 level tbsp) marmalade
2.5 ml ($\frac{1}{2}$ level tsp) bicarbonate of soda
30 ml (2 tbsp) milk or water
a few drops of gravy browning

Grease and line a 20.5-cm (8-inch) cake tin, using a double thickness of grease-proof paper and tie a double band of brown paper round the outside. Wash and dry all the fruit if necessary. Mix the prepared sultanas, currants and raisins. Sift the flour and spices, then mix with the fruit. Cream the margarine, sugar, lemon rind and essences together until pale and fluffy. Add the egg a little at a time, beating well after each addition. Add the marmalade and mix thoroughly. Fold in half the flour

and fruit with a metal spoon, then fold in the remainder. Dissolve the bicarbonate of soda in the milk or water and stir into the mixture, with a few drops of gravy browning. The mixture should be of a soft dropping consistency. Turn the mixture into the prepared tin, make a hollow in the centre and bake in the oven at 150°C (300°F) mark 2 for about 4 hours. Leave the cake to cool in the tin. Store wrapped in several layers of greaseproof paper and put in an airtight tin.

Fruity slab cake

100 g (4 oz) shelled Brazil nuts
100 g (4 oz) angelica
100 g (4 oz) glacé cherries
100 g (4 oz) glacé pineapple
225 g (8 oz) butter or margarine
225 g (8 oz) caster sugar
4 eggs, size 2, beaten
275 g (10 oz) plain flour
grated rind of 1 orange

Grease and line a tin measuring 28 × 19 cm ($11 \times 7\frac{1}{2}$ inches) across the top and 3.5 cm ($1\frac{1}{2}$ inches) deep.

Coarsely grate the Brazil nuts. Chop the angelica, discarding any excess sugar. Halve the cherries and roughly chop the pineapple. Cream the fat and sugar together until pale and fluffy. Add the egg a little at a time, beating well after each addition. Sift the flour over the mixture and fold in lightly with a metal spoon. Fold in the nuts, angelica, cherries, pineapple and orange rind. Turn the mixture into the prepared tin and bake in the oven at 180°C (350°F) mark 4 for about 1 hour. Turn out the cake and leave to cool on a wire rack.

Note If wished, decorate the cake mixture before baking with some of the nuts, coarsely grated, or additional nuts (also grated) and pieces of glacé pineapple.

Genoa cake

225 g (8 oz) sultanas
225 g (8 oz) currants
50 g (2 oz) chopped mixed peel
100 g (4 oz) glacé cherries
40 g (1½ oz) blanched almonds
225 g (8 oz) plain flour
pinch of salt
5 ml (1 level tsp) mixed spice
5 ml (1 level tsp) baking powder
200 g (7 oz) butter or margarine
175 g (6 oz) caster sugar
grated rind of 1 lemon
3 eggs, beaten
15–30 ml (1–2 tbsp) milk

Grease and line an 18-cm (7-inch) cake tin. Wash and dry the sultanas and currants if necessary. Mix together the fruit and mixed peel. Halve the cherries, then wash and dry them well. Chop the almonds, reserving a few for decoration. Sift together the flour, salt, spice and baking powder into a bowl. Cream the fat, sugar and lemon rind together until pale and fluffy. Add the egg a little at a time, beating well after each addition. Fold in the flour, the fruit and almonds, adding milk if necessary to give a dropping consistency. Turn the mixture into the prepared tin and decorate with the remaining almonds, halved. Bake in the oven at 150°C (300°F) mark 2 for 3–3¼ hours. Turn out and leave to cool on a wire rack.

Half-pound cake

A practical version of the traditional English pound cake – so called because most of the ingredients were added in 450-g (1-lb) quantities.

225 g (8 oz) butter or margarine
225 g (8 oz) caster sugar
4 eggs, beaten
225 g (8 oz) plain flour
2.5 ml (½ level tsp) salt
2.5 ml (½ level tsp) mixed spice
225 g (8 oz) seedless raisins
225 g (8 oz) mixed currants and sultanas
100 g (4 oz) glacé cherries, halved
15 ml (1 tbsp) brandy
a few walnut halves

Grease and line a 20.5-cm (8-inch) round cake tin. Cream the fat and sugar together until pale and fluffy. Add the egg a little at a time, beating well after each addition. Sift the flour, salt and spice together into a bowl and stir in the raisins, mixed fruit and cherries. Fold the flour and fruit into the creamed mixture with a metal spoon. Add the brandy and mix to a soft dropping consistency. Turn the mixture into the prepared tin, level the surface and arrange the nuts on top. Bake in the oven at 150°C (300°F) mark 2 for about 2½ hours. Leave the cake to cool slightly in the tin, then turn out on to a wire rack and leave to cool completely.

QUICK-MIX CAKES

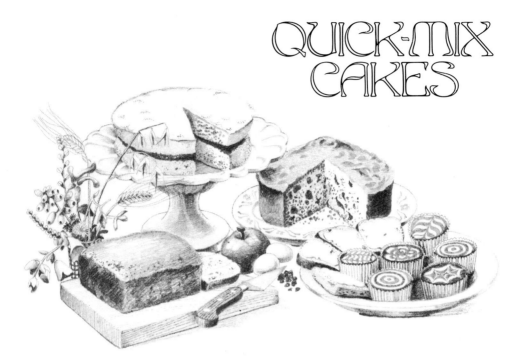

When you need to whip up something special at short notice, a quick-mix cake is the perfect solution. Made by the modern 'one-stage' method based on soft tub margarine, this type of cake is wonderfully quick and easy to prepare. There is no need for any creaming or rubbing in: the ingredients are simply beaten together with a wooden spoon for 2–3 minutes, until well blended and slightly glossy. This method is also ideal for making cakes in an electric mixer but be careful not to overbeat.

Soft margarine is the best choice as it blends easily with other ingredients even when taken straight from the refrigerator. You can use butter or margarine instead, but these must be allowed to soften at room temperature for about an hour beforehand. Self raising flour is invariably used – sometimes with the addition of a little extra baking powder to boost the rise. You can use either caster or brown soft sugar for these quick cakes because their fine crystals dissolve easily. Brown soft sugar produces a slightly darker, richer cake.

Quick-mix cakes are similar to those made by the creaming method, but their texture is more open and they do not keep so well. Store them as soon as they are cold to prevent them going stale. Keep them in an airtight container or wrap them tightly in foil.

One-stage sandwich cake

This is a very quick method of making a cake without rubbing in or creaming the fat first, but you must use a soft tub margarine.

100 g (4 oz) self raising flour
5 ml (1 level tsp) baking powder
100 g (4 oz) soft tub margarine
100 g (4 oz) caster sugar
2 eggs
jam or lemon curd to fill
caster sugar to dredge

Grease two 18-cm (7-inch) sandwich tins and line the base of each with greased greaseproof paper. Sift the flour and baking powder into a large mixing bowl.

Add the remaining ingredients, except the filling and caster sugar to dredge, mix well and beat for 2–3 minutes until well blended.

Divide the mixture equally between the two prepared tins, smoothing the surface with a palette knife. Bake in the oven at 170°C (325°F) mark 3 for 25–35 minutes until well risen and firm to the touch.

Turn the cakes out on to a tea towel, remove the lining paper, turn on to a wire rack and leave to cool. When cool, sandwich the sponges together with jam or lemon curd and dredge the top with caster sugar.

VARIATIONS

One-stage orange sandwich Add the grated rind and juice of one orange and use orange butter cream (*see page 170*) for filling.

One-stage mocha sandwich Replace 25 g (1 oz) flour with 30 ml (2 level tbsp) cocoa powder and 15 ml (1 level tbsp) instant coffee powder. Use chocolate, coffee or mocha butter cream (*see page 170*) for filling.

One-stage chocolate, cherry and nut sandwich Replace 30 ml (2 level tbsp) sugar with 60 ml (4 level tbsp) grated plain chocolate, 75 g (3 oz) chopped glacé cherries and 30 ml (2 level tbsp) chopped walnuts. Use chocolate butter cream (*see page 170*) for filling.

One-stage small cakes Divide the mixture between 18–20 paper cases. Bake in the oven at 200°C (400°F) mark 6 for 15–20 minutes until risen and firm to the touch. When cool, decorate with a selection from the following: glacé icing (*see page 171*), piped butter cream (*see page 170*), glacé cherries, chopped nuts, grated chocolate and crystallised orange and lemon slices.
Illustrated in colour on page 76

One-stage Victoria sandwich made with oil

150 g (5 oz) self raising flour
5 ml (1 level tsp) baking powder
pinch of salt
125 g (4½ oz) caster sugar
105 ml (7 tbsp) vegetable oil
2 eggs
45 ml (3 tbsp) milk
a few drops of vanilla essence
jam

Grease and line two 18-cm (7-inch) sandwich tins. Sift together the flour, baking powder and salt into a large bowl and stir in the sugar. Add the remaining ingredients, except the jam, mix well and beat for 2–3 minutes until well blended. Turn the mixture into the prepared tins and bake in the oven at 180°C (350°F) mark 4 for 35–40 minutes until risen, golden brown and firm to the touch. Turn out and leave to cool on a wire rack. When cold, sandwich the sponges together with jam.

Dark honey teabread

100 g (4 oz) plain flour
5 ml (1 level tsp) ground cinnamon
5 ml (1 level tsp) bicarbonate of soda
pinch of salt
45 ml (3 tbsp) vegetable oil
30 ml (2 tbsp) clear honey
30 ml (2 tbsp) golden syrup
50 g (2 oz) demerara sugar
1 egg
30 ml (2 tbsp) milk
75 g (3 oz) sultanas

For the topping
15 g (½ oz) glacé cherries
15 g (½ oz) walnuts
15 ml (1 tbsp) clear honey

Lightly grease and line a 750-ml (1¼-pint) loaf tin measuring 15 × 7.5 cm (6 × 3 inches) across the top. Sift together the flour, cinnamon, bicarbonate of soda and salt into a large bowl. Add the remaining ingredients, except the topping ingredients, mix well and beat for 2–3 minutes until well blended. Pour the mixture into the prepared tin and bake in the oven at 180°C (350°F) mark 4 for 1 hour. Cool in the tin for a few minutes, then turn out and leave to cool on a wire rack.

Roughly chop the cherries and walnuts for the topping. Brush the top of the cake with honey, then sprinkle over the cherries and nuts. Serve sliced and spread with butter.

One-stage marmalade cake

100 g (4 oz) self raising flour
100 g (4 oz) soft tub margarine
100 g (4 oz) caster sugar
2 eggs
15 ml (1 tbsp) hot water
75 ml (5 level tbsp) chunky marmalade
100 g (4 oz) icing sugar

Grease and line a 20.5-cm (8-inch) round cake tin with greaseproof paper cut deep enough to make a 2.5-cm (1-inch) collar above the top of the tin. Sift the flour into a large bowl. Add the remaining ingredients except the icing sugar, using only 45 ml (3 level tbsp) of the marmalade, mix well and beat for 2–3 minutes until well blended. Turn the mixture into the prepared tin and bake at 180°C (350°F) mark 4 for 35–40 minutes. Turn out and leave to cool on a wire rack. Spread with the remaining marmalade. Sift the icing sugar into a bowl and gradually add enough warm water to give a coating consistency. Spread the icing over the top of the cake and leave to set.

One-stage fruit cake

225 g (8 oz) self raising flour
10 ml (2 level tsp) mixed spice
5 ml (1 level tsp) baking powder
100 g (4 oz) soft tub margarine
100 g (4 oz) dark brown soft sugar
225 g (8 oz) mixed dried fruit
2 eggs
30 ml (2 tbsp) milk

Grease and line an 18-cm (7-inch) round cake tin. Sift together the flour, spice and baking powder into a large bowl. Add the remaining ingredients, mix well and beat for 2–3 minutes until well blended. Turn the mixture into the prepared tin and bake in the oven at 170°C (325°F) mark 3 for $1\frac{3}{4}$ hours. Turn out to cool on a wire rack.

One-stage fruit cake made with oil

225 g (8 oz) plain flour
10 ml (2 level tsp) baking powder
1.25 ml ($\frac{1}{4}$ level tsp) salt
150 g (5 oz) caster sugar
150 ml ($\frac{1}{4}$ pint) vegetable oil
2 eggs
45 ml (3 tbsp) milk
275 g (10 oz) mixed dried fruit
100 g (4 oz) glacé cherries, quartered
50 g (2 oz) chopped mixed peel

Grease and line an 18-cm (7-inch) round cake tin. Sift together the flour, baking powder and salt into a large bowl. Stir in the sugar. Add the remaining ingredients, mix well and beat for 2–3 minutes until well blended. Turn the mixture into the prepared tin and bake in the oven at 170°C (325°F) mark 3 for 1 hour. Reduce the oven temperature to 150°C (300°F) mark 2 and bake for a further $1\frac{1}{4}$–$1\frac{1}{2}$ hours. Leave the cake in the tin to cool for 1 hour, then turn it out. When the cake is cold, store in an airtight tin for at least a day before cutting.

Apple and walnut teabread

Illustrated in colour on page 76

225 g (8 oz) self raising flour
pinch of salt
5 ml (1 level tsp) mixed spice
100 g (4 oz) soft tub margarine
100 g (4 oz) caster sugar
2 eggs, size 2
15 ml (1 tbsp) honey or golden syrup
100 g (4 oz) sultanas
50 g (2 oz) walnuts, chopped
1 medium cooking apple, peeled, cored
 and chopped

Grease and line a 1.4-litre ($2\frac{1}{2}$-pint) loaf tin measuring 19 × 11 cm ($7\frac{1}{2}$ × $4\frac{1}{2}$ inches) across the top. Sift together the flour, salt and mixed spice into a large bowl. Add the remaining ingredients and beat together until well blended. Turn the mixture into the prepared tin and bake in the oven at 180°C (350°F) mark 4 for 1 hour. Reduce the oven temperature to 170°C (325°F) mark 3 and bake for a further 20 minutes. Turn out and leave to cool on a wire rack. Serve thickly sliced and buttered.

Chocolate and blackcurrant gâteau

50 g (2 oz) plain chocolate
100 g (4 oz) self raising flour
2 eggs
100 g (4 oz) soft tub margarine
100 g (4 oz) caster sugar
225 g (8 oz) blackcurrants, washed and strung
50 g (2 oz) granulated sugar
15 ml (1 level tbsp) arrowroot
150 ml ($\frac{1}{4}$ pint) whipping cream
icing sugar to decorate

Grease and line a 21.5-cm (8$\frac{1}{2}$-inch) sandwich tin. Break up the chocolate and put it in a bowl with 30 ml (2 tbsp) water. Stand the bowl over a pan of hot water and heat gently, stirring, until the chocolate has melted. Remove the bowl from the heat and leave to cool slightly.

Sift the flour into a large bowl. Add the chocolate, eggs, margarine and sugar, mix well and beat for 2–3 minutes until well blended. Pour the mixture into the prepared tin and bake in the oven at 190°C (375°F) mark 5 for about 30 minutes until risen and firm to the touch. Turn out and leave to cool on a wire rack.

Meanwhile, cook the blackcurrants with the granulated sugar and 150 ml ($\frac{1}{4}$ pint) water in a pan until soft. Blend the arrowroot with a little water, stir into the black-

currant purée and boil until transparent. Leave to cool.

Split the chocolate cake in half. Whip the cream until stiff. Fold the blackcurrant mixture into the whipped cream and sandwich the two layers of sponge together with the mixture. Place a pretty doily on top of the cake and then sprinkle with sifted icing sugar. Carefully remove the doily to leave a pretty decoration on the top of the cake. Serve this gâteau while it is still fresh.

Walnut coffee cake

100 g (4 oz) self raising flour
5 ml (1 level tsp) baking powder
100 g (4 oz) soft tub margarine
100 g (4 oz) caster sugar
2 eggs, size 2
50 g (2 oz) walnuts, chopped
15 ml (1 tbsp) coffee essence
walnut halves to decorate

For the coffee filling
225 g (8 oz) icing sugar
75 g (3 oz) soft tub margarine
30 ml (2 tbsp) milk
10 ml (2 tsp) coffee essence

Grease and line two 18-cm (7-inch) sandwich tins. Sift together the flour and baking powder into a large bowl. Add the remaining ingredients, except the filling and decoration, mix well and beat for 2–3 minutes until well blended. Turn the mixture into the prepared tins and level the surface. Bake in the oven at 170°C (325°F) mark 3 for 35–40 minutes. Turn the cake out and leave to cool on a wire rack.

To make the filling, sift the icing sugar into a bowl, add the margarine, milk and coffee essence and beat thoroughly. Sandwich the cakes together with some of the filling. Use the remainder to cover the top of the cake. Arrange walnut halves in the icing to decorate.

Chocolate nut bars

Illustrated in colour on page 76

100 g (4 oz) self raising flour
90 ml (6 level tbsp) rolled oats
100 g (4 oz) soft tub margarine
50 g (2 oz) caster sugar
50 g (2 oz) dark brown soft sugar
1.25 ml ($\frac{1}{4}$ level tsp) salt
5 ml (1 tsp) vanilla essence
1 egg
75 g (3 oz) plain chocolate
50 g (2 oz) chopped mixed nuts

Grease and line a 23-cm (9-inch) square shallow cake tin. Sift the flour into a large bowl and mix in the oats. Beat the fat, sugars, salt, essence and egg together until pale and fluffy. Stir in the flour and oats thoroughly. Spread the mixture in the tin and bake in the oven at 180°C (350°F) mark 4 for 30 minutes. Turn out and leave to cool on a wire rack.

Break the chocolate into pieces and put it in a small bowl. Stand the bowl over a pan of hot water and heat gently, stirring, until melted. Spread on the cake and sprinkle with nuts. Cut into bars.
Makes about 16 bars

Chocolate cake

100 g (4 oz) self raising flour
5 ml (1 level tsp) baking powder
30 ml (2 level tbsp) cocoa powder
225 g (8 oz) soft tub margarine
100 g (4 oz) caster sugar
2 eggs
75 g (3 oz) icing sugar, sifted
45 ml (3 level tbsp) chocolate nut spread

Grease and line two 18-cm (7-inch) sandwich tins. Sift together the flour, baking powder and cocoa powder into a large bowl. Add half the margarine, the sugar and eggs, mix well and beat for 2–3 minutes until well blended. Turn the mixture into the prepared tins. Bake in the oven at 170°C (325°F) mark 3 for about 25 minutes until well risen and firm. Turn the cake out of the tin and leave to cool on a wire rack.

Stir the icing sugar into the remaining margarine. Beat together until creamy. Add the chocolate nut spread, a tablespoon at a time, beating well. Sandwich the cakes together with about half the icing. Swirl the rest of the icing on top of the cake with a palette knife.

MELT-IN-THE-MOUTH CAKES

Gingerbreads and other cakes made by the 'melting' method have a deliciously moist and sticky texture which even dedicated slimmers find hard to resist.

The inviting texture and rich dark colour of these cakes are due to the high proportion of sugary ingredients, including liquid sweeteners such as syrup or black treacle. To ensure the liquid sweetener is easily incorporated, it is warmed with the fat and sugar until blended and then added to the dry ingredients together with any eggs and the liquid.

Bicarbonate of soda is often used to raise these cakes – it reacts with natural acids present in liquid sweeteners. Spices are frequently added; they enhance the flavour of the sweetener and also counteract the faintly bitter taste bicarbonate of soda is apt to leave.

Measure the sweetener carefully; too much can cause a heavy, sunken cake. Warm it very gently, just until the sugar has dissolved and the fat has melted. If allowed to boil, the mixture will become an unusable toffee-like mess. Allow the mixture to cool slightly before pouring it on to the dry ingredients, or it will begin to cook the flour and a hard tough cake will result. The blended mixture should have the consistency of heavy batter; it can be poured into the prepared tin and will find its own level.

Most cakes made by the melting method should be stored for a day or so before cutting to allow the crust to soften and the flavour to mellow.

Gingerbread

This moist cake is best eaten two or three days after baking. Wrap in foil and store in an airtight tin. For a smaller cake, use half the quantities given here and bake in a prepared 18-cm (7-inch) square tin for about 1 hour.

450 g (1 lb) plain flour
5 ml (1 level tsp) salt
15 ml (1 level tbsp) ground ginger
15 ml (3 level tsp) baking powder
5 ml (1 level tsp) bicarbonate of soda
225 g (8 oz) demerara sugar
175 g (6 oz) butter or margarine
175 g (6 oz) black treacle
175 g (6 oz) golden syrup
300 ml ($\frac{1}{2}$ pint) milk
1 egg, beaten

Grease and line a 23-cm (9-inch) square tin. Sift together the flour, salt, ginger, baking powder and bicarbonate of soda into a large mixing bowl. Put the sugar, fat, treacle and syrup in a pan and warm gently over a low heat until melted and well blended. Do not allow the mixture to boil.

Remove the pan from the heat and leave to cool slightly, until you can hold your hand comfortably against the side of the pan. Mix in the milk and beaten egg.

Make a well in the centre of the dry ingredients, pour in the liquid and mix very thoroughly.

Pour the mixture into the prepared tin and bake in the oven at 170°C (325°F) mark 3 for about 1½ hours until firm but springy to the touch. Leave the gingerbread in the tin for about 10 minutes after baking, then turn out on to a wire rack, remove the lining paper and leave to cool.

Spiced carrot cake

Illustrated in colour on page 93

450 g (1 lb) plain wholemeal flour
large pinch of salt
2.5 ml ($\frac{1}{2}$ level tsp) bicarbonate of soda
15 ml (1 level tbsp) ground cinnamon
2.5 ml ($\frac{1}{2}$ level tsp) grated nutmeg
1.25 ml ($\frac{1}{4}$ level tsp) ground cloves
100 g (4 oz) butter
450 g (1 lb) carrots, trimmed and scraped
100 g (4 oz) dark brown soft sugar
75 g (3 oz) clear honey
75 g (3 oz) black treacle
about 30 ml (2 tbsp) milk
30 ml (2 level tbsp) demerara sugar

Grease and line a 20.5-cm (8-inch) round cake tin. Sift together the flour, salt, bicarbonate of soda and spices into a large bowl. Rub in the butter. Coarsely grate in the carrots, then make a well in the centre. Warm the sugar, honey and treacle together over a low heat, and pour into the dry ingredients. Mix to a stiff dropping consistency with the milk. Turn the mixture into the prepared tin. Level the surface and sprinkle over the demerara sugar. Bake in the oven at 190°C (375°F) mark 5 for 1–1$\frac{1}{4}$ hours until a fine, warmed skewer inserted in the centre of the cake comes out clean. Turn the cake out of the tin and leave to cool on a wire rack.

Grandmother's boiled fruit cake

275 g (10 oz) plain flour
10 ml (2 level tsp) bicarbonate of soda
300 ml ($\frac{1}{2}$ pint) freshly made tea
100 g (4 oz) margarine
150 g (5 oz) light brown soft sugar
175 g (6 oz) currants
175 g (6 oz) sultanas
15 ml (1 level tbsp) mixed spice
1 egg, size 2, beaten

Grease and line an 18-cm (7-inch) round cake tin. Sift together the flour and bicarbonate of soda into a large bowl. Make a well in the centre. Put the tea, margarine, sugar, currants, sultanas and spice in a pan and bring to the boil. Reduce the heat and simmer for 20 minutes. Remove from the heat and leave to cool. When cold, pour into the dry ingredients, add the egg and mix thoroughly. Turn the mixture into the prepared tin and bake in the oven at 180°C (350°F) mark 4 for about 1 hour. When the cake is beginning to brown, cover with a piece of greaseproof paper. Turn out and leave to cool on a wire rack.

Boston brownies

Illustrated in colour on page 93

These are traditional American cookies which keep well if stored in an airtight container.

50 g (2 oz) plain chocolate
65 g (2$\frac{1}{2}$ oz) butter or margarine
175 g (6 oz) caster sugar
65 g (2$\frac{1}{2}$ oz) self raising flour
1.25 ml ($\frac{1}{4}$ level tsp) salt
2 eggs, beaten
2.5 ml ($\frac{1}{2}$ tsp) vanilla essence
50 g (2 oz) walnuts, roughly chopped

Grease and line a shallow 20.5-cm (8-inch) square cake tin. Break up the chocolate and put it in a bowl with the fat. Stand the bowl over a pan of hot water and heat gently, stirring, until melted. Add the sugar. Sift together the flour and salt into a bowl. Add the chocolate mixture, eggs, vanilla essence and walnuts. Mix thoroughly. Pour the mixture into the prepared tin and bake in the oven at 180°C (350°F) mark 4 for 35–40 minutes until the mixture is risen and beginning to leave the sides of the tin. Leave in the tin to cool, then cut into squares.
Makes about 12

Shaping Brandy snaps round a spoon handle

Brandy snaps

These crisp, lacy biscuits can be stored, unfilled, for about a week in an airtight tin.

50 g (2 oz) butter or margarine
50 g (2 oz) caster sugar
30 ml (2 level tbsp) golden syrup
50 g (2 oz) plain flour
2.5 ml ($\frac{1}{2}$ level tsp) ground ginger
5 ml (1 tsp) brandy
grated rind of $\frac{1}{2}$ a lemon
150 ml ($\frac{1}{4}$ pint) double cream

Grease the handles of several wooden spoons and line two or three baking sheets with non-stick paper. Melt the fat with the sugar and syrup in a small pan over a low heat. Remove the pan from the heat and sift in the flour and ground ginger. Add the brandy and lemon rind and stir until the ingredients are evenly blended.

Drop small spoonfuls of the mixture on to the prepared baking sheets, spacing them about 10 cm (4 inches) apart to allow room for spreading. Bake in rotation in the oven at 180°C (350°F) mark 4 for 7–10 minutes until bubbly and golden. Allow the biscuits to cool for 1–2 minutes, then loosen with a palette knife and roll them around the spoon handles. Leave until set, then twist gently to remove. (If the biscuits cool too much while still on the sheets and become too brittle to roll, return the sheet to the oven for a moment to soften them.)

Just before serving, whisk the cream until thick and use to fill the brandy snaps. *Makes 10*

VARIATION

Illustrated in colour on page 29

For brandy cornets, grease several metal cream horn tins. Prepare and bake the mixture as above. Allow the biscuits to cool for 1–2 minutes, then roll around the tins. Leave until set, then twist gently to remove from the tins.

Fluted gingerbread loaf

Illustrated in colour on page 40

225 g (8 oz) plain flour
2.5 ml ($\frac{1}{2}$ level tsp) salt
20 ml (4 level tsp) ground ginger
2.5 ml ($\frac{1}{2}$ level tsp) baking powder
2.5 ml ($\frac{1}{2}$ level tsp) bicarbonate of soda
100 g (4 oz) light brown soft sugar
75 g (3 oz) butter
30 ml (2 level tbsp) black treacle
150 ml (10 level tbsp) golden syrup
150 ml ($\frac{1}{4}$ pint) milk
1 egg, beaten
4–5 pieces of stem ginger

Thoroughly grease a 28.5 × 10-cm (11 × 4-inch) ridged oblong (Balmoral) tin with 1.1-litre (2-pint) capacity. Sift together the flour, salt, ground ginger, baking powder and bicarbonate of soda into a bowl. Make a well in the centre. Put the sugar, butter, treacle and golden syrup in a pan and warm gently over a low heat until melted and well blended. Leave to cool slightly. Pour into the dry ingredients, add the milk and egg and mix thoroughly. Turn the mixture into the prepared tin and bake in the oven at 170°C (325°F) mark 3 for about 1 hour 10 minutes. Allow to cool slightly in the tin, before turning out on to a wire rack. Decorate with the pieces of stem ginger, sliced and chopped.

Flapjack

Illustrated in colour on pages 93 and 168

50 g (2 oz) butter or block margarine
50 g (2 oz) demerara sugar
45 ml (3 level tbsp) golden syrup
100 g (4 oz) rolled oats

Grease an 18-cm (7-inch) square cake tin. Melt the butter with the sugar and syrup and pour it on to the rolled oats. Mix well, turn the mixture into the prepared tin and press down well. Bake in the oven at 180°C (350°F) mark 4 for 20–25 minutes until golden brown. Cool slightly in the tin, mark into fingers with a sharp knife and loosen round the edges. When firm, remove from the tin and break the flapjack into fingers. The flapjack may be stored in an airtight container for up to a week.
Makes 6–8

Florentines

Illustrated in colour on page 94

90 g (3½ oz) butter
100 g (4 oz) caster sugar
100 g (4 oz) flaked almonds, roughly
  chopped
25 g (1 oz) sultanas
5 glacé cherries, chopped
25 g (1 oz) chopped mixed peel
15 ml (1 tbsp) single cream or top of the
  milk
175 g (6 oz) plain chocolate

Line three baking sheets with non-stick paper. Melt the butter in a saucepan over a low heat, add the sugar and boil the mixture for 1 minute. Remove the pan from the heat and add all the remaining ingredients, except the chocolate, stirring well to mix. Drop the mixture in small, well-rounded heaps on to the prepared sheets, spacing them very well apart to allow room for spreading. Bake in the oven at 180°C (350°F) mark 4 for about 10 minutes until golden brown.

Remove the baking sheets from the oven and press around the edges of the biscuits with the blade of a knife to neaten the shape. Leave on the sheets until beginning to firm, then carefully lift on to a wire rack and leave to cool.

Break the chocolate into pieces and place in a bowl over a pan of hot water. Heat gently, stirring, until the chocolate has melted. Remove the bowl from the heat. Leave to cool and just as the chocolate is beginning to set, spread over the backs of the biscuits. Draw the prongs of a fork across the chocolate to mark wavy lines and leave to set.
Makes about 12

Oatmeal parkin

225 g (8 oz) plain flour
10 ml (2 level tsp) baking powder
20 ml (4 level tsp) ground ginger
100 g (4 oz) lard or margarine
225 g (8 oz) medium oatmeal
100 g (4 oz) caster sugar
175 g (6 oz) golden syrup
175 g (6 oz) black treacle
1 egg, beaten
60 ml (4 tbsp) milk

Grease and line a 23-cm (9-inch) square cake tin. Sift together the flour, baking powder and ginger into a large bowl. Rub in the fat and add the oatmeal and sugar. Make a well in the centre. Put the syrup and treacle in a pan and warm gently over a low heat. Leave to cool slightly. Pour into the dry ingredients, add the egg and milk and mix thoroughly. Pour the mixture into the prepared tin and bake in the oven at 180°C (350°F) mark 4 for 45 minutes–1 hour. Allow to cool a little in the tin, then turn out and finish cooling on a wire rack. Oatmeal parkin is best kept for about a week before eating. Serve cut into squares or fingers.

Swedish cardamom cake

Illustrated in colour on page 58

100 g (4 oz) butter
225 g (8 oz) caster sugar
10 ml (2 level tsp) ground cardamom
1 egg, size 2, beaten
150 ml ($\frac{1}{4}$ pint) single cream
350 g (12 oz) self raising flour

For the icing
75 g (3 oz) icing sugar
10 ml (2 tsp) lemon juice
grated lemon rind to decorate

Grease and dust with flour a 23-cm (9-inch), 1.7-litre (3-pint) ring mould. Melt the butter and pour it over the sugar in a bowl. Beat in the cardamom, egg and cream, then sift the flour over the mixture and fold in with a metal spoon. Turn the mixture into the prepared tin and level the surface. Bake in the oven at 180°C (350°F) mark 4 for 40–50 minutes until golden and firm to the touch. Turn out and leave to cool on a wire rack.

To make the icing, sift the icing sugar into a bowl and gradually add the lemon juice. Spoon the icing on to the top of the cake and allow to run down the sides. Decorate at once with lemon rind and leave to set.

Belgian cake

190 g (6$\frac{1}{2}$ oz) plain flour
5 ml (1 level tsp) bicarbonate of soda
5 ml (1 level tsp) baking powder
5 ml (1 level tsp) mixed spice
115 g (4$\frac{1}{2}$ oz) caster sugar
100 g (4 oz) currants
200 ml (7 fl oz) water
100 g (4 oz) butter

Grease and line an 18-cm (7-inch) round cake tin. Sift together the flour, bicarbonate of soda, baking powder and mixed spice into a bowl. Make a well in the centre. Place the sugar, currants, water and butter in a pan, bring to the boil and simmer for 10 minutes. Cool thoroughly. When cold, pour the currant mixture into the dry ingredients and mix thoroughly. Turn the mixture into the prepared tin and bake in the oven at 180°C (350°F) mark 4 for about 50 minutes. Turn out and leave to cool on a wire rack.

Note The cake may dip slightly in the centre during cooking.

From top: Spiced carrot cake, Boston brownies (*page 89*), Flapjack (*page 91*)

NO-BAKE CAKES

By using certain ingredients which become firm when cooled and act as a binding agent, you can make a variety of mouthwatering confections without the need for baking. No single common method is used, but generally no-bake cakes are set by chilling or by using gelatine. They are particularly popular with children and many will double equally well as a dessert.

Melted chocolate or melted butter can be combined with ready-cooked cereals (such as cornflakes or rice crispies) or crushed biscuits (plain, crumbly biscuits are best) and the mixture used to line a flan or sandwich tin. Flavourings, such as ground almonds or cinnamon, can also be added. Stale, broken biscuits can be used as long as they are not soggy. Leave the case to become firm in the refrigerator for about 1 hour before removing it from the tin and adding the filling. (Use a loose-bottomed tin for easy removal of the case.) Biscuit crust flan cases will store well for up to a week if wrapped in foil and kept in an airtight container. They can also be frozen and stored in the freezer for up to six months.

Gelatine is often used to set the filling in a no-bake cake – especially an uncooked cheesecake mixture. Nowadays gelatine is mostly sold in powdered form, although it may sometimes be found in sheets. Both powdered and sheet gelatine must be dissolved in a little measured liquid. Sheet gelatine may need preliminary soaking to make it pliable. Some cake recipes are made with tablet jelly instead of gelatine.

Florentines (*page 91*)

Chocolate peppermint crisp flan

175 g (6 oz) gingernut biscuits
75 g (3 oz) plain chocolate
3 egg yolks
100 g (4 oz) caster sugar
30 ml (2 tbsp) peppermint flavoured liqueur
10 ml (2 level tsp) powdered gelatine
a few drops of green food colouring
150 ml ($\frac{1}{4}$ pint) double or whipping cream, whipped

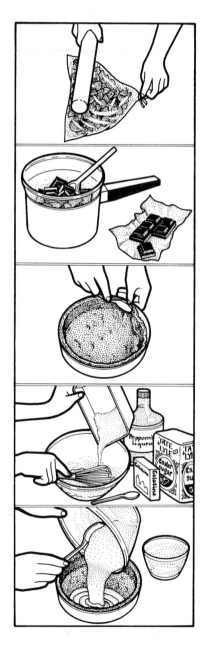

Grease a shallow 20.5-cm (8-inch) sandwich tin. Break the biscuits up, put them in a strong polythene bag and crush them with a rolling pin. Alternatively, crush the biscuit pieces, a few at a time, in a blender.

Break the chocolate into small pieces and place in a bowl. Stand the bowl over a pan of hot, not boiling, water and heat gently, stirring, until the chocolate has melted. Remove from the heat and stir in the biscuit crumbs until they bind together.

Spoon the mixture into the prepared tin, pressing the mixture into shape to make a shell with the back of a teaspoon. Chill or leave in a cool place until set.

Put the egg yolks in a bowl and whisk together. Add the sugar and liqueur and continue whisking until the mixture thickens. Put 30 ml (2 tbsp) water in a bowl and sprinkle in the gelatine. Stand the bowl over a pan of hot water and heat gently until the gelatine has dissolved. Remove from the heat and leave to cool slightly.

Gradually whisk the gelatine into the egg and liqueur mixture and fold in the food colouring and whipped cream. Just as the mixture is beginning to set, pour it into the biscuit crust case. Leave in the refrigerator to chill before serving.

Chocolate cornflake cakes

Illustrated in colour on page 168

225 g (8 oz) plain chocolate
15 ml (1 tbsp) golden syrup
50 g (2 oz) butter or margarine
50 g (2 oz) cornflakes

Place twelve paper cases on a baking sheet. Break the chocolate into pieces, put in a pan with the golden syrup and fat and melt together over a low heat. Remove the pan from the heat and stir in the cornflakes, mixing well. Divide the mixture equally between the paper cases and leave to set.
Makes 12

VARIATIONS

Add some finely chopped nuts, glacé cherries, sultanas or dates and stir in with the cornflakes. Alternatively, melt some chocolate and drizzle over the top, or decorate with a glacé cherry.

Uncooked chocolate cake

175 g (6 oz) digestive biscuits
25 g (1 oz) walnuts, coarsely chopped
25 g (1 oz) seedless raisins
90 g (3½ oz) butter or margarine
25 g (1 oz) caster sugar
75 g (3 oz) golden syrup
50 g (2 oz) cocoa powder

For the icing
50 g (2 oz) plain chocolate
15 ml (1 tbsp) hot water
65 g (2½ oz) icing sugar
a knob of butter

Place a 19 or 20.5-cm (7½ or 8-inch) flan ring on a flat serving plate. Roughly crush the biscuits, then combine with the walnuts and raisins. Cream the fat, sugar and syrup together until pale and fluffy.

Sift and beat in the cocoa, then stir in the biscuit mixture. When the ingredients are well mixed, press evenly into the flan ring and chill for 8 hours or overnight.

To make the icing, break the chocolate into pieces and place in a small pan with the hot water. Sift in the icing sugar, add the butter and stir together over a very low heat until melted and blended. Remove from the heat and allow to cool slightly. Remove the flan ring and spread the chocolate icing all over the cake. Leave in a cool place to set.

Coffee brandy cake

175 g (6 oz) butter
175 g (6 oz) caster sugar
3 eggs, size 2
30 ml (2 tbsp) coffee essence
15 ml (1 tbsp) brandy
12 trifle sponges
150 ml (¼ pint) double cream
25 g (1 oz) walnuts, finely chopped

Grease and line a 20.5-cm (8-inch) loose-bottomed cake tin.

Cream the butter and sugar together until pale and fluffy. Beat in the eggs, coffee essence and brandy. Cut the sponges in half lengthways and arrange eight pieces in the base of the prepared tin. Pour in half the coffee mixture. Cover with a further eight pieces of sponge, then pour over the remaining coffee mixture. Arrange the rest of the sponge pieces on top. Press down well and cover with greaseproof paper and a small plate with a weight on top. Leave in the refrigerator for about 3 hours until set.

Turn the cake out on to a plate. Whisk the cream until stiff and use some to cover the top of the cake. Fill a piping bag fitted with a medium star nozzle with the remaining cream and pipe a shell border around the top and bottom edges of the cake. Sprinkle the centre with nuts.

Chocolate and hazelnut ice cream cake

568 ml (1 pint) milk
75 g (3 oz) caster sugar
4 eggs, beaten
a few drops of vanilla essence
50 g (2 oz) hazelnuts, toasted and finely
  chopped
175 g (6 oz) plain chocolate
30 ml (2 tbsp) coffee cream liqueur
  (optional)
750 ml (1¼ pints) double cream
a few hazelnuts, toasted
a little grated chocolate

Heat the milk and sugar together in a saucepan until it just begins to boil. Pour on to the eggs, stirring all the time. Return the mixture to the pan and stir over a low heat until the custard thickens. Strain into a bowl. Add the vanilla essence and hazelnuts to 300 ml (½ pint) of the custard and pour into a freezing container. Break the chocolate into pieces, place in a bowl over a pan of hot water and stir until melted. Fold the melted chocolate into the remaining custard with the liqueur, if used, and pour into a freezing container. Leave to cool.

Lightly whisk 600 ml (1 pint) cream. Fold three quarters of the cream into the chocolate custard and the remaining quarter into the nut custard. Place the ice creams in the freezer or ice compartment of the refrigerator and freeze for about 45 minutes until frozen about 1 cm (½ inch) around the edges. Remove from the freezer and whisk well. Place half the chocolate cream in the base of a 19-cm (7½-inch) round, loose-bottomed cake tin. Spoon over the nut cream and finish with a layer of the remaining chocolate. Return to the freezer for about 2 hours until firm. Remove from the tin. Whisk the remaining cream until thick, spoon into a piping bag fitted with a large star nozzle and pipe on the top of the cake. Decorate with the hazelnuts and chocolate. Leave in the refrigerator for 15 minutes to 'come to' before serving.
Serves 10–12

Chocolate refrigerator cake

24–26 soft sponge fingers
175 g (6 oz) caster sugar
30 ml (2 level tbsp) cornflour
450 ml (¾ pint) milk
300 ml (½ pint) double or whipping cream
50 g (2 oz) plain chocolate
2 egg yolks
25 g (1 oz) butter
5 ml (1 level tsp) powdered gelatine
toasted flaked almonds to decorate

Line a 2-litre (3½-pint) loaf tin measuring 24 × 13.5 cm (9½ × 5½ inches) across the top with non-stick paper. Arrange a layer of sponge fingers to cover the base and sides. Blend the sugar and cornflour in a pan; gradually stir in the milk and half the cream. Break up the chocolate, add to the milk and bring slowly to the boil, stirring. Boil gently for 2–3 minutes, stirring, cool for a few minutes and beat in the egg yolks. Cook for 1 minute and beat in the butter. Put 10 ml (2 tsp) water in a small bowl and sprinkle in the gelatine. Stand the bowl over a pan of hot water and heat gently until the gelatine has dissolved. Cool and stir into the mixture. Cool, stirring occasionally. When the mixture is beginning to thicken, pour half of it over the sponge fingers. Cover with another layer of sponge fingers, then spoon the remaining mixture over these. Trim the tops of the fingers level with the filling and use the trimmings to make a final layer.

Leave overnight in the refrigerator. To serve, turn out on to a flat dish. Whip the rest of the cream, cover the top of the cake with it and sprinkle with the almonds.

Truffle cakes

100 g (4 oz) dry sponge cake or trimmings
100 g (4 oz) caster sugar
100 g (4 oz) ground almonds
about 275 g (10 oz) apricot jam, melted
5 ml (1 tsp) sherry or rum
chocolate vermicelli

Rub the cake through a fairly coarse sieve, add the sugar and ground almonds and stir well to mix. Add enough jam to bind and flavour with sherry or rum. Shape into sixteen or eighteen small balls and leave to become firm. Dip each ball in jam and roll in chocolate vermicelli to coat. Leave to dry, then place the cakes into small paper cases.

Makes 16–18

Coffee crackle

65 g (2½ oz) butter
30 ml (2 level tbsp) golden syrup
75 g (3 oz) rice crispies
30 ml (2 tbsp) coffee essence
15 ml (1 level tbsp) powdered gelatine
450 ml (¾ pint) milk
150 ml (¼ pint) single cream
two 300-ml (½-pint) packets coffee instant
    dessert
150 ml (¼ pint) double cream
15 ml (1 tbsp) milk
bought chocolate sauce

Grease and line the base and sides of a 2.3-litre (4-pint) charlotte mould. In a pan, melt the butter and golden syrup together. Add the rice crispies. Toss together until the crispies are evenly coated. Press the crispies mixture on to the base and sides of the tin with the back of a spoon – tilt the mould at an angle to do this satisfactorily. Chill until firm, then turn out the mould carefully and gently peel off the paper. Place the shell on a serving plate.

Put the coffee essence and 15 ml (1 tbsp) water in a small bowl and sprinkle in the gelatine. Stand the bowl over a pan of hot water and heat gently until the gelatine has dissolved. Whisk the milk, single cream and dessert mix until thick. Fold the cooled gelatine into a little of the whisked mixture. Put this back into the mixture and chill for 1 hour. Carefully spoon it into the crispy shell and level the surface. Lightly tie a band of ribbon round for support. Whip the double cream with 15 ml (1 tbsp) milk until it just holds its shape. Spread this over the filling. Drizzle some chocolate sauce over the top and draw a skewer through to give a 'marbling' effect. Serve this gâteau on the day it is made.

Collettes

190 g (6½ oz) plain chocolate
25 g (1 oz) butter
10 ml (2 tsp) brandy
60 ml (4 tbsp) double cream
flaked almonds and glacé cherries to
    decorate

Arrange sixteen small paper cases on a baking sheet. Break 100 g (4 oz) chocolate into pieces and place in a bowl over a pan of hot water. Heat gently, stirring, until the chocolate has melted, then remove the bowl from the heat. Using a clean paint brush, coat the inside of each paper case with the melted chocolate. Leave to set. Repeat at least twice. Chill until quite firm, then carefully peel away the paper from the chocolate cases.

Melt the remaining chocolate with the butter and leave until cool but not set, then stir in the brandy. Whisk the cream until stiff and fold into the chocolate mixture. Leave to set until thick enough for piping. Spoon the chocolate cream into a piping bag fitted with a small star nozzle and pipe into the chocolate cases. Decorate with a flaked almond or a piece of cherry.

Makes 16

Refrigerated cheesecake

225 g (8 oz) digestive biscuits
175 g (6 oz) butter
2.5 ml ($\frac{1}{2}$ level tsp) ground mixed spice
225 g (8 oz) cottage cheese
225 g (8 oz) cream cheese
grated rind and juice of 2 small lemons
2 eggs, separated
75 g (3 oz) caster sugar
15 ml (1 level tbsp) powdered gelatine
150 ml ($\frac{1}{4}$ pint) double cream

For the topping
50 g (2 oz) caster sugar
3–4 peaches, skinned, quartered, stoned
  and sliced
45 ml (3 level tbsp) apricot jam

Line the base of a 20.5-cm (8-inch) spring release cake tin with a round of non-stick paper. Crush the biscuits finely. Melt the butter in a pan and stir in the biscuit crumbs with the spice until well mixed. Use this mixture to line the base and sides of the prepared tin. Leave in the refrigerator for about 30 minutes until set.

Sieve the cottage cheese into a bowl and gradually beat in the cream cheese until smooth. Add the lemon rind and slowly work in 75 ml (5 tbsp) lemon juice. Whisk until smooth. Place the egg yolks and caster sugar in a small bowl and whisk together until pale and thick, then gradually fold them into the cheese mixture.

Place 45 ml (3 tbsp) water in a small bowl and sprinkle the gelatine on top. Stand the bowl over a pan of hot water and heat gently until the gelatine dissolves. Stir into the cheese mixture. Whip the cream until stiff and fold into the cheese mixture. Finally, whisk the egg whites until stiff and fold into the mixture. Pour into the biscuit case, smooth the surface and leave in the refrigerator to set.

To prepare the topping, dissolve the sugar in 150 ml ($\frac{1}{4}$ pint) water and bring to the boil. Add the peach slices and poach until tender. Drain, cool and arrange on top of the cheesecake. Add the jam to the syrup and boil to reduce to a glaze. Cool, then brush over the peaches. Chill in the refrigerator.

About 20 minutes before serving, carefully remove the cheesecake from the tin to 'come to' at room temperature.

Choco-mint swirl

Illustrated in colour on page 112

4 eggs, separated
50–75 g (2–3 oz) caster sugar
20 ml (4 level tsp) powdered gelatine
1.25 ml ($\frac{1}{4}$ tsp) peppermint essence
1.25 ml ($\frac{1}{4}$ tsp) sap green food colouring
50 g (2 oz) plain chocolate, melted
300 ml ($\frac{1}{2}$ pint) double cream
chocolate finger biscuits
whipped cream and shavings of chocolate
  to decorate

Place the egg yolks and sugar in a bowl. Whisk together over hot water until thick and creamy. Remove from the heat, whisking from time to time until cool. Put 45 ml (3 tbsp) water in a small bowl and sprinkle in the gelatine. Stand the bowl over a pan of hot water and heat gently until the gelatine has dissolved. Cool and stir into the egg mixture. Stir in the peppermint essence and green food colouring. Divide the peppermint mixture between two basins. Stir melted chocolate into one portion. Lightly whip the cream and fold half into each portion of mixture.

Stiffly whisk the egg whites and fold half through each mixture. Spoon alternately into a 900-ml (1$\frac{1}{2}$-pint) Balmoral mould. Top with the chocolate finger biscuits, cut to fit. Chill until set. Unmould and decorate with whipped cream, swirling with the back of a spoon, and chocolate.

Note The gelatine gels quickly, so have

the other ingredients ready. If sap green colouring is not available then omit it – do *not* substitute other greens.

Coffee-chocolate slice

Illustrated in colour on page 123

30 ml (2 level tbsp) granulated sugar
75 g (3 oz) butter
100 g (4 oz) icing sugar
225 g (8 oz) cream cheese
4 glacé cherries, chopped
25 g (1 oz) walnut halves, chopped
30 ml (2 level tbsp) nibbed almonds, toasted
15 ml (1 tbsp) coffee essence
two 184-g (6½-oz) packets Nice biscuits (small size)

For the icing
100 g (4 oz) caster sugar
45 ml (3 level tbsp) cocoa powder
5 ml (1 tsp) coffee essence
75 g (3 oz) butter

In a pan, dissolve the sugar in 60 ml (4 tbsp) water, bring to the boil, then leave to cool. Meanwhile, put the butter in a bowl, sift in the icing sugar and cream together. Add the cheese and beat well. Spoon one third of the mixture into another bowl and add the cherries and nuts. Beat the coffee essence into the remainder. Dip fifteen biscuits, one at a time, in the sugar syrup and arrange them in three rows of five on a sheet of foil. Spread each row with the coffee mixture. Add a second and third layer of biscuits and filling. Pile the cherry and nut cheese along the centre row only. Put your hands under the foil and bring up the outer rows of biscuits to meet in the centre, forming a triangle. Secure the foil and chill.

For the icing, blend the sugar and cocoa with 30 ml (2 tbsp) water and the coffee essence in a pan, then bring to the boil. Remove from the heat, add the butter in small pieces, beat well and cool. The icing should be of a coating consistency. Unwrap the cake, place on a wire rack over a tray and coat with icing. Chill overnight.

Apricot cheesecake

Illustrated in colour on page 111

450 g (1 lb) fresh apricots
75 g (3 oz) granulated sugar
225 g (8 oz) digestive biscuits
175 g (6 oz) butter or margarine
5 ml (1 level tsp) ground mixed spice
50 g (2 oz) caster sugar
2 large thin-skinned lemons
20 ml (4 level tsp) powdered gelatine
225 g (8 oz) cream cheese
225 g (8 oz) cottage cheese
397-g (14-oz) can condensed milk
icing sugar

Grease and line the base of a 21.5-cm (8½-inch) spring release tin. Halve and stone the apricots and poach gently in a syrup of the sugar and 200 ml (7 fl oz) water. When tender, drain and cool. Finely crush the biscuits. Melt the fat and stir in the biscuit crumbs, spice and sugar. Use three quarters of the crumbs to line the base and sides of the prepared tin. Set in the refrigerator for 30 minutes.

Grate the rind of both lemons and squeeze out the juice. Put the juice in a small bowl and sprinkle in the gelatine. Stand the bowl over a pan of hot water and heat gently until the gelatine has dissolved. Blend together the rind, cheeses, condensed milk and cooled gelatine until smooth. Roughly chop the apricots, then fold into the mixture. Pour the mixture into the crumb case, scatter the remaining crumbs over the top and place in the refrigerator for 2–3 hours. Turn out, upside down and dredge heavily with sifted icing sugar. Mark on a lattice design with a knife.
Serves 10–12

Florida cheesecake

100 g (4 oz) digestive biscuits
50 g (2 oz) butter or margarine
175 ml (6 fl oz) frozen concentrated
   orange juice
30 ml (2 level tbsp) powdered gelatine
100 g (4 oz) caster sugar
350 g (12 oz) cottage cheese
200 ml (7 fl oz) milk
2 egg whites
226-g (8-oz) can pineapple rings, drained
a few walnut halves to decorate

Crush the biscuits finely. Melt the fat and stir in the biscuit crumbs. Press into the base of a 21.5-cm (8½-inch) spring release cake tin. Pour the orange juice into a bowl and sprinkle in the gelatine. Stand the bowl over a pan of hot water and heat gently until the gelatine has dissolved. Cool and stir in the sugar. Cool slightly. Blend the cottage cheese and milk to form a purée. Stir into the cooled orange mixture. On the point of setting, fold in stiffly whisked egg whites. Turn the mixture into the prepared tin and leave to chill in the refrigerator.

Remove from the tin and decorate with the quartered pineapple rings and walnuts.

Gooseberry cheesecake

150 g (5 oz) digestive biscuits
65 g (2½ oz) butter
5 ml (1 level tsp) ground cinnamon
700 g (1½ lb) gooseberries, topped and
   tailed
175 g (6 oz) caster sugar
25 ml (5 level tsp) powdered gelatine
350 g (12 oz) cream cheese
300 ml (½ pint) double cream
1.25 ml (¼ level tsp) arrowroot

Grease and line a 20.5-cm (8-inch) spring-release cake tin. Finely crush the biscuits. Melt the butter in a pan and stir in the biscuit crumbs and cinnamon. Mix well together, then press into the prepared tin and chill in the refrigerator.

Place the gooseberries in a pan with the sugar, stir over a gentle heat until the juice runs, then cover and simmer to a pulp. Sieve to remove the pips; there should be 600 ml (1 pint) purée. Put 30 ml (2 tbsp) water in a small bowl and sprinkle in the gelatine. Stand the bowl over a pan of hot water and heat gently until the gelatine has dissolved. Cool and stir into 450 ml (¾ pint) of the purée, allow to cool but not set. Beat the cream cheese until smooth, then gradually beat in the jellied purée. Whisk the cream until it holds its shape but not stiff. Fold into the mixture then turn into the tin. Chill until firm.

In a pan, blend the arrowroot with the remaining purée, bring to boil and cook for 1 minute. Cool. When lukewarm, spread over the cheesecake. Leave to set.

Chocolate cases

175 g (6 oz) plain chocolate

For the filling and decoration
100 g (4 oz) sponge cake crumbs
15 ml (1 level tbsp) raspberry jam
a little sherry
150 ml (¼ pint) double cream
8 maraschino cherries

Break the chocolate into pieces and place in a bowl over a pan of hot water. Heat gently, stirring, until the chocolate has melted, then remove the bowl from the

*Making
Chocolate
cases*

heat. Using a clean paint brush, coat the inside of eight small paper cases with the melted chocolate. Leave to set and then repeat. Chill until quite firm, then carefully peel away the paper cases.

Mix together the cake crumbs, jam and sherry to taste and fill the cases with this mixture. Whisk the cream until stiff and divide equally between the cases, spooning it over the filling. Top each chocolate case with a cherry.

Makes 8

Coffee crunch cheesecake

Choose a pretty fluted china flan dish as this cheesecake is served directly from it.

175 g (6 oz) plain chocolate digestive biscuits
75 g (3 oz) butter
100 g (4 oz) curd cheese
150 ml ($\frac{1}{4}$ pint) whipping cream
2 egg yolks
50 g (2 oz) caster sugar
45 ml (3 tbsp) coffee essence
30 ml (2 tbsp) coffee flavoured liqueur
10 ml (2 level tsp) powdered gelatine
1 egg white
25 g (1 oz) plain chocolate, grated, to decorate

Grease a 23-cm (9-inch) china fluted flan dish. Finely crush the biscuits. Melt the butter and stir in the biscuit crumbs. Press into the prepared dish and chill until firm. Beat the curd cheese and cream together until smooth. Whisk the egg yolks and sugar until thick and light in colour and stir into the cheese mixture. Mix in the coffee essence and liqueur. Put 30 ml (2 tbsp) water in a small bowl and sprinkle in the gelatine. Stand the bowl over a pan of water and heat gently until the gelatine has dissolved. Whisk the egg white until stiff. Stir the cooled gelatine into the

cheesecake mixture and lastly fold in the stiffly whisked egg white. Pour into the flan case and place in the refrigerator to set. Remove from the refrigerator about 10 minutes before serving. Decorate with coarsely grated chocolate.

Lemon cheesecake

1$\frac{1}{2}$ packets of lemon jelly
60 ml (4 tbsp) water
2 eggs, separated
300 ml ($\frac{1}{2}$ pint) milk
grated rind of 2 lemons
90 ml (6 tbsp) lemon juice
450 g (1 lb) cottage cheese
15 ml (1 level tbsp) caster sugar
150 ml ($\frac{1}{4}$ pint) double cream
fresh lemon slices to decorate

For the crumb base
100 g (4 oz) digestive biscuits
50 g (2 oz) butter
50 g (2 oz) caster sugar

Put the jelly and water in a small pan and warm gently over a low heat, stirring until dissolved. Beat together the egg yolks and milk, pour on to the jelly, stir and return the mixture to the heat for a few minutes without boiling. Remove from the heat and add the lemon rind and juice. Sieve the cottage cheese and stir into the jelly or put jelly and cottage cheese in an electric blender and purée until smooth; turn the mixture into a bowl. Whisk the egg whites stiffly, add the 15 ml (1 level tbsp) sugar and whisk again until stiff. Fold into the cool cheese mixture. Whisk the cream until stiff and fold into the mixture. Turn into a 20.5-cm (8-inch) spring-release cake tin fitted with a tubular base.

Crush the biscuits finely. Melt the butter in a pan and stir in the sugar and biscuit crumbs. Use to cover the cheesecake mixture, pressing it on lightly; chill. Turn the cheesecake out carefully and decorate with the slices of lemon.

Strawberry refrigerator cake

225 g (8 oz) strawberries, hulled
150 ml ($\frac{1}{4}$ pint) fresh orange juice
45 ml (3 tbsp) orange flavoured liqueur
30 ml (2 level tbsp) icing sugar
30 ml (2 level tbsp) golden syrup
2 egg yolks, beaten
75 g (3 oz) butter
30 boudoir biscuits (sponge fingers)
150 ml ($\frac{1}{4}$ pint) double cream
60 ml (4 tbsp) single cream
whole strawberries to decorate

Slice the strawberries. Mix the orange juice, liqueur and sugar, pour over the strawberries and leave for 30 minutes. Heat the syrup over a gentle heat, bring to the boil, then allow to cool for 1 minute.

Pour in a thin stream on to the egg yolks, whisking all the time; continue to whisk until pale and creamy. Cream the butter until soft, then beat in the egg syrup, a little at a time. Drain the fruit.

Dip ten boudoir biscuits in the orange marinade and arrange them side by side on a sheet of non-stick paper. Cover with a layer of half the butter filling. Top with half the marinated strawberries. Add another layer of ten biscuits and top with the remaining butter mixture and strawberries. Finally, top with a layer of biscuits (all the marinade should now have been used up). Wrap the cake in paper and chill. Thirty minutes before it is required, whisk the creams together until thick enough to hold its shape; cover the cake and decorate with whole strawberries.

PASTRY CAKES

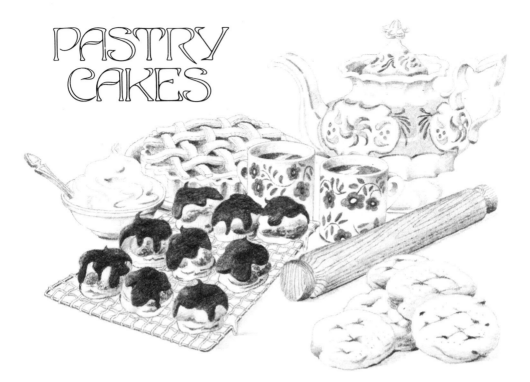

Pastries of various kinds provide the base for many luscious European confections, such as flaky Mille feuilles, mouthwatering Cream puffs and rich cheesecakes. The crispness of pastry perfectly offsets the soft creamy fillings and sweet rich icings which feature in so many of these celebrated gâteaux and small cakes.

Despite the mystique attached to pastry-making, the only secrets to success are patience, practice and care. Unless you are making choux pastry, the golden rule is to keep everything cool – kitchen, work surface, utensils, ingredients and yourself. Handle the pastry as little as possible and use just your fingertips for rubbing in the fat. If the mixture shows signs of becoming the least bit sticky and unmanageable, chill it briefly in the refrigerator.

Always add liquid gradually, using just enough to bind the mixture – a too wet or sticky dough will shrink badly during cooking and give a tough pastry. Use the minimum of flour for dusting the work surface and rolling pin, otherwise the balance of ingredients will be upset and the pastry may have a hard crust.

Flaked pastries are improved if you allow them to 'rest' in a cool place between the successive rollings and foldings. Leave prepared doughs in a cool place for about 30 minutes before rolling out and shaping. This makes them easier to handle and less prone to shrinking. Roll out and handle pastry as lightly and as little as possible. Avoid stretching pastry when putting it into a tin for it will shrink back during the baking and spoil the finished shape.

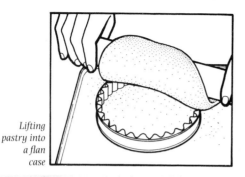

Lifting pastry into a flan case

Trimming off the surplus pastry

Lining a flan case

Use a plain or fluted flan ring placed on a baking sheet, or a loose-bottomed flan tin or sandwich tin. Thinly roll out the pastry to a circle about 5 cm (2 inches) wider all round than the diameter of the tin. Roll the pastry very loosely round the rolling pin and lift it on to the tin. Carefully unroll the pastry into position.

Lift the edges of the pastry and gently coax it into the shape of the ring or tin. Starting at the centre of the base, gently press the pastry into shape with your fingertips. Take care no pockets of air are trapped between the container and the pastry. Lightly press the pastry against the edges of the container. With a fluted ring or tin, press the pastry into each flute to ensure it will have a good shape. Then turn any surplus pastry outwards over the rim and roll across the top with the rolling pin to trim the edges.

Lining small moulds and tartlet tins

Arrange the moulds or tins close together on a baking sheet. Thinly roll out the pastry to a size sufficiently large to comfortably cover the area of the tins. Lay the pastry loosely over the tins. Break off a small knob of dough from the edge and use this to ease the pastry into each tin. Roll the rolling pin across the surface, then lift away the surplus pastry. With your fingertips, mould the pastry neatly in each tin.

If using a sheet of patty tins, thinly roll out the pastry and stamp out rounds about 1.5 cm ($\frac{3}{4}$ inch) larger than the diameter of the top of each tin. Gently press one round of dough into each tin and mould it into shape with your fingertips.

Baking blind

Pastry cases which are baked without the filling are said to be 'baked blind'. A lining of greaseproof paper and dried beans, or

Lining patty tins with pastry rounds

Baking blind

foil, is used to keep the pastry in good shape.

For large cases, cut a round of greaseproof paper rather larger than the ring or tin. Use this to line the pastry case and weigh it down with some dried beans, pasta or rice. Alternatively, screw up a piece of foil and use to line the base of the pastry case. Bake the pastry as directed for 10–15 minutes, then remove the baking beans and paper or foil lining and return the tin to the oven for a further 5 minutes to crisp the pastry. Leave the baked case to cool and shrink slightly before removing it from the tin. (It is worth keeping some dried beans specially for baking blind as they can be used over and over again.)

For small cases, it is usually sufficient to prick the pastry well with a fork before baking as directed.

Pastry cases which have been baked blind keep for a few days in an airtight tin.

Pastry making

The ingredients
Flour Plain flour is generally recommended, but you can obtain quite good results with a shortcrust pastry by using self raising flour, though this will give a softer, more crumbly texture.

Fat Butter, margarine and lard are the fats most commonly used, but proprietary vegetable shortenings (both blended and whipped up) and pure vegetable oils can give excellent results. Remember to follow the maker's directions, as sometimes a smaller quantity is recommended in proportion to the flour than is usual with other kinds of fat. Generally speaking the firmer block margarines should be used for traditional rubbing in.

For shortcrust pastry, butter, margarine, lard or vegetable fat can be used alone but margarine tends to give a firmer pastry which is more yellow in colour. Good results are achieved with a mixture of fats – butter or margarine with lard. For the richer pastries it is better to keep to the fat specified in the recipe.

Liquid Generally, allow about 5 ml (1 tsp) liquid per 25 g (1 oz) flour to bind short pastry to a stiff dough and about 15 ml (1 tbsp) liquid to bind flaky pastries to an elastic dough.

Short pastries

Shortcrust pastry
This, which is probably the most widely used pastry, is made by the rubbing in method. It is quick and simple to produce and forms the basis of a wide range of pastry cakes.

Flan pastry
A slightly richer pastry, made by the same method as shortcrust. It is usually sweetened and is ideal for flan cases, small tartlets and other sweet pastries.

Pâte sucrée (sugar pastry)
The French equivalent to enriched shortcrust, this is thin, crisp yet melting in texture and keeps its shape well. It is the best choice for continental pâtisserie.

Shortcrust pastry

*This pastry is quick and easy
to prepare and, if you follow
the basic steps carefully, you
can be sure of success.*

**175 g (6 oz) plain flour
pinch of salt
75 g (3 oz) butter or block margarine and lard**

Note For shortcrust pastry, the proportion of fat
to flour is half the quantity. Therefore, for a recipe
using 225 g (8 oz) shortcrust pastry, use 225 g
(8 oz) flour and 100 g (4 oz) fat.

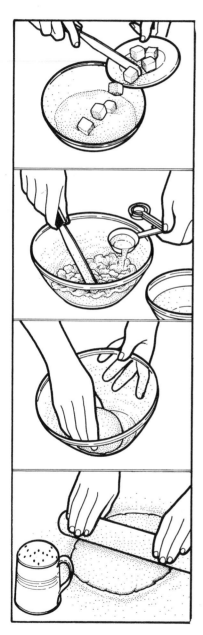

Mix the flour and salt together in a bowl. Cut the
fat into small pieces and add it to the flour. Using
both hands, rub the fat into the flour between
finger and thumb tips until the mixture resembles
fine breadcrumbs.

As far as possible, add 30 ml (2 tbsp) water at
once, sprinkling it evenly over the surface. (Uneven addition may cause blistering when the
pastry is cooked.) Stir it in with a round-bladed
knife until the mixture begins to stick together in
large lumps.

With one hand, collect the mixture together and
knead lightly for a few seconds to give a firm,
smooth dough. The pastry can be used straight
away, but is better allowed to 'rest' for about 30
minutes. It can also be wrapped in cling film and
kept in the refrigerator for a day or two.

When the pastry is required, sprinkle a very little
flour on a working surface and the rolling pin, not
on the pastry, and roll out the dough evenly in
one direction only, turning it occasionally. The
ideal thickness is usually about 0.3 cm ($\frac{1}{8}$ inch).
Do not pull or stretch the pastry. When cooking
shortcrust pastry, the usual oven temperature is
200–220°C (400–425°F) mark 6–7.

Flan pastry

100 g (4 oz) plain flour
pinch of salt
75 g (3 oz) butter or block margarine and
  lard
5 ml (1 level tsp) caster sugar
1 egg, beaten

Mix the flour and salt together in a bowl. Cut the fat into small pieces, add it to the flour and rub it in as for shortcrust pastry until the mixture resembles fine breadcrumbs. Stir in the sugar.

Add the egg, stirring with a round-bladed knife until the ingredients begin to stick together in large lumps. With one hand, collect the mixture together and knead lightly for a few seconds to give a firm, smooth dough. Roll out as for shortcrust pastry and use as required. When cooking flan pastry, the usual oven temperature is 200°C (400°F) mark 6.

Pâte sucrée

Note Pâte sucrée is a very rich short pastry. If a less rich pastry is required, substitute either shortcrust (page 108) or flan (page 109) pastry.

100 g (4 oz) plain flour
pinch of salt
50 g (2 oz) caster sugar
50 g (2 oz) butter (at room temperature)
2 egg yolks

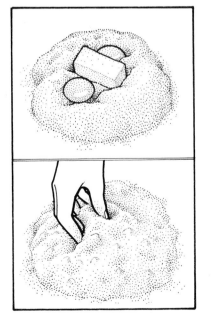

Sift the flour and salt together on to a working surface or, preferably, a marble slab. Make a well in the centre and add the sugar, butter and egg yolks.

Using the fingertips of one hand, pinch and work the sugar, butter and egg yolks together until well blended. Gradually work in all the flour, adding a little water if necessary to bind the mixture together. Knead lightly until smooth. Wrap the pastry in foil or cling film and leave to 'rest' in the refrigerator or a cool place for about 1 hour. Roll out the pastry on a lightly floured surface and use as required. Pâte sucrée is usually cooked at 190°C (375°F) mark 5.

'Flaked' pastries

Puff pastry
The richest of all the pastries, puff gives the most even rising, the most flaky effect and the crispest texture, but because of the time it takes, most people make it only occasionally. It requires very careful handling and whenever possible should be made the day before it is to be used, so that it has time to become firm and cool before it is shaped and baked. If you have a freezer, it's well worthwhile to make up a bulk batch and pack it in amounts that are practical to thaw and use. Bought puff pastry, either chilled or frozen, is very satisfactory, but remember to only roll it out to a maximum thickness of 0.3 cm ($\frac{1}{8}$ inch), as it rises very well.

'First rollings' are used where appearance is important. 'Second rollings' (usually the trimmings) can be used where appearance is not so important.

Flaky pastry
This can be used instead of puff pastry if a great rise is not needed. The instructions may seem rather complicated at first reading, but are less difficult than they appear and if you follow them carefully, you should be able to obtain really good results.

Rough puff pastry
This is similar in appearance and texture to Flaky pastry, though perhaps not so even, but it is quicker and easier to make and can be used instead of flaky except when even rising and appearance are particularly important, *eg.* when making Tarte Française and Mille Feuilles. Today, bought ready-made puff pastry is frequently used to replace home-made rough puff. Buy a 215-g ($7\frac{1}{2}$-oz) packet to replace home-made pastry made with 100 g (4 oz) flour and a 370-g (13-oz) packet to replace home-made pastry made with 200 g (7 oz) flour. Bought pastry should be rolled out slightly thinner than your own.

General points for flaked pastries
1. Always handle lightly and as little as possible.
2. The fat for flaky and puff pastries should be of about the same consistency as the dough with which it is to be combined. This is the reason for 'working' it on a plate beforehand. The fat for rough puff pastry should be firm so that the cubes of fat retain their shape while being mixed into the dry ingredients.
3. Remember to 'rest' all flaked pastries, *ie* cover and leave them in a cool place or the refrigerator for about 15 minutes, both during and after the making and also after shaping and before baking. This will prevent the fat from melting and spoiling the flaked texture when the pastry is cooked.
4. Always roll out lightly and evenly, without taking the rolling pin over the edges of the pastry. Never stretch the dough during shaping, or the finished dish will tend to be misshapen.

Apricot cheesecake (*page 101*)

Puff pastry

Although it is the richest of the pastries, puff is crispier, lighter and more delicate than any other.

200 g (7 oz) strong plain flour
pinch of salt
200 g (7 oz) butter
about 105 ml (7 tbsp) cold water and a squeeze of
    lemon juice
beaten egg to glaze

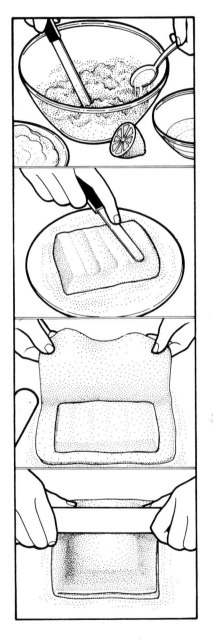

Mix the flour and salt together in a bowl. Put the butter on a plate and 'work' it with a knife until soft. Put a knob of butter into the flour and rub it in between finger and thumb tips. Using a round-bladed knife, stir in enough water and lemon juice to mix to a fairly soft, elastic dough. Turn the dough out on to a lightly floured surface and knead until smooth.

Form the rest of the softened butter into an oblong and roll the pastry out into a square.

Place the butter on one half of the pastry and enclose it by folding over the other half of the pastry and sealing the edges with a rolling pin.

Turn the pastry so that the folded edge is at the side and roll out into an oblong three times as long as it is wide. Fold the bottom third up and the top third down and seal the edges by pressing lightly with a rolling pin. Wrap the pastry loosely in greaseproof paper and leave in a cool place or in the refrigerator to 'rest' for about 30 minutes.

Arrange the pastry on a lightly floured working surface with the folded edges to the sides and repeat the rolling, folding and resting sequence until it has been completed six times altogether. After the final resting, shape the pastry as required. Brush with beaten egg before cooking to give the characteristic glaze of puff pastry. When cooking puff pastry, the usual oven temperature is 230°C (450°F) mark 8.

Note Uncooked home-made puff pastry will keep for 2–3 days if wrapped in foil or cling film and stored in the refrigerator.

Choco-mint swirl (*page 100*)

Flaky pastry

Follow these basic steps carefully for perfect flaky pastry.

200 g (7 oz) plain flour
pinch of salt
150 g (5 oz) butter or a mixture of butter and lard
about 105 ml (7 tbsp) cold water and a squeeze of lemon juice
beaten egg to glaze

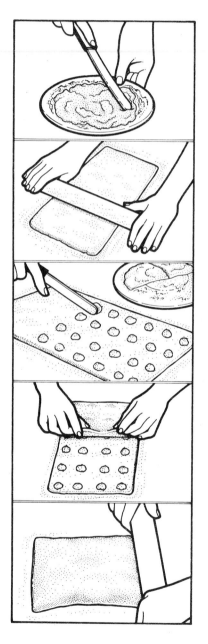

Mix the flour and salt together in a bowl. Soften the fat by 'working' it with a knife on a plate, then divide it into four equal portions. Add one quarter of the fat to the flour and rub it into the flour between finger and thumb tips until the mixture resembles fine breadcrumbs.

Add enough water and lemon juice, stirring with a round-bladed knife, to make a soft, elastic dough. Turn the dough on to a lightly floured surface and roll out into an oblong three times as long as it is wide.

Using a round-bladed knife, dot another quarter of the fat over the top two thirds of the pastry in flakes, so that it looks like buttons on a card.

Fold the bottom third of the pastry up and the top third down and turn it so that the folded edges are at the sides.

Seal the edges of the pastry by pressing with a rolling pin. Re-roll as before and repeat the process twice more until the remaining portions of fat have been used up. Wrap the pastry loosely in greaseproof paper and leave it to 'rest' in the refrigerator or a cool place for at least 30 minutes before using. This makes handling and shaping the pastry easier and gives a more evenly flaked texture.

Roll out the pastry on a lightly floured working surface to 0.3 cm ($\frac{1}{8}$ inch) thick and use as required. Brush with beaten egg before baking to give the characteristic glaze. When cooking flaky pastry, the usual oven temperature is 220°C (425°F) mark 7.

Rough puff pastry

This makes a good alternative to flaky pastry as it is quicker and easier to make and is suited to most flaky pastry recipes.

200 g (7 oz) plain flour
pinch of salt
150 g (5 oz) butter or block margarine
 and lard
about 105 ml (7 tbsp) cold water and a
 squeeze of lemon juice
beaten egg to glaze

Mix the flour and salt together in a bowl. Cut the fat (which should be quite firm) into cubes about 2 cm ($\frac{3}{4}$ inch) across. Stir the fat into the flour without breaking up the pieces and add enough water and lemon juice to mix to a fairly stiff dough. Turn on to a lightly floured surface and roll into an oblong three times as long as it is wide. Fold the bottom third up and the top third down, then turn the pastry so that the folded edges are at the sides. Seal the ends of the pastry by pressing lightly with a rolling pin. Repeat this rolling and folding process three more times. Wrap the pastry in greaseproof paper and leave to 'rest' in the refrigerator or a cool place for about 30 minutes before using.

Roll out the pastry to 0.3 cm ($\frac{1}{8}$ inch) thick and use as required. Brush with beaten egg before baking. When cooking rough puff pastry, the usual oven temperature is 220°C (425°F) mark 7.

Choux pastry

To ensure a good result with this special type of pastry, used for making éclairs, profiteroles and churros, there are a few points worth observing:

1. Remove the pan from the heat before adding the flour which must be added all at once.

2. After adding the flour, return the pan to the heat and continue beating until the mixture comes away from the sides of the pan and forms a ball in the centre.

3. Add the beaten egg gradually to the mixture, taking care to add only just enough to give a piping consistency. When beating by hand with a wooden spoon the arm tends to tire, the beating speed is reduced and the final consistency is often too slack to retain its shape. In this case a little less egg should be added. Use a size 4 egg if beating by hand and a size 2 egg when using an electric mixer.

4. To make the choux pastry a little easier to handle, chill it in the piping bag in the refrigerator for about 30 minutes before piping.

5. The oven door must not be opened during cooking.

6. Éclairs and profiteroles should be split open as soon as they are cooked to allow the steam to escape and the inside of the pastry to dry out.

7. Dampen baking sheets slightly with water before piping choux pastry on to them. This helps prevent sticking.

Choux pastry

*Light and airy, choux pastry
makes an ideal basis for many
delicious dessert cakes.*

50 g (2 oz) butter or block margarine
150 ml ($\frac{1}{4}$ pint) water
65 g ($2\frac{1}{2}$ oz) plain flour, sifted
2 eggs, lightly beaten

Put the fat and water together in a pan, heat gently until the fat has melted, then bring to the boil. Remove the pan from the heat.

Tip all the flour at once into the hot liquid. Beat thoroughly with a wooden spoon, then return the pan to the heat.

Continue beating the mixture until it is smooth and forms a ball in the centre of the pan. (Take care not to over-beat or the mixture will become fatty.) Remove from the heat and leave the mixture to cool for a minute or two.

Beat in the egg, a little at a time, adding only just enough to give a piping consistency. It is important to beat the mixture vigorously at this stage to trap in as much air as possible. A hand-held electric mixer is ideal for this purpose. Continue beating until the mixture develops an obvious sheen and then use as required. When cooking choux pastry, the usual oven temperature is 200–220°C (400–425°F) mark 6–7.

Black bun

This traditional Hogmanay cake should be made several weeks or even months before it is eaten, so that it has time to mature and mellow.

225 g (8 oz) shortcrust pastry (*see page 108*)
225 g (8 oz) plain flour
5 ml (1 level tsp) ground cinnamon
5 ml (1 level tsp) ground ginger
5 ml (1 level tsp) ground allspice
5 ml (1 level tsp) cream of tartar
5 ml (1 level tsp) bicarbonate of soda
450 g (1 lb) seedless raisins
450 g (1 lb) currants
50 g (2 oz) chopped mixed peel
100 g (4 oz) nibbed almonds
100 g (4 oz) dark brown soft sugar
1 egg
150 ml ($\frac{1}{4}$ pint) whisky
about 60 ml (4 tbsp) milk
beaten egg to glaze

Grease a 20.5-cm (8-inch) cake tin. Roll out two thirds of the pastry on a lightly floured working surface into a round about 35 cm (14 inches) in diameter. Use to line the prepared tin, making sure the pastry comes above the top of the sides of the cake tin and distributing the fullness evenly round the sides.

For the filling, sift together the flour, spices, cream of tartar and bicarbonate of soda into a large bowl and mix in the raisins, currants, mixed peel, almonds and sugar. Add the egg, whisky and milk and stir until the mixture is evenly moistened. Pack it into the pastry case and fold the top of the pastry over. Roll out the remaining dough to a 20.5-cm (8-inch) round. Moisten the edges of the pastry case, put the pastry round on top and seal the edges firmly together. With a skewer, make four or five holes right down to the bottom of the cake, then prick all over the top with a fork and brush with beaten egg. Bake in the oven at 180°C (350°F) mark 4 for 2½–3 hours. Cover with brown paper if the pastry becomes too brown. Turn out and leave to cool on a wire rack.

Strawberry shortcakes

Illustrated in colour on page 27

225 g (8 oz) plain flour
10 ml (2 level tsp) baking powder
50 g (2 oz) butter
25 g (1 oz) caster sugar
1 egg, beaten
a little milk

For the filling and topping
350 g (12 oz) strawberries, hulled
caster sugar
150 ml ($\frac{1}{4}$ pint) double cream

Lightly grease a large baking sheet. Sift together the flour and baking powder into a bowl. Rub in the butter until the mixture resembles fine breadcrumbs. Stir in the sugar and mix to a stiff dough with the egg and a little milk. Turn out the dough on to a working surface and roll out to a thickness of 1–2 cm ($\frac{1}{2}$–$\frac{3}{4}$ inch). With a 7.5-cm (3-inch) plain cutter, cut out six rounds. Place the rounds on the prepared baking sheet and bake in the oven at 230°C (450°F) mark 8 for 7–8 minutes until well risen and golden brown.

Crush 225 g (8 oz) strawberries very lightly and sweeten to taste with caster sugar. Whisk the cream until thick and spoon into a piping bag fitted with a medium star nozzle. Split the warm shortcakes in half and sandwich back together with the crushed berries. Top with a whirl of cream and decorate with whole berries.
Makes 6

Linzertorte

A classic Austrian torte, named after the town of Linz. Serve warm or cold as a dessert or with morning or afternoon coffee. It is traditionally served with Schlagsahne (see opposite).

150 g (5 oz) plain flour
2.5 ml ($\frac{1}{2}$ level tsp) ground cinnamon
75 g (3 oz) butter
50 g (2 oz) caster sugar
50 g (2 oz) ground almonds
grated rind of 1 lemon
2 egg yolks
15 ml (1 tbsp) lemon juice
350 g (12 oz) raspberry jam or fresh or
  frozen raspberries *(see below)*

Sift the flour and cinnamon into a bowl. Cut the butter into small pieces, add to the flour and rub in until the mixture resembles fine breadcrumbs. Add the sugar, ground almonds and lemon rind. Beat the egg yolks and add to the mixture with the lemon juice to make a stiff dough. Knead lightly and leave in a cool place for about 30 minutes.

Roll out approximately two thirds of the pastry on a lightly floured working surface and use to line a 21.5-cm (8$\frac{1}{2}$-inch) fluted flan ring on a baking sheet. Fill with raspberry jam or purée made from fresh or frozen raspberries *(see below)*. Roll out the remaining pastry and cut into 1-cm ($\frac{1}{2}$-inch) strips with a pastry wheel. Use to make a lattice design over the jam. Bake in the oven at 190°C (375°F) mark 5 for 25–30 minutes until golden brown. Remove from the flan ring and serve with whipped cream or Schlagsahne.

Note To use fresh or frozen raspberries instead of the jam, put 450 g (1 lb) raspberries with 15 ml (1 tbsp) water and a knob of butter in a pan, add a little sugar to taste and boil to reduce to a thick purée. Cool before using.

Schlagsahne

Whip 150 ml ($\frac{1}{4}$ pint) double cream until stiff. Sweeten with caster sugar to taste. Just before serving, whisk 1 egg white until stiff and fold lightly into the cream and sugar mixture.

Orange liqueur cheesecake

100 g (4 oz) plain flour
75 g (3 oz) butter or margarine
50 g (2 oz) caster sugar
1 egg, size 2, separated
225 g (8 oz) cream cheese
150 ml ($\frac{1}{4}$ pint) natural yogurt
grated rind and juice of 1 medium orange
30 ml (2 tbsp) lemon juice
10 ml (2 level tsp) powdered gelatine
45 ml (3 tbsp) orange flavoured liqueur
grated chocolate to decorate

Sift the flour into a bowl. Rub in the fat until the mixture resembles fine breadcrumbs. Stir in 25 g (1 oz) sugar and bind with the egg yolk and 10 ml (2 tsp) water. Roll out on a lightly floured working surface and use to line the base of a 20.5-cm (8-inch) fluted flan tin. Bake 'blind' in the oven at 200°C (400°F) mark 6 for about 25 minutes. Leave to cool slightly before removing from the tin.

Beat the cream cheese in a bowl and gradually beat in the yogurt. Stir in the remaining sugar, the orange rind and 60 ml (4 tbsp) orange juice. Put the lemon juice in a small bowl and sprinkle over the gelatine. Stand the bowl over a pan of hot water and heat gently until the gelatine has dissolved. Cool and stir into the cheese mixture with the liqueur. Whisk the egg white until stiff and fold in. Turn into the cold flan case and leave to set. Decorate the top of the cheesecake with grated chocolate.

Apfel strüdel

225 g (8 oz) plain flour
2.5 ml ($\frac{1}{2}$ level tsp) salt
1 egg, slightly beaten
30 ml (2 tbsp) oil
60 ml (4 tbsp) lukewarm water
45 ml (3 level tbsp) seedless raisins
45 ml (3 level tbsp) currants
75 g (3 oz) caster sugar
2.5 ml ($\frac{1}{2}$ level tsp) ground cinnamon
1 kg ($2\frac{1}{4}$ lb) cooking apples, peeled, cored
  and grated
45 ml (3 tbsp) melted butter
100 g (4 oz) ground almonds
icing sugar to decorate

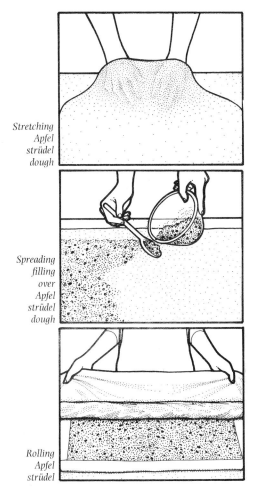

Stretching Apfel strüdel dough

Spreading filling over Apfel strüdel dough

Rolling Apfel strüdel

Lightly butter a baking sheet. Sift the flour and salt together into a large bowl, make a well in the centre and pour in the egg and oil. Add the water gradually, stirring with a fork to make a soft, sticky dough. Work the dough in the bowl until it leaves the sides, turn it out on to a lightly floured surface and knead for 15 minutes. Form into a ball, place on a cloth and cover with a warmed bowl. Leave to 'rest' in a warm place for 1 hour. Put the raisins, currants, sugar, cinnamon and apple together in a bowl and mix thoroughly.

Warm the rolling pin. Spread a clean cotton cloth on the table and sprinkle lightly with 15–30 ml (1–2 level tbsp) flour. Place the dough on the cloth and roll out into a rectangle about 0.3 cm ($\frac{1}{8}$ inch) thick, lifting and turning it to prevent it sticking to the cloth. Gently stretch the dough, working from the centre to the outside and using the backs of the hands, until it is paper-thin. Trim the edges to form a rectangle about 68 × 60 cm (27 × 24 inches). Leave the strüdel dough on the cloth to dry and 'rest' for about 15 minutes before filling and rolling.

Position the dough with one of the long sides towards you, brush with melted butter and sprinkle with ground almonds. Spread the apple mixture over the dough, leaving a 5-cm (2-inch) border uncovered all round the edge. Fold these pastry edges over the apple mixture, towards the centre. Lift the corners of the cloth nearest to you and over the pastry, causing the strüdel to roll up, but stop after each turn to pat into shape and to keep the roll even. Form the roll into a horseshoe shape, brush it with melted butter and slide it on to the prepared baking sheet. Bake in the oven at 190°C (375°F) mark 5 for about 40 minutes or until golden brown. Dredge the strüdel with icing sugar. Serve hot or cold, in slices, with cream as a tea-time speciality or a dinner dessert.

Honey cheesecake flan

175 g (6 oz) plain flour
pinch of salt
100 g (4 oz) butter or block margarine
50 g (2 oz) icing sugar
1 egg yolk
175 g (6 oz) cream cheese
60 ml (4 level tbsp) thick honey
2 eggs, beaten
1.25 ml ($\frac{1}{4}$ level tsp) ground nutmeg
25 g (1 oz) walnuts, chopped

To make the pastry, sift together the flour and salt into a large bowl. Rub in the fat until the mixture resembles fine breadcrumbs. Sift in the icing sugar and bind with the egg yolk and about 15 ml (1 tbsp) water. Roll out the pastry on a floured working surface and use to line an 18-cm (7-inch) flan ring placed on a baking sheet. Bake 'blind' in the oven for about 20 minutes at 200°C (400°F) mark 6 until firm but not brown.

Beat the cream cheese and honey until smooth. Add the eggs and nutmeg, mixing well. Pour the egg mixture into the flan case. Bake at 180°C (350°F) mark 4 for about 20 minutes or until a skin has formed. Sprinkle with the chopped walnuts. Return to the oven for a further 10–15 minutes until set. Serve cold.

Yorkshire cheesecake

450 g (1 lb) curd cheese
150 ml ($\frac{1}{4}$ pint) double cream
75 g (3 oz) caster sugar
grated rind of 1 lemon
15 ml (1 tbsp) lemon juice
40 g (1$\frac{1}{2}$ oz) cornflour
2 eggs, beaten
100 g (4 oz) shortcrust pastry (*see page 108*)
50 g (2 oz) seedless raisins

Beat the curd cheese until smooth and mix with the cream. Add the sugar, lemon rind and juice and the cornflour. Beat in the egg, a little at a time.

Roll out the pastry on a lightly floured working surface and use to line the base and 0.5 cm ($\frac{1}{4}$ inch) up the sides of a loose-bottomed 20.5-cm (8-inch) flan tin. Prick the base all over with a fork. Bake 'blind' in the oven at 190°C (375°F) mark 5 for 20 minutes. Roll out the pastry trimmings and cut into thin strips. Cover the baked pastry with a layer of raisins, then spoon in the cheese mixture. Make a lattice over the filling with the pastry strips. Reduce the oven temperature to 180°C (350°F) mark 4 and bake the cheesecake in the oven for about 35 minutes until the filling is just set. Leave the cheesecake in the oven until cold.

Moist almond butter tart

Illustrated in colour on page 122

175 g (6 oz) flan pastry (*see page 109*)
apricot jam or raspberry jelly

For the filling
100 g (4 oz) butter
100 g (4 oz) caster sugar
2 eggs, beaten
100 g (4 oz) cake crumbs
100 g (4 oz) ground almonds
a few drops of almond essence

Roll out the pastry on a lightly floured working surface and use to line a 24-cm (9$\frac{1}{2}$-inch) fluted flan tin. Reserve the trimmings. Spread the base with the jam or jelly.

For the filling, cream together the butter and sugar until pale and fluffy. Beat in the egg, cake crumbs, ground almonds and essence. Spread over the pastry. Decorate with shapes cut from the pastry trimmings. Bake in the oven at 200°C (400°F) mark 6 for 30 minutes. Reduce the oven temperature to 170°C (325°F) mark 3 for

Clockwise from top: Tartelettes aux fruits (*page 125*), Maids of honour (*page 129*), Cream horns, Palmiers (*page 126*), Mille feuilles (*page 128*)

Pages 122 and 123 (Clockwise from top left): Light fruit cake (*page 66*), Coffee chocolate slice (*page 101*), Coffee almond layer (*page 50*), Date ripple loaf (*page 65*), Orange and pineapple cake (*page 66*), Moist almond butter tart (*page 120*)

a further 30 minutes. Leave the tart to cool in the tin.

Note Crumbled trifle sponges or plain sandwich or madeira cake make the best crumbs. The same mixture can be baked in two 18-cm (7-inch) fluted china flan dishes, if preferred.

Glazed almond flan

1 quantity pâte sucrée (*see page 109*)
apricot or raspberry jam
75 g (3 oz) butter
75 g (3 oz) caster sugar
2 eggs, size 5, beaten
75 g (3 oz) ground almonds
50 g (2 oz) icing sugar
15 ml (1 level tbsp) flaked almonds, toasted

Roll out the pâte sucrée on a lightly floured working surface and use to line a 19-cm (7½-inch) loose-bottomed fluted flan ring. Trim the edges and keep the trimmings for decoration. Spread a thin layer of jam over the base.

Cream together the butter and sugar until pale and fluffy. Beat in the eggs and stir in the ground almonds. Turn the mixture into the pastry case and level the surface. Roll the trimmings into a narrow strip, cut thin 'laces' and use to lattice the top. Bake in the oven at 180°C (350°F) mark 5 for 45–50 minutes, until golden brown. Remove from the oven and glaze roughly with 'dribbles' of glacé icing made by combining the sifted icing sugar with a little water until of a coating consistency. Return the flan to the oven for 5 minutes. Sprinkle with flaked almonds. Remove the flan ring and cool the flan on a wire rack.

Tartelettes aux fruits

Illustrated in colour on page 121

1 quantity pâte sucrée (*see page 109*)
1 quantity crème pâtissière (*see page 176*)
425-g (15-oz) can black cherries, stoned
5 ml (1 level tsp) arrowroot
150 ml (¼ pint) double cream
50 ml (2 fl oz) single cream

Roll out the pâte sucrée on a lightly floured working surface and use to line eight 8.5-cm (3½-inch) shallow patty tins. Bake 'blind' in the oven at 190°C (375°F) mark 5 for 15–20 minutes until pale golden. Turn out and leave to cool on a wire rack.

Before serving, spread a layer of crème pâtissière over the tart bases. Drain the cherries, reserving 150 ml (¼ pint) juice. Blend the arrowroot with a little of the juice, then add the remaining juice. Heat, stirring all the time until thickened, and leave to cool. Whisk the double and single cream together until stiff. Fill a piping bag fitted with a small star nozzle and pipe stars of cream round the edge of the pastry. Arrange the cherries in the centre and glaze with the thickened juice.

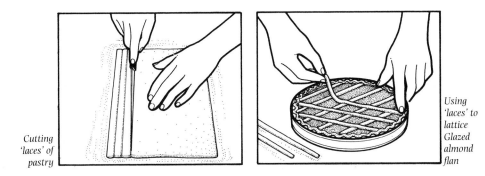

Cutting 'laces' of pastry

Using 'laces' to lattice Glazed almond flan

Gâteau St. Honoré (*page 130*)

Palmiers

Illustrated in colour on page 121

$\frac{1}{2}$ **quantity puff pastry** (*see page 113*) **or
215-g (7$\frac{1}{2}$-oz) packet frozen puff pastry,
thawed**
caster sugar
150 ml ($\frac{1}{4}$ pint) double cream
75 ml (3 fl oz) single cream

Dampen the surface of a baking sheet
with water. Roll out the pastry on a
lightly floured working surface to a rectangle measuring 30.5 × 25.5 cm (12 × 10
inches). Dredge with caster sugar. Fold the
long sides halfway towards the centre.
Dredge with more sugar and repeat,
folding right to the centre. Dredge with
sugar again and fold in half lengthways,
hiding the first folds and pressing lightly
and evenly. Cut into twelve equal-sized
slices. Place the palmiers on the baking
sheet, cut side down and flatten slightly
with a round-bladed knife. Bake in the
oven at 220°C (425°F) mark 7 for 8

minutes until golden brown. Turn each
over and bake for a further 4 minutes.
Remove from the baking sheet and leave
to cool on a wire rack.

Whisk the creams together with a little
caster sugar, until lightly peaked. Sandwich the palmiers together with the cream
before serving. Sprinkle with caster sugar.

Cream horns

Illustrated in colour on page 121

$\frac{1}{2}$ **quantity puff pastry** (*see page 113*) **or
215-g (7$\frac{1}{2}$-oz) packet frozen puff pastry,
thawed**
beaten egg to glaze
raspberry jam
150 ml ($\frac{1}{4}$ pint) double cream
75 ml (3 fl oz) single cream
icing sugar to decorate

Roll out the pastry on a lightly floured
working surface to a strip measuring 66 ×
10–11.5 cm (26 × 4–4$\frac{1}{2}$ inches). Cut the
pastry lengthways into 1-cm ($\frac{1}{2}$-inch) rib-

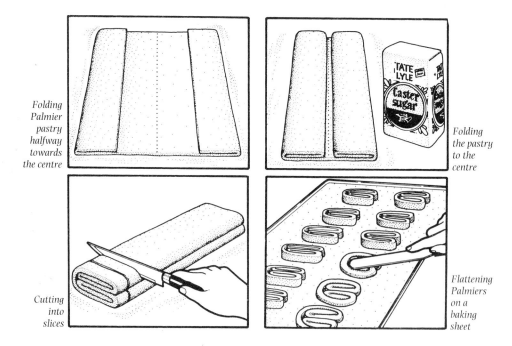

*Folding
Palmier
pastry
halfway
towards
the centre*

*Folding
the pastry
to the
centre*

*Cutting
into
slices*

*Flattening
Palmiers
on a
baking
sheet*

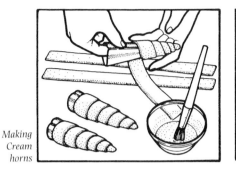

Making Cream horns

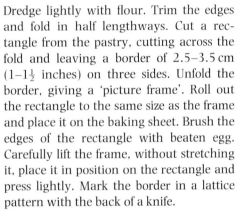

Marking the border of Tarte Française

bons with a sharp knife. Moisten one edge of each strip and wind each round a cream horn tin starting at the tip, overlapping 0.3 cm ($\frac{1}{8}$ inch), and finishing neatly on the underside. The pastry should not overlap the metal rim. Brush with beaten egg to glaze. Dampen the surface of a baking sheet with water and arrange the cream horns on it, join-side down. Bake in the oven at 220°C (425°F) mark 7 for 10 minutes until golden brown. Cool for a few minutes then carefully twist each tin, holding the pastry lightly in the other hand, to ease it out of the pastry horn. When cold, fill the tip of each horn with a little jam. Whisk the two creams together until stiff and fill the horns down to the jam. Dredge with sifted icing sugar.

Tarte Française

1 quantity puff pastry (*see page 113*) **or 370-g (13-oz) packet frozen puff pastry, thawed**
plain flour to dredge
beaten egg to glaze
apricot glaze (*see page 176*)
canned or fresh fruit (*see opposite*)

Dampen the surface of a baking sheet with water. Roll out the pastry on a lightly floured working surface into an oblong measuring about 30.5 × 15 cm (12 × 6 inches) and 0.5–1 cm ($\frac{1}{4}$–$\frac{1}{2}$ inch) thick.

Dredge lightly with flour. Trim the edges and fold in half lengthways. Cut a rectangle from the pastry, cutting across the fold and leaving a border of 2.5–3.5 cm (1–1$\frac{1}{2}$ inches) on three sides. Unfold the border, giving a 'picture frame'. Roll out the rectangle to the same size as the frame and place it on the baking sheet. Brush the edges of the rectangle with beaten egg. Carefully lift the frame, without stretching it, place it in position on the rectangle and press lightly. Mark the border in a lattice pattern with the back of a knife.

Prick the base of the tart and brush the border with beaten egg, being careful not to let any drip down the sides. Put in the refrigerator to chill for 10 minutes. Bake in the oven at 220°C (425°F) mark 7 for about 20 minutes until well risen, crisp and golden. If the edges show signs of over-browning, cover with damp grease-proof paper. Remove from the baking sheet and leave to cool on a wire rack.

To finish, brush the centre of the tart with apricot glaze, arrange the drained canned fruit or prepared fresh fruit in rows over it and brush again with glaze.

Note Apricots, grapes, peaches, stoned cherries, mandarins and strawberries are all suitable. If canned fruit is used, the juice may be thickened with arrowroot and sharpened with lemon juice to use as a glaze, or make up a jelly glaze, to use instead of apricot glaze.

Galette jalousie

The regular cuts across the top of the jalousie represent the slats of wooden shutters, which in French are known as 'jalousies'.

$\frac{1}{2}$ **quantity puff pastry** (*see page 113*) **or 215-g (7$\frac{1}{2}$-oz) packet frozen puff pastry, thawed**
beaten egg to glaze
225 g (8 oz) apricot jam
beaten egg white and caster sugar to coat

Dampen the surface of a baking sheet with water. Roll out the pastry on a lightly floured working surface into a strip measuring 46 × 10 cm (18 × 4 inches). Cut into

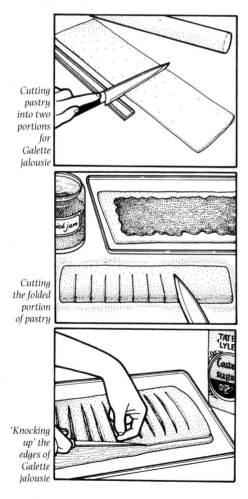

Cutting pastry into two portions for Galette jalousie

Cutting the folded portion of pastry

'Knocking up' the edges of Galette jalousie

two portions, one 5 cm (2 inches) shorter than the other. Roll out the smaller piece to the same size as the other and place it on the dampened baking sheet. Brush a border 1 cm ($\frac{1}{2}$ inch) wide up each side of the strip with beaten egg. Spread the jam over the centre of the pastry.

Fold the thicker piece of pastry in half lengthways. Using a sharp knife, cut across the fold at intervals to within 1 cm ($\frac{1}{2}$ inch) of the other edge. Unfold the pastry and lift it carefully on to the portion on the baking sheet. Press the edges well together and 'knock up' with a knife. Bake in the oven at 220°C (425°F) mark 7 for about 20 minutes until golden brown. Remove from the oven, brush with egg white, dredge with caster sugar and return to the oven for a further 5 minutes to 'frost' the top. Serve hot or cold.

Mille feuilles

Illustrated in colour on page 121

$\frac{1}{2}$ **quantity puff pastry** (*see page 113*) **or 215-g (7$\frac{1}{2}$-oz) packet frozen puff pastry, thawed**
100 g (4 oz) raspberry jam
1 quantity crème pâtissière (*see page 176*) **or 300 ml ($\frac{1}{2}$ pint) double cream, whipped**
175 g (6 oz) glacé icing (*see page 171*)
red food colouring

Dampen the surface of a baking sheet with water. Roll out the pastry on a lightly floured working surface into a rectangle measuring 25.5 × 23 cm (10 × 9 inches) and prick all over with a fork. Place on the baking sheet and bake in the oven at 230°C (450°F) mark 8 for 25 minutes, until well risen and golden brown. Remove from the baking sheet and leave to cool on a wire rack.

When cold, trim the edges, cut in half lengthways and cut each half into six slices. Spread half with raspberry jam, then cover with the crème pâtissière or cream. Spread raspberry jam on to the bases of the remaining pieces of pastry and place on top of the first layers. Make the glacé icing and mix 15 ml (1 tbsp) icing with a few drops of red colouring to make a deep pink colour. Pour this into a grease-proof paper piping bag (*see page 165*) and cut the tip off the bag just before it is required. Spread the remaining white icing over the tops of the pastries. With the pink icing, pipe lines across the Mille feuilles, 1 cm ($\frac{1}{2}$ inch) apart. Draw a skewer down the length of the Mille feuilles at 1-cm ($\frac{1}{2}$-inch) intervals to make a 'feathering' design. Leave to set.

Maids of honour

Illustrated in colour on page 121

These little cakes were first made in Henry VIII's palace at Hampton Court where they proved so popular with the Queen's maids of honour that they were named after them.

568 ml (1 pint) milk
15 ml (1 tbsp) rennet
$\frac{1}{2}$ quantity puff pastry (*see page 113*) or
 215-g (7$\frac{1}{2}$-oz) packet frozen puff pastry, thawed
1 egg, beaten
15 g ($\frac{1}{2}$ oz) butter, melted
50 g (2 oz) caster sugar

Warm the milk in a saucepan over a low heat to 37°C (98°F). Pour into a bowl and quickly stir in the rennet. Leave at room temperature for 1$\frac{1}{2}$–2 hours until set, then put the junket into a muslin bag and leave to drain overnight. Chill the curd until very firm.

Have ready twelve deep 6.5-cm (2$\frac{1}{2}$-inch) patty tins. Roll out the pastry very thinly on a lightly floured working surface and, with a 7.5-cm (3-inch) plain cutter, stamp out twelve rounds. Line the patty tins with the pastry rounds and prick well with a fork.

Stir the egg, butter and sugar into the drained curd. Divide the mixture between the pastry cases and bake in the oven at 200°C (400°F) mark 6 for 30 minutes until well risen and just firm to the touch. Maids of honour are best served whilst still warm.
Makes 12

Gâteau Pithiviers

This recipe was created in the 19th century and became the speciality of the small town it was named after, just south of Paris.

$\frac{1}{2}$ quantity puff pastry (*see page 113*) or
 215-g (7$\frac{1}{2}$-oz) packet frozen puff pastry, thawed
beaten egg to glaze
caster sugar to decorate

For the filling
100 g (4 oz) ground almonds
100 g (4 oz) caster sugar
40 g (1$\frac{1}{2}$ oz) butter
2 egg yolks
15 ml (1 tbsp) rum

Dampen the surface of a baking sheet with water. Cut off one third of the pastry, roll out on a lightly floured working surface and shape into a 15-cm (6-inch) round. Roll out the remaining pastry and shape into an 18-cm (7-inch) round twice as thick as the first. Beat together the filling ingredients. Place the thinner round of pastry on the baking sheet and spread the filling over the centre. Brush the edge of the pastry with water and cover with the thicker round. Pinch the edges together to seal. With the point of a sharp knife, mark six curved lines from the centre to the outside edge. Brush with the beaten egg and bake in the oven at 200°C (400°F) mark 6 for 30 minutes until risen and golden brown. Sprinkle the top with caster sugar and serve warm.

Eccles cakes

½ **quantity puff or flaky pastry** (*see pages 113 and 114*) **or 215-g (7½-oz) packet frozen puff pastry, thawed**

For the filling
25 g (1 oz) butter, softened
25 g (1 oz) dark brown soft sugar
25 g (1 oz) finely chopped mixed peel
50 g (2 oz) currants

For the glaze
egg white, lightly whipped
caster sugar

Roll out the pastry thinly on a lightly floured working surface and cut into 9-cm (3½-inch) rounds. Mix together the ingredients for the filling and place a small spoonful of mixture in the centre of each pastry round. Draw up the pastry edges together and re-shape into a round. Turn it over and roll lightly until the currants just show through. Score in a lattice pattern with a knife. Allow the cakes to 'rest' on a baking sheet for about 10 minutes in a cool place. Brush with egg white and dredge with caster sugar. Bake in the oven at 230°C (450°F) mark 8 for about 15 minutes until golden. Leave to cool on a wire rack.

Sacristains

100 g (4 oz) puff or flaky pastry trimmings (*see pages 113 and 114*)
1 egg white, lightly beaten
25 g (1 oz) caster sugar
7.5 ml (1½ level tsp) ground cinnamon
25 g (1 oz) blanched almonds, chopped

Knead the pastry trimmings together very lightly and roll out on a lightly floured surface to an oblong measuring 10 × 35.5 cm (4 × 14 inches). Brush the egg white over the pastry to within 1 cm (½ inch) of the edge. Mix the sugar and

cinnamon and sprinkle with the nuts over the pastry. Cut the pastry crossways to give strips 1 cm (½ inch) wide and 10 cm (4 inches) long. Sacristains can then be shaped in many ways. The strips can be twisted, shaped into circles or tied into knots. Place them on a baking sheet and bake in the oven at 220°C (425°F) mark 4 for about 10 minutes until golden brown.

Gâteau St. Honoré

Illustrated in colour on page 124

Dedicated to the patron saint of pastry cooks, this is a speciality of Paris.

1 quantity pâte sucrée (*see page 109*)
beaten egg to glaze
1 quantity choux pastry (*see page 116*)
300 ml (½ pint) double cream
45 ml (3 level tbsp) caster sugar
1 quantity crème pâtissière (*see page 176*)
angelica and glacé cherries to decorate

Roll out the pâte sucrée on a lightly floured working surface into an 18-cm (7-inch) round, put on a baking sheet and prick all over the surface with a fork. Brush a 1-cm (½-inch) band round the edge with beaten egg. Fill a piping bag fitted with a medium plain nozzle with choux pastry. Pipe a circle round the edge of the pastry and brush with beaten egg. With the remaining choux pastry pipe about twenty walnut-sized rounds on to the baking sheet. Brush these with beaten egg and bake both the flan and the choux balls in the oven at 190°C (375°F) mark 5 for about 35 minutes or until well risen and golden brown. Split the choux balls to release the steam, then leave them with the flan to cool on a wire rack.

Whisk the cream until stiff. Reserving a little cream for the top of the gâteau, fill a piping bag fitted with a medium plain

Dipping choux buns in syrup for Gâteau St. Honoré

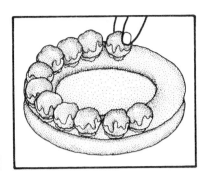

Sticking choux buns on to Gâteau St. Honoré

nozzle and pipe some into each of the cold choux buns. Dissolve the sugar in 45 ml (3 tbsp) water and boil until the edge just begins to turn straw-coloured. Dip the tops of the choux buns in this syrup, using a skewer or tongs to hold them.

Use the remainder of the syrup to stick the buns on to the choux pastry border to form a wall. Fill the centre of the gâteau with the crème pâtissière mixture. Pipe the reserved cream around the edge, in between the choux balls. Decorate with angelica and cherries.
Serves 6

Choux à l'orange

double quantity choux pastry (*see page 116*)
60–75 ml (4–5 tbsp) orange flavoured liqueur
double quantity crème pâtissière (*see page 176*)
icing sugar to decorate

Dampen the surface of two baking sheets with water. Place small spoonfuls of the choux pastry, about the size of walnuts, well spaced out on the baking sheets. Bake in the oven at 200°C (400°F) mark 6 for 10–15 minutes until well risen and golden brown. Make a slit in the side of each choux to release the steam and leave to cool on a wire rack. Beat the liqueur into the crème pâtissière and use to fill a piping bag fitted with a large plain nozzle. Pipe

the mixture into the choux. Dredge with icing sugar and serve.

Redcurrant choux puff

double quantity choux pastry (*see page 116*)
450 ml (¾ pint) double cream
225 g (8 oz) fresh redcurrants, strung and washed
60 ml (4 level tbsp) caster sugar
15 ml (1 tbsp) brandy
icing sugar and redcurrants on the stem to decorate

Line two baking sheets with non-stick paper and draw one 20.5-cm (8-inch) circle on each. Fill a piping bag fitted with a large star nozzle with two thirds of the choux mixture and pipe rosettes very close together around the inside edge of one of the circles. Pipe the remaining mixture through a plain nozzle around the second circle. Bake in the oven at 200°C (400°F) mark 6 for 30 minutes until well risen and golden brown. Slit to release the steam and leave to cool on a wire rack.

Whisk the cream until stiff and use one third to sandwich the two rings together. Place on a serving plate. Crush the redcurrants lightly and sprinkle over half the sugar. Fold the brandy and remaining sugar into the remaining cream and fill the choux ring with alternate layers of fruit and cream. Dredge with icing sugar and decorate with redcurrants.
Serves 6

Tabatières

These traditional French pastries are called 'tabatières' because the piped choux forms a similar shape to that of a tobacco pouch or snuff box.

1 quantity choux pastry (*see page 116*)
150 ml (¼ pint) double cream
1 quantity crème pâtissière (*see page 176*)
50 g (2 oz) praline (*see page 176*)
45 ml (3 level tbsp) apricot glaze (*see page 176*)
225 g (8 oz) fresh strawberries or raspberries

Dampen the surface of a baking sheet with water. Fill a piping bag fitted with a small plain nozzle with choux pastry and pipe eight small triangular shapes on to the baking sheet. Bake in the oven at 200°C (400°F) mark 6 for 25–30 minutes until well risen and crisp. Split the pastries to release the steam and leave to cool on a wire rack. Whisk the cream until stiff and fold in the crème pâtissière and praline. Fill the pastries with the cream filling. Brush the tops with glaze and arrange some fruit on top of each.

Profiteroles

1 quantity choux pastry (*see page 116*)
150 ml (¼ pint) double cream
icing sugar to decorate

For the chocolate sauce
50 g (2 oz) plain chocolate
knob of butter
15 ml (1 tbsp) milk
5 ml (1 tsp) vanilla essence

Dampen the surface of two or three baking sheets with water. Fill a piping bag fitted with a medium plain nozzle with choux pastry and pipe small balls, about the size of walnuts, on to the baking sheets. Bake in the oven at 200°C (400°F) mark 6 for 25–30 minutes until crisp. Make a hole in

the bottom of each profiterole to release the steam and leave to cool on a wire rack.

Whisk the cream until stiff and fill a piping bag fitted with a medium plain nozzle. Use to fill the profiteroles. Dredge with icing sugar and pile them into a pyramid.

To make the chocolate sauce, break up the chocolate and put it in a small bowl with the butter. Stand the bowl over a pan of warm water and heat gently, stirring until the chocolate has melted. Stir in the milk and vanilla essence. Pour a little chocolate sauce over the profiteroles and serve the rest separately. Serve immediately.

VARIATION

For an alternative sauce, melt 100 g (4 oz) plain chocolate as above, gradually stirring in a small can of evaporated milk and beat well.

Chocolate praline choux buns

1 quantity choux pastry (*see page 116*)
beaten egg to glaze
15 g (½ oz) flaked almonds
icing sugar to decorate

For the filling
150 ml (¼ pint) milk
15 ml (1 level tbsp) custard powder
75 g (3 oz) plain chocolate
150 ml (¼ pint) double cream
75 g (3 oz) praline (*see page 176*)

Dampen the surface of a baking sheet with water. Place ten spoonfuls of the choux mixture on to the baking sheet, brush with beaten egg and sprinkle with flaked almonds. Bake in the oven at 200°C (400°F) mark 6 for 25–30 minutes until well risen and crisp. Slit the sides to release the steam and leave to cool on a wire rack.

For the filling, blend together the milk and custard powder in a pan. Bring to the boil, stirring, to thicken. Remove from the heat, cover with damp greaseproof paper and leave to cool. Break up the chocolate and put it in a bowl, stand this over a pan of hot water and heat gently, stirring, until the chocolate has melted. Stir into the cold custard. Whisk the cream until stiff and fold carefully into the custard with the praline, using a metal spoon. Fill the choux buns, using a teaspoon or a piping bag fitted with a medium plain nozzle, and dredge with sifted icing sugar.

Éclairs

Illustrated in colour on page 29

1 quantity choux pastry (*see page 116*)
300 ml ($\frac{1}{2}$ pint) double cream
1 quantity chocolate or coffee glacé icing
   (*see page 171*) **or 50 g (2 oz) plain**
   chocolate

Dampen the surface of a baking sheet with water. Put the choux pastry into a piping bag fitted with a medium plain nozzle and pipe in fingers, 9 cm (3$\frac{1}{2}$ inches) long, on to the baking sheet, keeping the lengths very even and cutting the pastry off with a wet knife against the edge of the nozzle. Bake in the oven at 200°C (400°F) mark 6 for about 35 minutes until well risen, crisp and golden. Remove from the baking sheet, slit down the sides with a sharp,

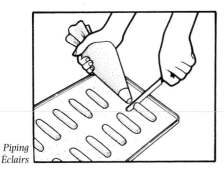

Piping
Éclairs

pointed knife to allow the steam to escape and leave on a wire rack to cool.

When the éclairs are cold, and shortly before serving, whisk the cream until stiff and use to fill the éclairs. Ice the tops with a little chocolate or coffee glacé icing or break up the chocolate, put it in a small bowl over a pan of hot water and heat gently, stirring, until the chocolate has melted. Pour into a shallow bowl and dip in the filled éclairs, drawing each one across the surface of the chocolate.

Churros

These fried choux pastries are delicious served as a dessert or like doughnuts at tea-time.

50 g (2 oz) butter
300 ml ($\frac{1}{2}$ pint) water
150 g (5 oz) plain flour
3 eggs, size 2
15 ml (1 tbsp) orange-flower water
oil for deep frying
caster sugar and icing sugar to decorate

Heat the butter and water in a saucepan and bring to the boil. Take off the heat, tip in all the flour at once and beat until smooth. Add the eggs one at a time and beat vigorously until well incorporated. Add the orange-flower water. Put the mixture into a piping bag fitted with a medium plain nozzle. Heat a pan of deep oil to 182°C (360°F) or until a 2.5-cm (1-inch) cube of bread will turn brown in 1 minute. Carefully pipe lengths of the churros mixture into the oil, in rings, spirals or horseshoes, cutting the mixture off to the required length with a knife. Fry until golden brown, turning them once. (Don't fry more than about three at a time, as the mixture swells during cooking.) Drain thoroughly on absorbent kitchen paper and keep warm. Before serving, dredge the churros heavily with a mixture of caster and icing sugar.

Paris–Brest

This pastry was created in the late 19th century to commemorate the famous bicycle race that took place between Paris and Brest, the race being run along a circular route.

1 quantity choux pastry (*see page 116*)
beaten egg to glaze
50 g (2 oz) flaked almonds
100 g (4 oz) caster sugar
2 egg whites
100 g (4 oz) butter
50 g (2 oz) praline (*see page 176*)
4 macaroon biscuits
45 ml (3 tbsp) brandy
icing sugar to decorate

Lightly dampen a baking sheet. Fill a piping bag fitted with a large plain nozzle with choux pastry and pipe into a 20.5-cm (8-inch) diameter ring. Brush the ring with beaten egg and sprinkle over the almonds. Bake in the oven at 200°C (400°F) mark 6 for 30 minutes until well risen and golden brown. Slit the ring to release the steam and leave to cool on a wire rack.

Dissolve the sugar in 75 ml (5 tbsp) water and bring to the boil. Boil until a thick syrup forms, at about 104°C (220°F). Whisk the egg whites until stiff and gradually beat in the sugar syrup. Continue beating until the mixture is cold. Cream the butter until soft and fold in the praline and egg white mixture. Cut the choux ring in half horizontally. Fill the bottom half with some of the filling mixture. Crush the macaroons and sprinkle them with the brandy. Spoon over the filling and top with the remaining cream filling. Cover with the top half of the choux ring and dredge with icing sugar.
Serves 6

RISING TO THE OCCASION

The soft, cake-like texture which distinguishes these special cakes from ordinary bread comes from the use of fat and/or eggs to enrich the mixture. Both fat and eggs retard the action of yeast, so the 'sponge batter' method is often employed. The yeast is allowed to start work in a batter made from about one third of the flour and all of the liquid before the other ingredients are added. This is convenient when using dried yeast as there is no need to reconstitute it first.

For less rich mixtures, the 'straight dough' method is generally used. Fresh yeast is simply blended with the warm liquid, then mixed with the dry ingredients for the dough. Dried yeast must be reconstituted in a proportion (usually one third) of the liquid before it is added to the dry ingredients.

Note To avoid repetition of instructions, the recipes in this chapter have been written using fresh yeast, but dried yeast can be used equally successfully. As it is more concentrated than fresh yeast, only half the amount of dried yeast is generally required. Sugar helps to activate dried yeast. Dissolve the sugar in tepid liquid, in the proportion of 5 ml (1 level tsp) to 300 ml ($\frac{1}{2}$ pint). Sprinkle the yeast granules over the surface of the liquid and leave the mixture to froth for about 15 minutes before using.

25 g (1 oz) fresh yeast is equivalent to 15 ml (1 level tbsp) dried yeast.

15 g ($\frac{1}{2}$ oz) fresh yeast is equivalent to 10 ml (2 level tsp) dried yeast.

Rum babas

Illustrated in colour on page 149

Soaked in spirit and decorated with a whirl of cream, these make a delicious dessert to serve at a dinner party.

25 g (1 oz) fresh yeast
90 ml (6 tbsp) tepid milk
225 g (8 oz) strong plain flour
2.5 ml ($\frac{1}{2}$ level tsp) salt
30 ml (2 level tbsp) caster sugar
4 eggs, beaten
100 g (4 oz) butter, softened but not melted
100 g (4 oz) currants
300 ml ($\frac{1}{2}$ pint) double cream

For the rum syrup
120 ml (8 tbsp) clear honey
120 ml (8 tbsp) water
a little rum

Lightly grease sixteen 9-cm ($3\frac{1}{2}$-inch) ring tins with lard and place them on baking sheets. Put the yeast, milk and 50 g (2 oz) flour into a bowl and blend until smooth. Cover with a clean cloth and leave in a warm place for about 15 minutes until frothy. Add the remaining flour, the salt, sugar, eggs, butter and currants and beat well with a wooden spoon for 3–4 minutes.

Half fill the prepared tins with the dough, cover with a clean cloth and leave to rise in a warm place until the tins are two-thirds full. Bake in the oven at 200°C (400°F) mark 6 for 15–20 minutes until well risen, golden and just beginning to shrink away from the sides of the tins. Leave to cool in the tins for a few minutes.

Meanwhile, make the rum syrup. Put the honey and water together in a pan and warm gently. Add rum to taste. Turn the rum babas out on to a wire rack and put a tray underneath. While the babas are still hot, spoon rum syrup over each one until well soaked. Leave to cool.

To serve, whisk the cream until thick and spoon or pipe some into the centre of each baba.

Lardy cake

*This traditional recipe from Wiltshire can be
served from the oven as a pudding or cold as a
cake for tea.*

15 g ($\frac{1}{2}$ oz) fresh yeast
300 ml ($\frac{1}{2}$ pint) tepid water
450 g (1 lb) strong plain flour
10 ml (2 level tsp) salt
cooking oil
50 g (2 oz) butter
100 g (4 oz) caster sugar
5 ml (1 level tsp) ground mixed spice
75 g (3 oz) sultanas or currants
50 g (2 oz) lard

Grease a 25.5×20.5-cm (10×8-inch)
cake tin. Blend the yeast with the water
and leave in a warm place for about 15
minutes until frothy. Sift together the flour
and salt into a large bowl and stir in the
yeast mixture and 15 ml (1 tbsp) oil. Beat
until smooth then cover and leave to rise
in a warm place for about 1 hour until
doubled in size.

Turn out the dough on to a lightly
floured working surface and knead for
5–10 minutes. Roll out to a rectangle
about 0.5 cm ($\frac{1}{4}$ inch) thick. Cover two
thirds of the dough with small flakes of
butter and sprinkle over 45 ml (3 level
tbsp) sugar, half the spice and half the
dried fruit. Fold and roll out as for flaky
pastry (*see page 114*). Repeat the process
with the lard, 45 ml (3 level tbsp) sugar
and the remaining spice and fruit. Fold
the dough again in the same way and roll
out once more.

Place the dough in the prepared tin,
pressing it well down into the corners.
Cover with a clean cloth and leave to rise
in a warm place for about 1 hour until
doubled in size. Brush the surface with oil,
sprinkle with the remaining caster sugar
and score the surface in a criss-cross
pattern with a sharp knife. Bake in the
oven at 220°C (425°F) mark 7 for about

30 minutes until well risen and golden.
Turn out and leave to cool on a wire rack.
Serve sliced, plain or with butter.

Sally Lunn

*Sally Lunn was an itinerant cake seller in
Bath during the 18th century and her cake,
or bun, became nationally famous.*

50 g (2 oz) butter
200 ml (7 fl oz) tepid milk
5 ml (1 level tsp) caster sugar
2 eggs
15 g ($\frac{1}{2}$ oz) fresh yeast
450 g (1 lb) strong plain flour
5 ml (1 level tsp) salt

For the glaze
60 ml (4 tbsp) water
30 ml (2 level tbsp) sugar

Grease two 12.5–15-cm (5–6-inch) round
cake tins. Melt the butter slowly in a pan,
remove from the heat and add the milk
and sugar. Beat the eggs and add with the
warm milk mixture to the yeast. Blend
well. Sift together the flour and salt, add
the yeast mixture and mix well. Knead on
a lightly floured working surface until
smooth. Put into the prepared tins, cover
with a clean cloth and leave to rise for
about 1 hour until the dough fills the tins.
Bake in the oven at 230°C (450°F) mark 8
for 15–20 minutes. Turn out and leave to
cool on a wire rack. Make the glaze by
heating the water and sugar to boiling
point. Boil for 2 minutes. Use at once to
glaze the hot buns.

Fruited Sally Lunn

Add 175 g (6 oz) mixed dried fruits, such
as currants, sultanas, seedless raisins and
chopped glacé cherries to the above
recipe. Stir the fruit into the flour and
continue as above. To glaze the buns,
brush with honey or golden syrup while
still warm.

Hungarian coffee cake

450 g (1 lb) strong plain flour
15 g ($\frac{1}{2}$ oz) fresh yeast
225 ml (8 fl oz) tepid milk
5 ml (1 level tsp) salt
50 g (2 oz) butter or block margarine
1 egg, beaten

For the topping
40 g (1$\frac{1}{2}$ oz) butter, melted
75 g (3 oz) caster sugar
5 ml (1 level tsp) ground cinnamon
25 g (1 oz) walnuts, chopped
25 g (1 oz) seedless raisins

Grease a 1.7-litre (3-pint) ring mould. Put 150 g (5 oz) of the flour, the yeast and milk in a bowl and blend until smooth. Cover with a clean cloth and leave in a warm place for about 15 minutes until frothy. Sift the remaining flour and salt into a bowl and rub in the fat. Add the beaten egg and the flour mixture to the yeast batter and mix well to give a soft dough. Turn the dough on to a lightly floured working surface and knead for

Rolling balls of dough for Hungarian coffee cake

Arranging dough balls in a ring mould

about 10 minutes until smooth. Cover the dough with a clean cloth and leave to rise in a warm place until doubled in size.

Knead the dough lightly. Divide into twenty-four equal-sized pieces about the size of walnuts and roll into balls. Roll each ball in the melted butter and then in a mixture of sugar, cinnamon, walnuts and raisins. Arrange a double row of dough balls in the prepared mould. Cover with a clean cloth and leave in a warm place to prove for about 45 minutes until the dough comes to the top of the ring mould. Bake in the oven at 200°C (400°F) mark 6 for about 25 minutes. Leave in the tin to cool for a few minutes before turning out carefully on to a wire rack.

Fruited butterscotch ring

For the enriched white dough
375 g (13 oz) strong plain flour
25 g (1 oz) fresh yeast
about 200 ml (7 fl oz) tepid milk
5 ml (1 level tsp) salt
40 g (1$\frac{1}{2}$ oz) butter
1 egg, beaten

For the topping
50 g (2 oz) butter
50 g (2 oz) light brown soft sugar
30 ml (2 level tbsp) golden syrup
50 g (2 oz) currants

Grease and line a 1.7-litre (3-pint) angel cake tin or plain ring mould. Put 200 g (7 oz) of the flour, the yeast and milk into a bowl and blend until smooth. Cover with a clean cloth and leave in a warm place for about 30 minutes until frothy. Sift together the remaining flour and salt and rub in the butter. Add this and the beaten egg to the yeast mixture. Mix well to a soft dough, adding a little more flour if the dough is too sticky. Turn on to a lightly floured working surface and knead for at least 10 minutes until smooth. Cover with a clean cloth and leave in a warm place for about 1 hour until doubled in size. Turn the dough out on to a lightly floured working surface and knead again for 4–5 minutes until smooth.

For the topping, melt together the butter, sugar and golden syrup and bring to the boil. Pour into the base of the prepared tin and sprinkle over half the currants. Shape the dough into about thirty-six small balls. Arrange the balls of dough in loose layers in the tin, sprinkling with the rest of the currants. Cover with a clean cloth and leave to prove until the dough almost reaches top of the tin. Place the tin on a baking sheet and bake in the oven at 220°C (425°F) mark 7 for about 40 minutes. Turn out and leave to cool on a wire rack before slicing, or pull apart to eat while still warm.

Granary tea cake

100 g (4 oz) butter
250 ml (9 fl oz) milk
750 g (1 lb 10 oz) granary flour
10 ml (2 level tsp) salt
25 g (1 oz) fresh yeast
2 eggs, size 2, beaten
50 g (2 oz) currants
25 g (1 oz) chopped mixed peel
beaten egg
barley kernels

Grease two baking sheets. In a pan, melt the butter in the milk. Leave to cool. Mix together the granary flour and salt. Blend the yeast with a little cool milk. Make a well in the centre of the dry ingredients and add the yeast mixture, remaining milk and egg. Mix to a soft dough, adding the currants and mixed peel. Knead for 10 minutes on a lightly floured working surface. Cover with a clean cloth and leave in a warm place for about 1 hour until doubled in size. Knead the dough for 2–3 minutes on the floured surface. Divide into sixteen flat ovals. Arrange on the baking sheets in overlapping rings of eight buns each. Cover with a clean cloth and leave to prove until doubled in size. Brush with beaten egg, scatter with barley kernels and bake in the oven at 200°C (400°F) mark 6 for about 25 minutes. Leave to cool on a wire rack.
Makes 2 tea cakes

Devonshire splits

15 g ($\frac{1}{2}$ oz) fresh yeast
about 300 ml ($\frac{1}{2}$ pint) tepid milk
450 g (1 lb) strong plain flour
5 ml (1 level tsp) salt
50 g (2 oz) butter
30 ml (2 level tbsp) caster sugar
icing sugar

For the filling
raspberry or strawberry jam
clotted or whipped cream

Grease a baking sheet. Blend the yeast with half the milk. Sift together the flour and salt into a bowl. Heat the butter and sugar in the remaining milk until tepid and stir into the flour with the yeast liquid. Beat well and turn on to a lightly floured working surface. Knead until smooth. Cover with a clean cloth and leave to rise in a warm place for about 1 hour until doubled in size.

Turn the dough on to the lightly floured surface and divide into fourteen to sixteen pieces. Knead lightly and shape into buns. Place on the baking sheet and flatten slightly with the hand. Cover with a clean cloth and leave to prove in a warm place for about 20 minutes. Bake in the oven at 220°C (425°F) mark 7 for 15–20 minutes. Turn out and leave to cool on a wire rack. Split the buns almost in half and fill with jam and cream. Dust the tops with sifted icing sugar.
Makes 14–16

Stollen

This is a traditional German Christmas cake.

15 g ($\frac{1}{2}$ oz) fresh yeast
100 ml (4 fl oz) tepid milk
225 g (8 oz) strong plain flour
1.25 ml ($\frac{1}{4}$ level tsp) salt
25 g (1 oz) margarine
grated rind of 1 small lemon
50 g (2 oz) chopped mixed peel
50 g (2 oz) currants
50 g (2 oz) sultanas
25 g (1 oz) blanched almonds, chopped
$\frac{1}{2}$ a beaten egg
icing sugar to dredge

Grease a large baking sheet. Put the yeast, milk and 50 g (2 oz) flour in a bowl and blend until smooth. Cover with a clean cloth and leave in a warm place for about 15 minutes until frothy. Sift together the remaining flour and salt into a bowl and rub in the margarine. Stir in the lemon rind, dried fruit and nuts. Add the yeast mixture and beaten egg and mix thoroughly to a soft dough. Turn on to a

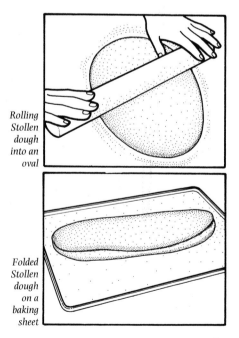

Rolling Stollen dough into an oval

Folded Stollen dough on a baking sheet

lightly floured working surface and knead for about 10 minutes until smooth. Cover with a clean cloth and leave to rise in a warm place for about 1 hour until doubled in size.

Knead the dough for 2–3 minutes, then roll into an oval shape about 23 × 18 cm (9 × 7 inches). Mark a line lengthways with the rolling pin and fold the dough in half along this line. Place on the baking sheet, cover with a clean cloth and leave to prove in a warm place for about 40 minutes until doubled in size. Bake in the oven at 200°C (400°F) mark 6 for 30 minutes until well risen and golden brown. Leave to cool on a wire rack. Before serving, dredge with icing sugar.

Streusel squares

225 g (8 oz) strong plain flour
50 g (2 oz) fine semolina
50 g (2 oz) caster sugar
75 g (3 oz) butter or margarine
25 g (1 oz) fresh yeast
2 eggs, beaten
45 ml (3 tbsp) milk
grated rind and juice of 1 orange
100 g (4 oz) currants
raspberry jam

For the topping
40 g ($1\frac{1}{2}$ oz) butter or margarine
50 g (2 oz) plain flour
50 g (2 oz) demerara sugar
pinch of ground cinnamon

Grease a 23 × 18-cm (9 × 7-inch) shallow tin. Sift together the flour, semolina and sugar. Rub in the fat and then rub in the yeast. Add the eggs, milk and 30 ml (2 tbsp) orange juice and mix to give a soft dough. Add the orange rind and currants to the dough. Put the dough in the prepared tin spreading it evenly. Cover with a layer of raspberry jam and leave to rise in a warm place for about 1 hour until doubled in size.

To make the topping, rub the fat into the flour and sugar and add the cinnamon. Cover the top of the dough with this mixture. Bake in the oven at 200°C (400°F) mark 6 for about 40 minutes until spongy and pale brown. Cool for a few minutes and loosen the edges. Turn out carefully on to a cloth or greaseproof paper, and then turn it over on to a wire rack, right side up. Serve warm, in squares, with coffee, or slice thinly to serve at tea-time.

Danish almond fingers

Illustrated in colour on page 149

15 g ($\frac{1}{2}$ oz) fresh yeast
75 ml (5 tbsp) tepid water
225 g (8 oz) plain flour
pinch of salt
25 g (1 oz) lard
1 egg, beaten
15 ml (1 level tbsp) caster sugar
150 g (5 oz) butter or margarine
350 g (12 oz) almond paste
beaten egg to glaze
1 quantity glacé icing (*see page 171*) to
    decorate

Grease a baking sheet. Blend the yeast with the water. Sift together the flour and salt into a bowl and rub in the lard. Make a well in the centre and add the blended yeast, egg and sugar. Mix to a soft dough. Turn on to a lightly floured working surface and knead until smooth. Cover with a clean cloth and leave in a cool place for 10 minutes.

Work the fat with a knife until soft, then form into a block of 23 × 7.5 cm (9 × 3 inches). Roll out the dough to a 25.5-cm (10-inch) square, place the butter in the centre, fold the sides up over it and seal. Roll out on the floured surface to 38 × 12.5 cm (15 × 5 inches). Fold the top third down and the bottom third up. Cover with a clean cloth and leave for 10 minutes in a

cool place. Repeat twice, resting finally for 30 minutes.

Roll out the dough to 30.5 × 20.5 cm (12 × 8 inches). Cut into twelve strips 2.5 cm (1 inch) wide. Cut the almond paste into twelve finger shapes and wrap a strip of dough round each. Place on the greased baking sheet, cover with a clean cloth and leave in a warm place for about 20 minutes until spongy. Brush with beaten egg and bake in the oven at 220°C (425°F) mark 7 for about 15 minutes. Brush the fingers with glacé icing while they are still warm.
Makes 12

Yeasted fruit cake

25 g (1 oz) fresh yeast
200 ml (7 fl oz) tepid milk
225 g (8 oz) strong plain flour
2.5 ml ($\frac{1}{2}$ level tsp) salt
50 g (2 oz) semolina
100 g (4 oz) caster sugar
100 g (4 oz) block margarine
200 g (7 oz) mixed dried fruit,
    eg. currants, sultanas, raisins, mixed
    peel
25 g (1 oz) glacé cherries, chopped
1 egg, beaten

Grease a 1.4-litre (2$\frac{1}{2}$-pint) ring tin. Put the yeast and milk in a small bowl and blend until smooth. Cover with a clean cloth and leave in a warm place for about 15 minutes until frothy. Mix together the flour, salt, semolina and caster sugar. Rub in the margarine and stir in the fruit. Add the egg and yeast mixture to the dry ingredients. Beat well for 5 minutes. Turn the mixture into the prepared tin and leave to rise in a warm place for 1 hour until doubled in size. Bake in the oven at 200°C (400°F) mark 6 for about 30 minutes until golden and firm. Turn out and leave to cool on a wire rack. Serve sliced, with or without butter.

Poppy seed yeast cake

Illustrated in colour on page 58

25 g (1 oz) fresh yeast
22 ml (1½ tbsp) tepid water
45 ml (3 tbsp) milk
50 g (2 oz) granulated sugar
275 g (10 oz) plain flour
1 egg
50 g (2 oz) butter, cut in small pieces and softened

For the filling
100 g (4 oz) poppy seeds
25 g (1 oz) almonds, chopped
50 g (2 oz) seedless raisins, chopped
grated rind of 2 lemons
grated rind of 1 medium orange
75 ml (5 tbsp) milk
100 g (4 oz) granulated sugar
15 ml (1 level tbsp) plain flour
1 egg, separated
15 ml (1 tbsp) single cream or top of the milk
15 ml (1 tbsp) melted butter

For the topping
milk
icing sugar

Lightly grease a 24×13×7.5-cm (9½× 5½×3-inch) loaf tin. Blend the yeast with the water and leave to stand for 5 minutes, then stir to dissolve the yeast completely and leave in a warm place for a further 3–5 minutes until beginning to froth. Meanwhile, pour the milk into a pan, add the sugar and stir over a low heat until the sugar is dissolved. Remove from the heat and leave to cool. Put the yeast mixture in a large bowl, stir in the milk and sugar and beat in 250 g (9 oz) flour alternately with the egg and butter. Mix until the dough can be gathered into a compact ball, then transfer to a working surface sprinkled with the remaining flour and knead until smooth. Shape into a ball and place in a mixing bowl. Add enough cold water to cover the dough by about 4 cm (1½ inches)

and leave for 15–45 minutes until the top of the ball has risen above the surface of the water.

Remove the dough from the water, pat dry with absorbent kitchen paper and knead for 5–10 minutes until smooth and elastic. Place the dough in a lightly greased bowl, cover with a clean cloth and leave to rise in a warm place for about 30 minutes until doubled in size.

To make the filling, grind the poppy seeds in a blender or use a pestle and mortar. Mix the ground poppy seeds with the almonds, raisins, lemon and orange rind. Whisk together the milk, sugar and flour, put into a pan and bring to the boil, stirring continuously. Remove from the heat and pour over the poppy seed mixture. Add the egg yolk and cream or top of the milk and mix together thoroughly. Whisk the egg white until stiff and fold into the mixture.

Knead the dough briefly, then place on a lightly floured working surface and roll out to a rectangle of about 20.5 × 30.5 cm

Spreading filling for Poppy seed yeast cake

Rolling Poppy seed yeast cake

(8 × 12 inches). Spread the filling evenly over the dough to within 1 cm ($\frac{1}{2}$ inch) of the edges and dribble over the melted butter. Roll one short side to the centre, like a Swiss roll, then roll the opposite side to the centre in the same way. Firmly holding both sides together, turn the cake over and place seam-side down in the prepared tin.

Brush the top with milk and bake in the oven at 190°C (375°F) mark 5 for about 1 hour until golden brown and crusty. Leave in the tin for 10–15 minutes then turn out on to a wire rack and dredge lightly with icing sugar. Leave to cool completely before slicing. Serve while very fresh.

Apricot savarin

Illustrated in colour on page 149

75 g (3 oz) dried apricots, soaked
   overnight
25 g (1 oz) fresh yeast
90 ml (6 tbsp) tepid milk
225 g (8 oz) strong plain flour
2.5 ml ($\frac{1}{2}$ level tsp) salt
30 ml (2 level tbsp) caster sugar
4 eggs, beaten
100 g (4 oz) butter, softened

For the syrup
90 ml (6 tbsp) clear honey
90 ml (6 tbsp) water
45 ml (3 tbsp) brandy

Grease a 1.4-litre (2$\frac{1}{2}$-pint) ring mould. Drain and chop the apricots. Put the yeast, milk and 50 g (2 oz) flour into a bowl and blend until smooth. Leave in a warm place for about 15 minutes until frothy. Add the remaining flour with the salt, sugar, egg, butter and apricots. Beat thoroughly for 3–4 minutes. Pour the mixture into the prepared tin, cover with a clean cloth and leave to rise for about 15 minutes in a warm place. Bake in the oven at 200°C (400°F) mark 6 for about 30 minutes. Turn out on to a serving dish.

Place the honey, water and brandy in a pan and bring to the boil. While the savarin is still hot, spoon over the syrup until it is all absorbed. You may fill the centre of the savarin with more poached dried or fresh or canned apricots. A fresh fruit salad also makes a pleasant combination. Serve pouring cream separately.
Serves 8

Saffron cake

The Phoenicians introduced saffron to Cornwall, from where this cake is believed to originate. Infuse the saffron overnight before you bake the cake.

25 g (1 oz) fresh yeast
150 ml ($\frac{1}{4}$ pint) tepid milk
450 g (1 lb) strong plain flour
5 ml (1 level tsp) salt
50 g (2 oz) butter
50 g (2 oz) lard
175 g (6 oz) currants
grated rind of $\frac{1}{2}$ a lemon
25 g (1 oz) caster sugar
2.5 ml ($\frac{1}{2}$ tsp) saffron strands, infused
   overnight in 150 ml ($\frac{1}{4}$ pint) boiling
   water

Grease a 20.5-cm (8-inch) round cake tin. Blend the yeast with the milk. Sift together the flour and salt into a bowl and rub in the butter and lard until the mixture resembles fine breadcrumbs. Stir in the currants, lemon rind and sugar. Strain the saffron infusion into a pan and warm slightly. Add to the dry ingredients with the yeast liquid and beat well. Turn the dough into the prepared tin, cover with a clean cloth and leave to rise in a warm place for about 1 hour until the dough comes to the top of the tin. Bake in the oven at 200°C (400°F) mark 6 for 30 minutes. Reduce the oven temperature to 180°C (350°F) mark 4 and bake for a further 30 minutes. Turn out and leave to cool on a wire rack.

Hot cross buns

These are traditionally eaten on Good Friday. The symbolic crosses are usually made of pastry, but if you prefer, mark them on with a sharp knife.

25 g (1 oz) fresh yeast
150 ml ($\frac{1}{4}$ pint) tepid milk
60 ml (4 tbsp) tepid water
450 g (1 lb) strong plain flour
5 ml (1 level tsp) salt
2.5 ml ($\frac{1}{2}$ level tsp) ground mixed spice
2.5 ml ($\frac{1}{2}$ level tsp) ground cinnamon
2.5 ml ($\frac{1}{2}$ level tsp) ground nutmeg
50 g (2 oz) caster sugar
50 g (2 oz) butter, melted and cooled
1 egg, beaten
100 g (4 oz) currants
25 g (1 oz) chopped mixed peel
50 g (2 oz) shortcrust pastry (*see page 108*)

For the glaze
60 ml (4 tbsp) milk and water
45 ml (3 level tbsp) caster sugar

Grease a baking sheet. Put the yeast, milk, water and 100 g (4 oz) of the flour into a bowl and blend until smooth. Cover with a clean cloth and leave in a warm place for about 15 minutes until frothy. Sift together the remaining flour, salt, spices and sugar into a bowl. Stir in the butter, egg, yeast mixture and fruit and mix to a soft dough. Turn on to a lightly floured working surface and knead until smooth. Cover with a clean cloth and leave to rise in a warm place for about 1 hour until doubled in size. Turn the dough out on to the floured surface and knead for 2–3 minutes. Divide the dough into twelve pieces and shape into round buns. Place on the baking sheet, cover with a clean cloth and leave to prove in a warm place until doubled in size.

Roll out the pastry thinly on a lightly floured working surface and cut into thin strips about 9 cm (3$\frac{1}{2}$ inches) long. Dampen the pastry strips and lay two on each bun to make a cross. Bake in the oven at 190°C (375°F) mark 5 for 15–20 minutes until golden brown. For the glaze, heat the milk, water and sugar gently together. Brush the hot buns twice with glaze then leave to cool on a wire rack.
Makes 12

Chelsea buns

These were an 18th-century speciality of the Old Chelsea Bun House in Pimlico which was then in the Borough of Chelsea.

15 g ($\frac{1}{2}$ oz) fresh yeast
100 ml (4 fl oz) tepid milk
225 g (8 oz) strong plain flour
2.5 ml ($\frac{1}{2}$ level tsp) salt
about 15 g ($\frac{1}{2}$ oz) butter or lard
1 egg, beaten
clear honey to glaze

For the filling
melted butter
75 g (3 oz) mixed dried fruit
25 g (1 oz) chopped mixed peel
50 g (2 oz) light brown soft sugar

Grease an 18-cm (7-inch) square cake tin. Put the yeast, milk and 50 g (2 oz) of the flour into a bowl and blend until smooth. Cover with a clean cloth and leave in a warm place for about 15 minutes until frothy. Sift together the remaining flour and salt into a bowl and rub in the fat. Add the yeast mixture and egg and mix to a soft dough. Turn on to a lightly floured working surface and knead for about 5 minutes until smooth. Cover with a clean cloth and leave to rise in a warm place for about 1 hour until doubled in size.

Knead the dough for 2–3 minutes on the floured surface and roll out to a rectangle of 30.5 × 23 cm (12 × 9 inches). Brush with melted butter and cover with a mixture of dried fruit, mixed peel and brown sugar. Roll up from the longest side like a Swiss roll and seal the edge with water. Cut into nine equal slices and place these, cut side down, in the prepared tin. Cover with a clean cloth and leave to prove in a warm place until doubled in size. Bake in the oven at 190°C (375°F) mark 5 for about 30 minutes. While still warm, brush the buns with a wet brush dipped in honey.

Makes 9

Butterscotch stickies

Illustrated in colour on page 149

225 g (8 oz) strong plain flour
15 g ($\frac{1}{2}$ oz) fresh yeast
100 ml (4 fl oz) tepid milk
2.5 ml ($\frac{1}{2}$ level tsp) salt
knob of butter or lard
1 egg, beaten
25 g (1 oz) butter
100 g (4 oz) dark brown soft sugar
50 g (2 oz) almonds, chopped
10 ml (2 level tsp) ground cinnamon

Lightly grease an 18-cm (7-inch) square cake tin. Put 50 g (2 oz) of the flour, the yeast and milk into a small bowl and blend until smooth. Cover with a clean cloth and leave in a warm place for about 20 minutes until frothy. Sift together the remaining flour and salt and rub in the fat. Mix with the yeast mixture and egg. Beat well. Turn on to a lightly floured working surface and knead for about 5 minutes. Cover with a clean cloth and leave to rise for 1–1$\frac{1}{2}$ hours until the dough has doubled in size.

Knead the dough lightly on the floured surface and roll out to an oblong of 30.5 × 23 cm (12 × 9 inches).

Melt the butter and stir in the remaining ingredients. Spread half in the base of the prepared tin and the rest over the rolled-out dough. Roll up the dough from the longest side, like a Swiss roll, and seal the edges. Cut into equal slices and place, cut side down, in the tin. Cover with a

clean cloth and leave to prove for about 30 minutes in a warm place. Bake in the oven at 190°C (375°F) mark 5 for 30–35 minutes. Turn out on to a wire rack immediately and leave to cool. Break into pieces to serve.

Makes 9

Orange streusel cake

225 g (8 oz) strong plain flour
2.5 ml ($\frac{1}{2}$ level tsp) salt
50 g (2 oz) semolina
75 g (3 oz) caster sugar
100 g (4 oz) margarine
25 g (1 oz) fresh yeast
100 g (4 oz) currants (optional)
grated rind and juice of 2 oranges
2 eggs, beaten
orange marmalade

For the topping
50 g (2 oz) margarine
75 g (3 oz) plain flour
50 g (2 oz) demerara sugar
2.5 ml ($\frac{1}{2}$ level tsp) ground cinnamon

Grease a shallow 27.5 × 18-cm (10$\frac{3}{4}$ × 7-inch) tin. Mix together the flour, salt, semolina and caster sugar. Rub in the margarine and the yeast. Add the currants, if liked, and the orange rind. Make the orange juice up to 90 ml (6 tbsp) with milk, if necessary, and add to the mixture with the eggs. Beat well for 3 minutes.

Turn the mixture into the prepared tin, cover with a layer of marmalade and leave to rise in a warm place until doubled in size.

For the topping, rub the margarine into the flour, stir in the sugar and cinnamon and sprinkle this mixture over the marmalade. Bake in the oven at 200°C (400°F) mark 6 for about 35 minutes. Turn out on to a piece of greaseproof paper, then invert on to a wire rack. Serve warm or cold, cut into squares or fingers.

Danish pastries

For the basic dough
25 g (1 oz) fresh yeast
about 150 ml ($\frac{1}{4}$ pint) tepid water
450 g (1 lb) plain flour (not strong)
5 ml (1 level tsp) salt
50 g (2 oz) lard
30 ml (2 level tbsp) caster sugar
2 eggs, beaten
275 g (10 oz) butter
beaten egg to glaze

For the fillings
1 quantity almond paste (*see page 175*)
1 quantity crème pâtissière (*see page 176*)
cinnamon butter (*see below*)
sultanas

For the toppings
1 quantity glacé icing (*see page 171*)
flaked or chopped almonds, toasted
redcurrant jelly (optional)

For the cinnamon butter
50 g (2 oz) butter
50 g (2 oz) caster sugar
10 ml (2 level tsp) ground cinnamon

Blend the yeast with the water. Mix the flour and salt together, rub in the lard and stir in the sugar. Add the yeast liquid and beaten eggs and mix to an elastic dough, adding a little more water if necessary. Knead lightly. Cover the bowl and leave the dough to 'rest' in the refrigerator for about 10 minutes.

Work the butter with a knife until soft and form it into an oblong. Roll the dough on a lightly floured surface into an oblong about three times the size of the butter, put the butter in the centre of the dough and enclose it by folding the sides of the dough over. Seal the edges with a rolling pin.

Turn the dough so that the folds are to the sides and roll into a strip three times as long as it is wide. Fold the bottom third up, and the top third down, cover and leave to 'rest' for 10 minutes. Repeat the turning,

rolling, folding and 'resting' twice more and then shape as required.

Crescents Roll out half the dough thinly and cut out two 23-cm (9-inch) rounds. Divide each into eight segments and put a little almond paste or crème pâtissière at the base of each. Roll up from the base and curl round to form a crescent. Place on a baking sheet.

Imperial stars Roll out half the dough thinly, cut into 7.5-cm (3-inch) squares and make diagonal cuts from each corner to within 1 cm ($\frac{1}{2}$ inch) of the centre. Put a piece of almond paste in the centre of the square and fold one corner of each cut section down to the centre, securing the tips with a little beaten egg. Place on a baking sheet.

Cushions Roll out half the dough thinly and cut into 7.5-cm (3-inch) squares. Put a little almond paste in the centre and either fold over two opposite corners to the centre or fold over all four corners, securing the tips with beaten egg. Place on a baking sheet.

Pinwheels Roll out half the dough into two oblongs 30 cm (12 inches) long and 20.5 cm (8 inches) wide. Cream all the cinnamon butter ingredients together and spread over the oblongs. Sprinkle with sultanas and roll up like Swiss rolls. Cut into 2.5-cm (1-inch) slices and place, cut side upwards, on a baking sheet.

Twists Roll out half the dough thinly and cut into two oblongs 30 cm (12 inches) long and 20.5 cm (8 inches) wide. Cut each oblong lengthways to give four pieces. Cream all the cinnamon butter ingredients together and spread over the pieces of dough. Fold the bottom third of each up and the top third down, seal and cut each across into thin slices. Twist these slices and put on a baking sheet.

Each of the above makes 16 pastries.

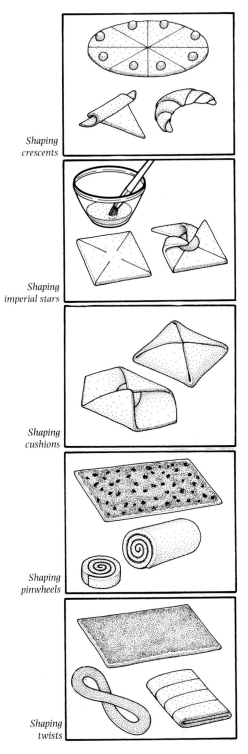

Shaping crescents

Shaping imperial stars

Shaping cushions

Shaping pinwheels

Shaping twists

To finish the pastries

After shaping, leave in a warm place for 20–30 minutes until doubled in size. Brush with beaten egg and bake in the oven at 220°C (425°F) mark 7 for about 15 minutes until golden brown. While they are still hot, brush with thin white glacé icing and sprinkle with toasted, flaked or chopped almonds. Finish the centres of imperial stars and cushions with a small spoonful of crème pâtissière or redcurrant jelly.

Coconut clusters

225 g (8 oz) strong plain flour
1.25 ml ($\frac{1}{4}$ level tsp) salt
75 g (3 oz) desiccated coconut
25 g (1 oz) caster sugar
15 g ($\frac{1}{2}$ oz) fresh yeast
150 ml ($\frac{1}{4}$ pint) tepid milk
finely grated rind of 1 lemon
milk or beaten egg to glaze
toasted long thread coconut to decorate

Grease a 21.5-cm ($8\frac{1}{2}$-inch) spring-release cake tin. Sift together the flour and salt and stir in the coconut and sugar. Blend the yeast and milk together and add to the dry ingredients with the lemon rind. Knead well until smooth on a lightly floured working surface, adding more flour if necessary. Cover with a clean cloth and leave to rise in a warm place for about 1 hour, until doubled in size.

Knead the dough on the floured surface and cut into eight even-sized pieces. Form into balls and place in the prepared tin. Cover and leave to prove for about 45 minutes in a warm place until doubled in size.

Brush with milk or beaten egg and bake in the oven at 200°C (400°F) mark 6 for about 25 minutes until golden and firm. Turn out and leave to cool on a wire rack. Sprinkle with the toasted coconut and break into pieces to serve.

Doughnuts

15 g (½ oz) fresh yeast
about 60 ml (4 tbsp) tepid milk
225 g (8 oz) strong plain flour
2.5 ml (½ level tsp) salt
knob of butter or margarine
1 egg, beaten
jam
fat for deep frying
sugar and ground cinnamon to coat

Blend the yeast with the milk. Sift together the flour and salt into a bowl and rub in the fat. Add the yeast liquid and egg and mix to a soft dough, adding a little more milk if necessary. Beat well until smooth, cover with a clean cloth and leave to rise in a warm place for about 1 hour until doubled in size. Knead lightly on a lightly floured working surface and divide into ten to twelve pieces. Shape each into a round, put 5 ml (1 level tsp) jam in the centre and draw up the edges to form a ball, pressing firmly to seal the edges together. Heat the fat to 180°C (360°F) or until it will brown a 2.5-cm (1-inch) cube of bread in 1 minute. Fry the doughnuts for 5–10 minutes until golden brown. Drain on crumpled absorbent kitchen paper and toss in sugar mixed with a little cinnamon. Eat the same day.
Makes 10–12

Doughnut ties

Illustrated in colour opposite

Make the dough as above, then divide into ten pieces. Shape each into a roll 18 cm (7 inches) long. Tie each into a knot. Deep fry as above until golden. Drain on absorbent kitchen paper. Toss in a mixture of caster sugar and poppy seeds to coat. Serve fresh.

Clockwise from top: Apricot savarin (*page 143*), Danish almond fingers (*page 141*), Doughnut ties (*above*), Butterscotch stickies (*page 145*), Rum babas (*page 136*)

MERINGUE CAKES

There are three basic types of meringue. Meringue Suisse, the easiest to make has a crisp texture and is used for shells and nests. Meringue cuite is a more stable mixture, ideal for piping fancy baskets and cases. It is more brittle and powdery than meringue Suisse. American meringue is used for pavlovas, layered tortes and party cakes. The unique texture of this meringue – crisp outside and marshmallowy within – is due to the addition of a little vinegar and cornflour.

For best results, use eggs that are 2–3 days old. If possible, keep the separated whites – which must be quite free of any yolk – in a covered container in the refrigerator for up to 24 hours before use. The whites will become more gelatinous and whisk more quickly to a greater volume. If you have to use the whites directly after separating, the colder they are the better. Sometimes a pinch of salt or cream of tartar is added to help the whites hold their shape.

When the mixture is stiff enough to stand in peaks, the sugar should be added. Caster or icing sugar give the best texture. Only half the sugar should be whisked in at first so that the meringue does not collapse. The remaining sugar is folded in with a metal spoon. The meringue must be used immediately otherwise the mixture will separate out. If a meringue goes soft after storing, dry it out in a very low oven for about 30 minutes until crisp. Unfilled meringue shells and nests keep well for 2–3 weeks in an airtight tin.

Strawberry vacherin (page 158)

Small meringues

Illustrated in colour on page 168

2 egg whites
100 g (4 oz) caster sugar
150 ml (¼ pint) double cream

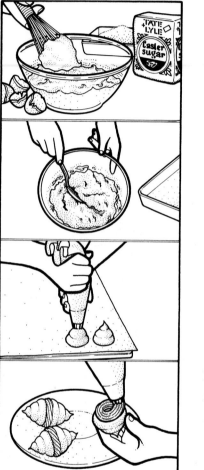

Line a large baking sheet with non-stick paper. Whisk the egg whites until very stiff. Add half the sugar to the egg whites and whisk again until the mixture regains its former stiffness.

Fold the remaining sugar into the mixture very lightly with a metal spoon.

Spoon the mixture into a piping bag fitted with a large star nozzle and pipe small rounds on to the prepared baking sheet. Alternatively, put the mixture in spoonfuls on to the baking sheet.

Dry out in the oven at 130°C (250°F) mark ½ for 2–3 hours until the meringues are firm and crisp but still white. If they begin to colour, prop the oven door slightly open. Ease the meringues off the paper and leave to cool on a wire rack. To serve, whisk the cream until stiff and use to sandwich the meringues together in pairs.

VARIATIONS

Pink meringues Tint the mixture pink by adding 1–2 drops of red food colouring when folding in the sugar.

Coffee meringues Fold in 10 ml (2 tsp) coffee essence with the sugar.

Chocolate meringues Fold in 10 ml (2 level tsp) cocoa powder with the sugar.

Filling variations Add finely chopped nuts, melted chocolate or a little liqueur to the whipped cream.

Chestnut vacherin

This is a classic French sweet made with mouthwatering meringues and chestnut flavoured cream.

6 egg whites
350 g (12 oz) caster sugar
300 ml ($\frac{1}{2}$ pint) double cream
30 ml (2 tbsp) milk
440-g (15$\frac{1}{2}$-oz) can sweetened chestnut purée
15 ml (1 tbsp) dry sherry
3 marrons glacés
25 g (1 oz) plain chocolate

Draw three 23-cm (9-inch) circles on non-stick paper and place on baking sheets.

Whisk the egg whites until very stiff and whisk in half the sugar. Carefully fold in the remaining sugar with a metal spoon. Spoon into a large piping bag fitted with a medium plain nozzle. Pipe the meringue mixture on to the circles, starting in the centre of each and working outwards in a coil to fill the circles. Alternatively, spoon the mixture on to the baking sheets and spread with a palette knife to fill the circles. Use slightly less than a third of the meringue for each circle. With the remaining meringue, pipe six shell shapes on to the paper in the corners of the baking sheets. Bake in the oven at 110°C (225°F) mark $\frac{1}{4}$ for 3 hours until crisp and dry. Leave to cool on the baking sheet and then carefully remove from the paper.

Place one meringue round on a flat serving plate. Whisk the cream with the milk until it just holds its shape and reserve 75 ml (5 level tbsp) for decoration. Fold the chestnut purée and sherry into the cream and spread half over the meringue base. Place the second meringue round on top and spread with the remaining chestnut cream. Top with the last meringue round. Position the meringue shells evenly around the top and secure with a little of the reserved cream. Place spoonfuls of the reserved cream between the shells. Place the marrons glacés in the centre of the meringue.

Break the chocolate into pieces and put in a bowl over a pan of hot water. Heat gently, stirring, until the chocolate has melted. Spoon into a small greaseproof paper piping bag (*see page 165*) and snip off the tip. Drizzle the chocolate over the cream. Chill for 1 hour before serving.

Hazelnut and chocolate meringue cake

3 egg whites
175 g (6 oz) caster sugar
2.5 ml ($\frac{1}{2}$ tsp) distilled white vinegar
100 g (4 oz) hazelnuts, skinned (*see page 19*) and finely chopped
100 g (4 oz) plain chocolate
30 ml (2 tbsp) brandy or rum
300 ml ($\frac{1}{2}$ pint) whipping cream
chocolate curls (*see page 164*) to decorate

Draw two 20.5-cm (8-inch) circles on non-stick paper and place on baking sheets.

Whisk the egg whites until very stiff and whisk in half the sugar. Carefully fold in the remaining sugar and the vinegar with a metal spoon. Lastly, fold in the nuts with 25 g (1 oz) chocolate, grated. Divide the meringue mixture between the baking sheets and spread to fill the circles.

Bake in the oven at 110°C (225°F) mark $\frac{1}{4}$ for about 1$\frac{3}{4}$ hours or until dry. Leave to cool on the baking sheets and then carefully remove from the paper.

Break the remaining chocolate into pieces and put, with the brandy or rum, in a small bowl over a pan of hot water. Heat gently, stirring, until the chocolate has melted, then remove from the heat. Leave until cool but not set. Lightly whisk the cream and stir in the cool chocolate mixture. Use to sandwich the meringue rounds together and decorate with chocolate curls before serving.

Pavlova

This classic meringue is named after Anna Pavlova, the famous Russian dancer.

3 egg whites
175 g (6 oz) caster sugar
2.5 ml (½ tsp) vanilla essence
2.5 ml (½ tsp) distilled white wine vinegar
5 ml (1 level tsp) cornflour
300 ml (½ pint) double cream
fresh strawberries, raspberries or Chinese
    gooseberries, or canned passion fruit,
    drained

Draw an 18-cm (7-inch) circle on non-stick paper and place the paper on a baking sheet. Whisk the egg whites until very stiff. Whisk in half the sugar then carefully fold in the remaining sugar, the vanilla essence, vinegar and cornflour with a metal spoon. Spread the meringue mixture over the circle and bake in the oven at 150°C (300°F) mark 2 for about 1 hour until crisp and dry. Leave to cool on the baking sheet then carefully remove from the paper.

Whisk the cream until stiff. Slide the meringue on to a flat plate, pile the cream on it and arrange the fruit on top.

Mocha meringue

3 egg whites
175 g (6 oz) sugar
15 ml (1 level tbsp) instant coffee powder

For the filling
300 ml (½ pint) double cream
2 egg whites
5 ml (1 level tsp) instant coffee powder
25 g (1 oz) chocolate, grated
25 g (1 oz) almonds, finely chopped
chopped almonds and grated chocolate to
    decorate

Draw two 20.5-cm (8-inch) circles on non-stick paper and place the paper on two baking sheets. Whisk the egg whites until very stiff. Whisk in half the sugar, add the instant coffee and whisk until the mixture is really stiff and no longer speckled with coffee. Carefully fold in the remaining sugar with a metal spoon. Divide the mixture between the baking sheets and spread evenly to fill the circles. Bake in the oven at 150°C (300°F) mark 2 for about 2 hours until dry. Leave the meringue rounds to cool on the baking sheets before very carefully lifting them off.

To make up the filling, whisk the cream until thick. Whisk the egg whites until stiff, then carefully fold the egg whites into the cream. Fold in the coffee powder, chocolate and nuts. Sandwich the meringue layers together with half the cream mixture. Spread the remainder on top and decorate with nuts and chocolate about 30 minutes before serving.

Rolla torte

3 egg whites
pinch of cream of tartar
pinch of salt
165 g (5½ oz) caster sugar
25 g (1 oz) ground almonds
25 g (1 oz) cornflour
1 quantity chocolate crème au beurre (*see
    page 171*)
50 g (2 oz) flaked almonds, lightly toasted
icing sugar to decorate

Draw three 18-cm (7-inch) circles on non-stick paper and place on baking sheets. Whisk the egg whites with the cream of tartar and salt until very stiff. Whisk in two thirds of the sugar, 15 ml (1 level tbsp) at a time. Mix together the remaining sugar, almonds and cornflour and fold carefully into the meringue mixture with a metal spoon. Using a piping bag fitted with a small plain nozzle, pipe the mixture on to the circles, starting from the centre and working outwards in a coil. Alternatively, spread the meringue with a palette knife in smooth layers. Bake in the oven at 170°C (325°F) mark 3 for 30 minutes until just coloured and dry. Leave to cool on the baking sheets before lifting off the paper.

Use the crème au beurre to sandwich the meringue layers together and to coat the sides. Decorate the sides with flaked almonds and dredge the top with icing sugar. Leave in a cool place for 24 hours before cutting, allowing the meringue layers to soften a little.

Raspberry meringue gâteau

1 egg white
50 g (2 oz) caster sugar

For the cake
3 eggs, size 2
115 g (4½ oz) caster sugar
75 g (3 oz) plain flour
450 ml (¾ pint) double cream
150 ml (¼ pint) soured cream
450 g (1 lb) fresh raspberries

Line a baking sheet with non-stick paper. Whisk the egg white until very stiff and whisk in half the sugar. Carefully fold in the remaining sugar with a metal spoon. Spoon into a large piping bag fitted with a 1-cm (½-inch) plain nozzle and pipe thumb-sized meringues on to the paper. Bake in the oven at 150°C (300°F) mark 2 for about 1 hour until crisp and dry. Cool on a wire rack.

Grease and line a 21.5-cm (8½-inch) round cake tin. Whisk the eggs and sugar together until thick. Sift the flour over the mixture and fold in with a metal spoon. Turn the mixture into the prepared tin. Bake in the oven at 180°C (350°F) mark 4 for about 35 minutes. Turn out and leave to cool on a wire rack.

Stiffly whisk 150 ml (¼ pint) double cream and whisk in the soured cream.

Split the cake in two and sandwich together with the whipped cream and raspberries, reserving a few raspberries for decoration. Whip the remaining cream and spread a thin layer over the cake. Press the meringues around the edge. Spoon the rest of the cream into a piping bag fitted with a plain nozzle and pipe a lattice pattern. Decorate with the reserved raspberries.

Chamonix

2 egg whites
100 g (4 oz) caster sugar

For the filling
225 g (8 oz) canned chestnut purée
30 ml (2 level tbsp) caster sugar
2.5 ml (½ tsp) vanilla essence
150 ml (¼ pint) double cream
25 g (1 oz) plain chocolate, grated

Line a baking sheet with non-stick paper. Whisk the egg whites until very stiff and whisk in half the sugar. Carefully fold in the remaining sugar with a metal spoon. Spoon the mixture into a piping bag fitted with a medium plain nozzle and pipe ten 6.5-cm (2½-inch) rounds on to the baking sheet. Bake in the oven at 130°C (250°F) mark ½ for 2½–3 hours until crisp and dry.

To make the filling, mix the chestnut purée with the sugar and vanilla essence. Spoon the chestnut purée mixture into a piping bag fitted with a small plain nozzle and pipe a line of purée around the top edge of each meringue. Whisk the cream until stiff. Fill the centres with a small blob of cream and sprinkle each with a little grated chocolate.
Makes 10

VARIATION

Meringue nests Make, pipe and bake the meringue cases as above. To serve, fill with whipped cream combined with chopped fresh fruits.

Walnut and brown sugar meringue

4 egg whites
100 g (4 oz) caster sugar
100 g (4 oz) light brown soft sugar
75 g (3 oz) walnuts, ground

For the filling
2.5 ml (½ level tsp) instant coffee
15 ml (1 level tbsp) light brown soft sugar
15 ml (1 tbsp) boiling water
300 ml (½ pint) double cream

For the decoration
icing sugar
150 ml (¼ pint) double cream, whipped
sugar coffee beans or walnut halves

Draw two 20.5-cm (8-inch) circles on non-stick paper and place on baking sheets.

Whisk the egg whites until very stiff. Sift the sugars together and whisk half into the egg whites, a little at a time. Carefully fold in the remainder and the walnuts with a metal spoon. Spoon into a piping bag fitted with a medium plain nozzle. Pipe meringue mixture on to the circles, starting in the centre of each and working outwards in a coil to fill the circles. Alternatively, spoon the mixture on to the baking sheets and spread with a palette knife to fill the circles. Bake in the oven at 140°C (275°F) mark 1 for about 1½ hours until dry. Turn off the oven and leave to get cold, then carefully remove the meringue from the paper.

For the filling, mix the coffee and brown sugar with the boiling water and allow to cool. Whisk the cream and, as it begins to thicken, add the coffee syrup, then continue whisking until thick. Sandwich the two meringue rounds together with the coffee cream. Dredge the centre of the top with icing sugar. Spoon the whipped cream into a piping bag fitted with a large star nozzle and pipe rosettes of cream round the edge. Decorate with the coffee beans or walnuts.

Vacherin aux cerises

225 g (8 oz) caster sugar
150 ml (¼ pint) water
4 egg whites
300 ml (½ pint) double cream
maraschino cherries
frosted cherries (*see opposite*) **to decorate**

Draw four 18-cm (7-inch) circles on non-stick paper and place on baking sheets.

Place the sugar and water in a saucepan and heat until dissolved. Bring to the boil and boil without stirring until the temperature reaches 120°C (248°F). While boiling, wash down any sugar crystals from the sides of the pan with a pastry brush dipped in water. Meanwhile, whisk the egg whites until very stiff. Gradually pour the hot syrup on to them, whisking all the time, until the meringue is cold. Using a large piping bag fitted with a small plain nozzle, pipe the mixture on to the circles, starting from the centre and working outwards in a coil, taking care that each coil of meringue just touches the previous one. Alternatively, spread the meringue on the paper in smooth layers with a palette knife. Bake in the oven at 140°C (275°F) mark 1 for about 1½ hours, until dry. Leave to cool on the baking sheets, then carefully remove from the paper.

Whisk the cream until it forms soft peaks and flavour with a little of the juice from the maraschino cherries. Drain some maraschino cherries and cut each in half. Layer up the meringue circles with some of the cream and cherries and press carefully to flatten slightly. Spoon the remaining whipped cream into a piping bag fitted with a medium star nozzle and pipe whirls of cream on top of the vacherin. Decorate with frosted cherries.

Frosted cherries Drain maraschino cherries (if possible use those with stems attached). Dip them in granulated sugar and leave to dry before using to decorate the vacherin.

Spiced blackcurrant meringue cake

100 g (4 oz) butter, softened
75 g (3 oz) caster sugar
4 egg yolks
90 ml (6 tbsp) milk
75 g (3 oz) plain flour
25 g (1 oz) cornflour
pinch of salt
1.25 ml ($\frac{1}{4}$ level tsp) mixed spice
5 ml (1 level tsp) baking powder
60 ml (4 level tbsp) blackcurrant jam

For the topping
4 egg whites
175 g (6 oz) caster sugar
pinch of ground cinnamon
25 g (1 oz) flaked almonds, toasted

Grease and line a 23-cm (9-inch) round cake tin. Cream the butter and sugar together until pale and fluffy, and gradually add the egg yolks and milk. Sift together the flours, salt, spice and baking powder and fold into the mixture thoroughly with a metal spoon. Turn the mixture into the prepared tin and bake in the oven at 180°C (350°F) mark 4 for 35 minutes until golden and firm to the touch. Turn the cake out on to a baking sheet and leave to cool slightly. Reduce the oven temperature to 150°C (300°F) mark 2. Spread the cake with jam.

For the meringue topping, whisk the egg whites until very stiff and whisk in half the sugar then carefully fold in the remaining sugar and the cinnamon with a metal spoon. Spoon the mixture into a piping bag fitted with a large star nozzle and pipe lines of meringue across the cake. Pipe more lines over the top in the opposite direction and finish by piping stars around the outer edge. Return to the oven for 20–25 minutes until the meringue is slightly coloured. Sprinkle with toasted almonds. This meringue cake is best served on the day of making.

Japonais

6 egg whites
350 g (12 oz) caster sugar
175 g (6 oz) ground almonds
1 quantity coffee crème au beurre (*see page 171*)
1 quantity praline (*see page 176*)
cocoa powder and sugar-coated chocolate sweets to decorate

Draw two 23-cm (9-inch) circles on non-stick paper and place on baking sheets.

Whisk the egg whites until very stiff and whisk in half the sugar. Carefully fold in the remaining sugar and the ground almonds with a metal spoon. Spoon into a large piping bag fitted with a medium plain nozzle. Pipe the meringue mixture on to the circles, starting in the centre and working outwards in a coil to fill the circles. Alternatively, spoon the mixture on to the baking sheets and spread with a palette knife to fill the circles. Bake in the oven at 170°C (325°F) mark 3 for about 1 hour until the meringue is crisp and golden. Leave to cool on the baking sheets. When the meringue rounds are cold, carefully remove the paper.

Use half the crème au beurre to sandwich the two meringue rounds together. Crush the praline finely and sprinkle over the top. Cut a 7.5-cm (3-inch) circle from the centre of a piece of card. Position the card over the top of the meringue and dredge the cocoa through a sieve to fill the cut-out centre. Remove the card. Spoon the remaining crème au beurre into a piping bag fitted with a medium star nozzle and pipe around the edge. Decorate with sugar-coated sweets.

Meringue basket

4 egg whites
225 g (8 oz) icing sugar
300 ml ($\frac{1}{2}$ pint) double cream
a few drops of vanilla essence (optional)
30 ml (2 tbsp) orange flavoured liqueur
225 g (8 oz) fruit, *eg.* **grapes, seeded;**
  cherries, stoned; strawberries and
  raspberries, hulled; peaches, sliced

Draw three 19-cm (7$\frac{1}{2}$-inch) circles on non-stick paper and place on baking sheets.

Place three egg whites and 175 g (6 oz) sugar in a deep bowl standing over hot water and whisk continuously until really thick. Spoon the mixture into a piping bag fitted with a large star nozzle and pipe a

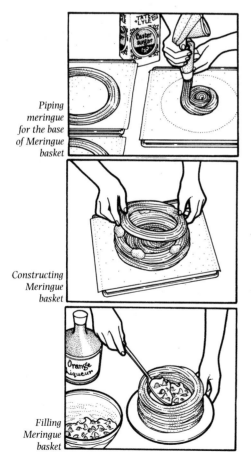

Piping meringue for the base of Meringue basket

Constructing Meringue basket

Filling Meringue basket

ring round the outlines of two of the circles. Pipe the remainder on to the third baking sheet in a coil to fill the circle. Bake in the oven at 110°C (225°F) mark $\frac{1}{4}$ for 2$\frac{1}{2}$–3 hours until crisp and dry. Leave the meringue to cool before carefully removing the paper.

Whisk the remaining egg white until stiff, then carefully fold in the remaining sugar with a metal spoon. Use this mixture to secure the meringue rings on to the round base, one on top of the other. Stand the basket on non-stick paper on a baking sheet and return to the oven to dry for a further 2 hours. Leave to cool, then carefully remove the paper.

Meanwhile, whisk the cream until stiff, adding a few drops of vanilla essence, if liked, and the orange liqueur. Fold in the prepared fruit, reserving some pieces for decoration. When the basket is cold, fill it with the cream and fruit mixture, and decorate with the remaining pieces of fruit.

Strawberry vacherin

Illustrated in colour on page 150

3 egg whites
175 g (6 oz) caster sugar
300 ml ($\frac{1}{2}$ pint) double cream
150 ml ($\frac{1}{4}$ pint) single cream
225 g (8 oz) strawberries, hulled

Draw a 20.5-cm (8-inch) circle on a piece of non-stick paper and place on a baking sheet. Line a second baking sheet with a plain piece of non-stick paper. Whisk the egg whites until very stiff and whisk in half the sugar. Carefully fold in the remaining sugar. Spoon half the mixture into a piping bag fitted with a large star nozzle and pipe twenty-four shell shapes on to the plain non-stick paper. Spoon the remainder of the meringue mixture on to the second baking sheet and spread to completely cover the circle.

Bake in the oven at 150°C (300°F) mark 2 for about 2 hours. Turn off the oven and leave until the oven is cold and the meringue is crisp and dry. Carefully peel off the paper, and store the meringue in an airtight container until needed. About 30 minutes to 1 hour before serving, whisk the creams together until stiff. Use some of the cream to build up a double row of meringue shells on the meringue round to form a basket. Spoon the remaining cream into the centre and top with strawberries. Leave in a cool place until ready to serve.

Pineapple meringue torte

4 egg whites
225 g (8 oz) caster sugar
pinch of cream of tartar
100 g (4 oz) blanched almonds, finely chopped
icing sugar to decorate

For the filling
567-g (1 lb 4-oz) can pineapple segments
300 ml ($\frac{1}{2}$ pint) double cream
45 ml (3 tbsp) milk

Several hours before required, empty the can of pineapple into a saucepan and boil until the juice is reduced almost entirely and the pineapple looks opaque, then leave to cool.

Draw two 20.5-cm (8-inch) circles on non-stick paper and place on a baking sheet. Whisk the egg whites in a bowl until very stiff, add 30 ml (2 level tbsp) sugar and the cream of tartar and whisk again until stiff. Using a metal spoon, carefully fold in the remaining sugar and the finely chopped nuts. Spread the meringue mixture over the circles.

Bake in the oven at 150°C (300°F) mark 2 for about $1\frac{1}{4}$ hours until the almond meringue is crisp and the paper peels away easily. Leave to cool on the baking sheet, then carefully remove from the paper.

To serve, whisk the cream and milk together until thick enough to spread. Set aside some of the cream for piping. Add almost all the pineapple pieces to most of the cream, reserving some for decoration. Use the pineapple cream to sandwich the meringue rounds together. Place on a serving plate and dredge the top with icing sugar. Spoon the remaining cream into a piping bag fitted with a medium star nozzle and pipe whirls of cream round the top edge of the torte. Finish with the reserved pineapple and leave in a cool place, preferably the refrigerator, for several hours before serving.

The decoration on an informal cake can be anything from a light dusting of caster sugar or a smooth covering of glacé icing to an elaborate coating of chopped nuts and a topping of whirls of butter cream.

When to decorate a cake
A cake looks freshest if iced on the day it is to be served, but it is often more convenient to do this the night or day before. Do not apply glacé icing more than 48 hours ahead as it will wrinkle or crack. Chocolate shapes will absorb moisture from the icing and lose their crispness and gloss if added too far ahead. The colouring in sugar-coated sweets tends to run and spoil the icing, so these too should be added just before serving. You can, of course, assemble and decorate the rest of the cake in advance. (Reserve a little icing to stick last-minute decorations in place.) Most of the decorated cakes featured in this book will store well in an airtight tin. Store cream-filled cakes in the refrigerator.

Cake boards
A silver cake board enhances any iced cake. Sometimes called 'drums', they are sold in large stationery shops and confectioner's. Whether round or square, the board should be large enough to project about 2.5 cm (1 inch) all round the iced cake, so choose one about 5 cm (2 inches) larger than the cake itself. The board can be used again provided the cake is carefully cut and the silver paper surface is not damaged. After use, clean the board with a damp cloth, then leave to dry before storing. If the board is damaged, re-cover it with a new piece of foil.

If the cake needs a base and you don't have a special cake board, you can improvise with a large flat plate or a baking sheet covered in foil.

Preparing a cake for decorating
Cool the cake completely. Make sure the surface is quite level for icing – if necessary, turn the cake upside-down and use the flat underside. With a pastry brush, brush away any crumbs or loose bits which might stick to the icing and spoil the effect.

If making a sandwich or layer cake, put in the filling. If the sides are to be coated with chopped nuts, coconut, etc, do this before icing the top (*see below*).

Place the cake on a wire rack so it can be easily moved when finished – newly applied icing may crack if you transfer the cake from one plate to another. Prepare any decoration required – chop nuts, toast flaked almonds, halve or quarter glacé cherries, cut slices of crystallised orange or lemon into triangles, grate chocolate and so forth. Have ready any sweets or candles.

Decorating the sides of a cake
Covering the sides with chopped nuts,

Decorating the sides of a cake

grated chocolate, chocolate vermicelli or desiccated coconut is a quick and easy way to give a cake a professional look. To make sure the decoration will stick, brush the sides of the cake with apricot glaze (*see page 176*) or coat with butter cream (*see page 170*). Spread a fairly thick layer of chopped nuts or other decoration down the centre of a piece of greaseproof paper. Hold the cake on its side between the palms of your hands and roll it in the nuts until the sides are completely coated.

Icing

Using butter cream

As a filling Slice the cake horizontally in half (*see page 19*). Spread butter cream over the cut surface of both cakes, then sandwich them together again and press down to prevent the layers sliding when cut.

As a side covering Spread butter cream evenly round the sides of the cake with a palette knife making sure there are no gaps. If decorating further (with chopped nuts, etc) hold the knife upright, at an angle of 45° to the cake, and draw it towards you to smooth the surface. Then roll in nuts etc. as described above.

As a topping Pile butter cream on top of the cake and spread it smoothly and evenly with a palette knife, right to the edges. For a more interesting effect, draw the prongs of a fork across the butter cream or make pronounced swirl marks with the flat blade of a knife before adding any other decoration.

Using glacé icing

Large cakes If coating both the top and sides of the cake, stand the cake on a wire rack with a large plate or tray underneath to catch the drips. As soon as the icing reaches a coating consistency and looks smooth and glossy, pour it from the bowl on to the centre of the cake. Allow the icing to run down the sides, guiding the flow with a palette knife. Keep a little icing in reserve to fill any gaps. An attractive effect, particularly suited to unfilled cakes and loaf cakes, can be achieved by simply allowing the icing to dribble naturally down the sides, leaving the gaps unfilled.

If the sides are decorated and only the top is to be glacé-iced, pour the icing on to the centre of the cake. Use a palette knife to spread the icing evenly over the surface, stopping just inside the top edges to prevent it dripping down the sides.

If the top of the cake is to be glacé-iced, but you wish to leave the sides plain, secure a double band of greaseproof paper

Decorating the top of a cake with a fork

Glacé icing the top of a cake

around the cake – the band should project about 2.5 cm (1 inch) above the top of the cake. Pour the icing on to the cake and allow it to find its own level. Leave until set, then peel away the paper with the aid of a palette knife.

Small cakes If the cakes are baked in paper cases, pour a small spoonful of icing on to the top and allow it to run over the surface. Fill in any gaps with a little extra icing.

Cakes that have been cut from a slab can be arranged on a wire rack (over a large plate or tray) and the icing poured over as described above. Alternatively, skewer each cake in turn on a fork and dip in the icing; drain, then leave to dry on a wire rack.

Adding decorations Arrange any prepared decorations (sweets, glacé cherries, nuts, etc) in position as soon as the icing has thickened and formed a slight skin. If added while the icing is still wet, decorations will slide out of position; if added when the icing is wet, they will cause the surface to crack. If you have to add decorations at the last minute, when the icing is hard, stick them on with a little extra icing or some apricot glaze.

Unless you are feather-icing a cake (*see below*), leave the icing until quite dry and set before applying any piped decoration.

Feather-icing Make up one quantity of glacé icing (*see page 171*) using 100 g (4 oz) icing sugar and about 15 ml (1 tbsp) warm water to mix to a coating consistency.

Make up a second quantity of glacé icing using 50 g (2 oz) icing sugar and gradually add enough warm water to mix to a thick consistency suitable for piping. Add enough red food colouring to tint the icing a dark pink. Spoon the pink icing into a greaseproof paper piping bag (*see page 165*) without a nozzle.

Pour the white icing on to the top of the cake and spread almost to the edges with a palette knife. Working quickly, before the white icing forms a skin, snip the end off the piping bag and pipe parallel lines of pink icing, about 1–2 cm ($\frac{1}{2}$–$\frac{3}{4}$ inch) apart, over the surface. Then quickly draw the point of a skewer or sharp knife across the piped lines, first in one direction and then in the other, spacing each stroke 1–2 cm ($\frac{1}{2}$–$\frac{3}{4}$ inch) apart, to give a feathered effect. Leave to set. Small cakes can also be decorated in this way, using a variety of different coloured glacé icing.

Quick ways with icing
Here are eight easy ways of 'dressing up' a pair of 18-cm (7-inch) cakes, using plain ones for some versions and chocolate or coffee-flavoured cakes for others. Instructions for making glacé icing are on page 171; butter cream on page 170.
1. Sandwich the cakes together with lemon curd. Make 350 g (12 oz) lemon

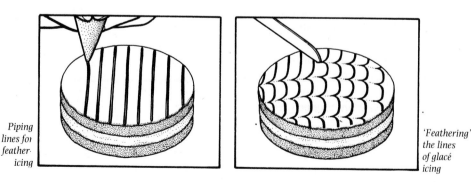

Piping lines for feather-icing

'Feathering' the lines of glacé icing

butter cream, and swirl it over the top and sides of the cake. Decorate the top of the cake with mimosa balls and pieces of cut angelica.

2. Make 350 g (12 oz) orange or lemon butter cream. Use half to sandwich the cakes together and the rest to cover the top smoothly. Mark the top in lines or squares with a fork and decorate with small pieces of crystallised orange or lemon slices.

3. Drain a can of pineapple, mandarins or peaches. Sandwich the cakes together with apricot jam. Make 350 g (12 oz) butter cream including a little of the fruit juice. Spread some butter cream round the sides and cover with chopped almonds. Spread the remaining butter cream over the top, mark with a fork, and decorate with pieces of drained fruit.

4. Make 250 g (9 oz) coffee butter cream and an equal amount of chocolate butter cream. Sandwich the cakes with some coffee butter cream. Spread some chocolate butter cream round the sides and swirl with a knife. Spread the remaining chocolate butter cream smoothly over the top. Use the remaining coffee butter cream to pipe a border of whirls around the top edge.

5. Sieve 90 ml (6 level tbsp) apricot or raspberry jam. Sandwich the cakes with some jam and use the rest to brush round the sides. Holding the cake on its side, roll it in desiccated coconut or chopped nuts until an even layer sticks to the jam. Make 100 g (4 oz) glacé icing and use to ice the top. Decorate with chocolate drops or halved nuts.

6. Sandwich the cakes together with 175 g (6 oz) walnut butter cream. Cover the top with 100 g (4 oz) chocolate glacé icing and decorate with chopped or halved walnuts.

7. Make 350 g (12 oz) butter cream. Use some to sandwich two chocolate layers together and spread the rest round the sides. Roll the sides in chocolate vermicelli. Cover the top of the cake with 100 g (4 oz) chocolate glacé icing. Melt 40 g (1½ oz) plain chocolate and drizzle over the surface.

8. Make 350 g (12 oz) chocolate butter cream. Use some of this to sandwich the cakes and spread the rest roughly round the sides. Cover the top of the cake with 100 g (4 oz) white glacé icing and decorate with chocolate drops.

Cake decorations

Here is a check-list; keep a selection and you will never be without an instant finish for your cakes. For even more ideas, look round sweet shops, confectionery counters or large department stores, grocers and supermarkets.

Nuts Shelled walnuts (refresh them in the oven if you've had them a little time), hazelnuts, pistachios (rather expensive; buy in small amounts as they tend to lose colour and always blanch before use), almonds (have a selection of types), pecans (a change from walnuts, smoother in texture, more bland in flavour).

Crystallised violets and roses Buy in small quantities and keep in a dark place or jar to avoid bleaching.

Angelica Look for a really good colour and not too much sugar. To remove sugar, soak briefly in hot water, then drain and dry well.

Chocolate and coloured vermicelli Buy in fairly small amounts, unless a favourite recipe needs a larger quantity for, say, coating the sides of a cake. Vermicelli stales and becomes speckled.

Silver dragees (balls) Keep in a dry place. It's useful to have two sizes. Use tweezers for handling, as the colour can come off and they are difficult to grip. Dragees also come in a variety of other colours.

Hundreds and thousands Popular with children and very useful as a quick decoration.

Glacé and candied fruits Cherries, ginger and pineapple are the most useful; others are generally left-overs after the Christmas season. Will go sugary if kept too long.

Sugar coffee beans Found in sweet shops, these are ideal for coffee cakes and gâteaux.

Chocolate Choose hard chocolate for chopping and grating; soft chocolate for scrolls and curls (*see below*). Soft chocolate coverings are useful for melting. For more advanced work, choose special couverture chocolate. Crumbled chocolate flake is a useful last-minute decoration.

Chocolate decorations

Chocolate caraque Break 100 g (4 oz) chocolate into pieces and put in a bowl over a pan of hot water. Heat gently, stirring, until the chocolate has melted. Pour it in a thin layer on to a marble slab and leave to set until it no longer sticks to the hand when touched. Holding a large knife with both hands, push the blade across the surface of the chocolate to roll pieces off in long curls.

Making chocolate caraque

Chocolate triangles Make a sheet of chocolate as above and cut it into 6–8 triangles.

Chocolate squares Make a sheet of chocolate as above and cut into 2.5-cm (1-inch) squares.

Chocolate curls Using a potato peeler, 'peel' thin layers straight from the block of chocolate.

Chocolate circles Make a sheet of chocolate as above and stamp out circles using a small round cutter.

Icing formal cakes

If you wish to make a Christmas cake or celebration cake for a special occasion, such as a Wedding, Christening or Anniversary, follow the recipe for Rich fruit cake on pages 72–73 to make the size and shape of cake of your choice. A rich fruit cake improves with keeping so can be made from 2–3 months in advance. After cooling and soaking with brandy, wrap the cake in greaseproof paper and then in a double thickness of foil. Store upside-down in an airtight tin in a cool, dry place.

12–20 days before Apply the almond paste (*see page 175*). You will find the quantity needed for the size of cake on the chart opposite. Loosely cover the cake and store in a cool, dry place for 2–5 days.

10–15 days before Apply the first coat of Royal icing (*see page 174*) and leave to dry for 1–2 days, then apply the second coat, if necessary. The chart opposite gives the quantity of icing required for the size of cake.

8–12 days before Assemble or make all the separate decorations required for the cake.

7 days before Complete all further decorating a week before the cake is to be served. Do not assemble a tiered cake, however, until the very last possible moment.

Icing and almond paste quantities

The almond paste quantities quoted in the following chart will give a thin covering. The amount of Royal icing should be enough for two coats.

Square tin size		15 cm (6 inches) square	18 cm (7 inches) square	20.5 cm (8 inches) square	23 cm (9 inches) square	25.5 cm (10 inches) square	28 cm (11 inches) square	30.5 cm (12 inches) square
Round tin size	15 cm (6 inches) round	18 cm (7 inches) round	20.5 cm (8 inches) round	23 cm (9 inches) round	25.5 cm (10 inches) round	28 cm (11 inches) round	30.5 cm (12 inches) round	
Almond paste	350 g 12 oz	450 g (1 lb)	550 g (1¼ lb)	800 g (1¾ lb)	900 g (2 lb)	1 kg (2¼ lb)	1.1 kg (2½ lb)	1.4 kg (3 lb)
Royal icing	450 g (1 lb)	550 g (1¼ lb)	700 g (1½ lb)	900 g (2 lb)	1 kg (2¼ lb)	1.1 kg (2½ lb)	1.4 kg (3 lb)	1.6 kg (3½ lb)

All about piping

Piping equipment and techniques

Butter cream, crème au beurre, stiff glacé icing and Royal icing can all be piped on to cakes. It is usual for each kind to be used on a base of the same type of icing, although butter cream can be piped on to glacé icing. Use butter cream or glacé icing for decorating sponge cakes, and Royal icing for formal decoration of fruit cakes.

The icing used for piping must be free of all lumps which might block the nozzles; it must also be of such a consistency that it can be forced easily through the nozzle but will retain its shape.

It is best to work with a small quantity of icing at a time. A large amount is difficult to pipe as unnecessary strain is put on the hand to push the icing through.

If you are a beginner, it is a good idea to practise piping on an up-turned plate to acquire confidence and skill. Remember that if the base icing is hard the piped icing can be carefully scraped off while still soft, so mistakes can be corrected.

Piping bags

Special icing pumps can be bought but paper piping bags or small ready-made fabric piping bags are very easy to use.

Paper piping bags are disposable, but a nylon bag must be thoroughly washed and dried after use. Nozzles must be cleaned scrupulously – push out any remaining icing and soak overnight in warm water. Dry thoroughly before storing.

To use a greaseproof paper piping bag Instructions for making a paper piping bag are on page 169. Avoid over-filling the bag – it should be no more than half full, or the icing may squeeze out of the top. Fold the top flap down, enclosing the front edge, until the bag is sealed and quite firm. Open one hand and place the icing bag across the palm. Place your thumb on the cushion of folded paper at the top of the bag. Fold over your four fingers and apply a steady, even pressure until the icing begins to come out of the nozzle.

To use a nylon piping bag Half fill the bag with icing. Place the thumb and forefinger at the point where the icing stops and twist the bag tightly two or three times. This stops the icing squeezing out of the top of the bag when pressure is applied.

Open one hand and place the icing bag across the palm. Clasp the bag where it is twisted with your thumb and forefinger and maintain an even grip. Fold over the other three fingers and apply a steady but even pressure until the icing begins to come out of the nozzle.

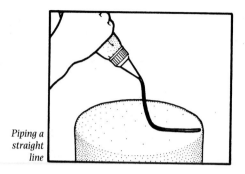

Piping a straight line

Piping a straight line

Place a plain nozzle in the icing bag and half fill it with icing. Wipe away any icing from the tip of the nozzle so you can start the piping neatly. Place the tip of the nozzle where the straight line is to begin. Apply slight pressure to the icing bag and as the icing starts to come from the nozzle, lift the icing bag about 2.5 cm (1 inch) above the surface. This allows even the shakiest of hands to pipe a perfectly straight line. Move your hand in the direction of the line, guiding the icing bag with the other hand if liked, allowing the icing to flow evenly. Stop squeezing the bag about 1 cm ($\frac{1}{2}$ inch) before the end of the line, and gently lower the tip of the nozzle to the surface. This action will end the line neatly. If you continue to squeeze the icing bag the line will end with an undesirable blob.

Piping dots

Only a slight pressure on the icing bag is required to pipe a dot. Place the tip of the nozzle on the surface and hold the bag almost upright. Squeeze the icing bag gently and at the same time lift the nozzle slightly. Stop squeezing the icing bag, move the nozzle slightly in a gentle shaking action to avoid a 'tail' and lift the nozzle. Practise piping rows of different sized dots. A larger dot can be achieved by moving the nozzle in a circular motion or by using a larger nozzle.

Piping stars

Place a five or eight-point star nozzle in the icing bag and half fill it with icing.

Star nozzles vary in the size of the tip of the nozzle and this determines the size of the piped star or rosette as well as the number of points to the star. Select a five or eight-point star to begin with, then progress to the larger and more complex nozzles.

Hold the icing bag upright and just above the surface of the cake. Squeeze the icing from the bag. Stop squeezing once the star is formed on the surface and lift the nozzle away sharply. A good star should sit reasonably squat on the surface of the cake and not be 'lifted' up into a point. Practise until you can achieve a perfect star.

Piping rosettes

A rosette is piped with a star nozzle but the pipe is moved in a circular motion – rather like piping a large dot.

Hold the icing bag upright, just above the surface of the cake; squeeze gently and move the nozzle in a complete circle, filling in the centre. Pull the nozzle sharply away from the rosette to avoid forming a point or tail.

Piping a shell border

A shell edging can be made with a star nozzle, or with a special shell nozzle. A shell nozzle will give a fatter, fuller shell with more ridges than a star nozzle.

In either case, the movement of the nozzle is the same. Hold the icing bag at an angle to the surface and just above it. Squeeze the icing bag until the icing begins to come from the nozzle and a head is formed. Pull the icing bag gently to the right and at the same time release pressure on the bag. The shell should be well formed and come to a neat point.

A shell border is achieved by piping a

Mocha refrigerator cake (page 52)

Use the right sugar for the job.

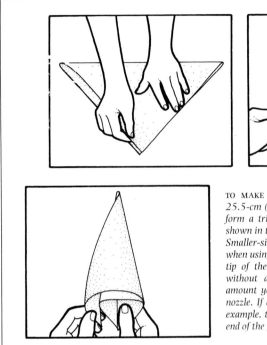
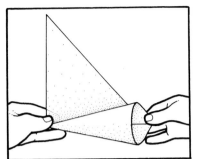

TO MAKE A GREASEPROOF PAPER PIPING BAG *Fold a 25.5-cm (10-inch) square of greaseproof paper in half to form a triangle and bring the points round together as shown in the drawings. Fold the points inwards to secure. Smaller-sized bags are often easier to handle, especially when using a writing nozzle. To insert a nozzle, snip off the tip of the bag and drop in the nozzle – preferably one without a screw band – before adding the icing. The amount you need to snip off depends on the size of the nozzle. If a very fine line is needed, for feather-icing, for example, there is no need to use a nozzle; just snip off the end of the paper piping bag.*

series of well-formed shells together, linked in a line. Each shell should be quite distinct in its shape with a head and pointed tail. Many beginners pipe a shell edge without releasing the pressure to form the point and the result is a very bulky edge which is not even in size.

Piping patterns with a star or shell nozzle
An effective border can be made with either the star or shell nozzle: pipe in a continuous line, moving the nozzle from side to side at the same time to give a zig-zag effect. If necessary, stop in the middle of the line to turn the cake. The break can be easily disguised if care is taken to match the pattern at the join.

Writing
Use a plain writing nozzle. Practise with simple capital letters to start with, piping straight lines. Before you attempt to pipe on the cake, draw the letters on grease-proof paper and prick them out on to the base icing with a pin. These letters can be piped like a series of straight lines, each ending without a blob.

Once you can control the icing bag, progress to fancier writing. Books and magazines always prove a useful source for stylised lettering.

Piping a rose
Roses are piped with a petal nozzle on to a piece of non-stick paper on an icing nail. Icing nails look like up-turned saucers of metal or polythene mounted on a nail and are easy to hold and rotate in the hand while piping. Place a little icing on the top of the icing nail and stick a small square of non-stick or waxed paper on top. Place a petal nozzle in an icing bag and half fill the

Clockwise from top left: Chocolate cornflake cakes (*page 97*), Small pink and coffee meringues (*page 152*), Butterfly cakes (*page 62*), Flapjack (*page 91*)

bag with icing. Hold the petal nozzle with the thin part uppermost. Pipe a cone of icing, twisting the nail between the thumb and forefinger, to form the centre of the rose. Pipe five or six petals around the centre of the rose, overlapping each and piping the outer petals so they are more open and lie flatter. Vary the shape of the roses by adding as many or few petals as you wish.

Lift the square of paper from the nail and leave the rose, uncovered, for about 24 hours or until completely dry before using to decorate a cake.

Basic icing recipes

Butter cream

The quantities given make sufficient to coat the sides of an 18-cm (7-inch) cake, or give a topping and a filling. If you wish to coat both the sides and give a topping or filling, increase the amounts of butter and sugar to 100 g (4 oz) and 225 g (8 oz) respectively. This will make a 325-g (12-oz) quantity.

75 g (3 oz) butter
175 g (6 oz) icing sugar
a few drops of vanilla essence
15–30 ml (1–2 tbsp) milk or warm water

Cream the butter until soft and gradually sift and beat in the sugar, adding a few drops of vanilla essence and the milk or water.

VARIATIONS

Orange or lemon Replace the vanilla essence with a little finely grated orange or lemon rind. Add a little juice from the fruit, beating well to avoid curdling the mixture.

Walnut Add 30 ml (2 level tbsp) finely chopped walnuts and mix well.

Almond Add 30 ml (2 level tbsp) finely chopped toasted almonds and mix well.

Coffee Replace the vanilla essence with 10 ml (2 level tsp) instant coffee powder blended with some of the liquid, or replace 15 ml (1 tbsp) of the liquid with the same amount of coffee essence.

Chocolate Replace 15 ml (1 tbsp) of the liquid with 25–40 g (1–1½ oz) chocolate, melted, or dissolve 15 ml (1 level tbsp) cocoa powder in a little hot water and cool before adding to the mixture.

Mocha Dissolve 5 ml (1 level tsp) cocoa powder and 10 ml (2 level tsp) instant coffee powder in a little warm water taken from the measured amount. Cool before adding to the mixture.

Makes 250 g (9 oz)

Crème au beurre (rich butter cream)

The quantities given make sufficient rich butter cream to fill or cover the sides of a 20.5-cm (8-inch) cake.

75 g (3 oz) caster sugar
2 egg yolks, beaten
175 g (6 oz) butter

Place the sugar in a heavy-based saucepan, add 60 ml (4 tbsp) water and heat very gently to dissolve the sugar without boiling. When completely dissolved, bring to boiling point and boil steadily for 2–3 minutes, to reach a temperature of 107°C (225°F). Pour the syrup in a thin stream on to the egg yolks in a deep bowl, whisking all the time. Continue to whisk until the mixture is thick and cold. Cream the butter until very soft and gradually beat in the mixture.

VARIATIONS

Chocolate Break 50 g (2 oz) plain chocolate into pieces and put in a small bowl with 15 ml (1 tbsp) water. Stand the bowl over a pan of hot water and heat gently, stirring, until the mixture is smooth and the chocolate melted. Cool slightly and beat into the basic Crème au beurre mixture.

Coffee Beat 15–30 ml (1–2 tbsp) coffee essence to taste into the basic Crème au beurre mixture.

Fruit Crush 225 g (8 oz) fresh strawberries, raspberries, etc, or thaw, drain and crush frozen fruit. Beat into the basic Crème au beurre mixture.

Orange or lemon Add freshly grated rind and juice to taste to the basic Crème au beurre mixture.

Makes about 200 g (7 oz)

Note Crème au beurre can be made a day in advance and stored in a cool place. If it separates out, place it in a slightly warmed bowl and beat until smooth.

Continental butter cream

15 ml (1 level tbsp) cornflour
40 g (1½ oz) caster sugar
150 ml (¼ pint) milk
1 egg yolk
75 g (3 oz) icing sugar
175 g (6 oz) butter, softened

Blend together the cornflour, sugar and a little of the milk. Bring the remaining milk to the boil and pour on to the cornflour mixture. Pour back into the pan and bring to the boil stirring all the time until thickened. Cool slightly, beat in the egg yolk and cook gently for 2–3 minutes. Leave until cold, covered with a piece of grease-proof paper. Sift the icing sugar into a bowl, add the butter and cream together, then fold in the cold custard.

Makes about 300 ml (½ pint)

Glacé icing

The quantities given make sufficient to cover the top of an 18-cm (7-inch) cake or up to eighteen small cakes. To cover the top of a 20.5-cm (8-inch) cake, increase the quantities to 175 g (6 oz) icing sugar and 30 ml (2 tbsp) warm water. This will give a 175-g (6-oz) quantity of icing.

100 g (4 oz) icing sugar
15 ml (1 tbsp) warm water

Sift the icing sugar into a bowl. If you wish, add a few drops of any flavouring and gradually add the warm water. The icing should be thick enough to coat the back of a spoon. If necessary add more water or sugar to adjust the consistency. Add colouring, if liked, and use at once.

For icing of a finer texture, put the sugar and water, and any flavouring, into a small pan and heat, stirring, until the mixture is warm – don't make it too hot. The icing should coat the back of a wooden spoon and be smooth and glossy.

VARIATIONS

Orange Replace the water with 15 ml (1 tbsp) strained orange juice.

Lemon Replace the water with 15 ml (1 tbsp) strained lemon juice.

Chocolate Dissolve 10 ml (2 level tsp) cocoa powder in a little hot water and use instead of the same amount of measured water.

Coffee Flavour with 5 ml (1 tsp) coffee essence or dissolve 10 ml (2 level tsp) instant coffee in a little hot water and use instead of the same amount of measured water.

Mocha Dissolve 5 ml (1 level tsp) cocoa powder and 10 ml (2 level tsp) instant coffee in a little hot water and use instead of the same amount of measured water.

Liqueur Replace 10–15 ml (2–3 tsp) of the measured water with the same amount of any liqueur.

Makes about 100 g (4 oz)

American frosting

The quantities given make sufficient frosting for an 18-cm (7-inch) cake.

1 egg white
225 g (8 oz) caster or granulated sugar
pinch of cream of tartar

Whisk the egg white until stiff. Gently heat the sugar in 60 ml (4 tbsp) water with the cream of tartar, stirring until dissolved. Then, without stirring, boil to 120°C (240°F). Remove the sugar syrup from the heat and, immediately the bubbles subside, pour it on to the egg white in a thin stream, beating the mixture continuously. When it thickens, shows signs of going dull round the edges and is almost cold, pour the frosting quickly over the cake and spread evenly with a palette knife.

VARIATIONS
Orange Beat in a few drops of orange essence and a little orange food colouring before the mixture thickens.

Lemon Beat in a little lemon juice before the mixture thickens.

Caramel Substitute demerara sugar for the white sugar, following the same method as above.

Coffee Beat in 5 ml (1 tsp) coffee essence before the mixture thickens.

Makes about 225 g (8 oz)

Note To make this frosting successfully it is necessary to use a sugar-boiling thermometer. If you do not possess one, you can make Seven-minute frosting (*see below*).

Seven-minute frosting

The quantities given make sufficient frosting to cover an 18-cm (7-inch) cake. To cover the top and sides of a three or four layer cake, double the quantities.

1 egg white
175 g (6 oz) caster sugar
pinch of salt
pinch of cream of tartar

This is an imitation American frosting that does not need a sugar-boiling thermometer.

Put all the ingredients into a bowl with 30 ml (2 tbsp) water and whisk lightly. Place the bowl over a pan of hot water and heat, whisking continuously, until the mixture thickens sufficiently to stand in peaks. This will take about 7 minutes depending on the whisk used and the heat of the water. Pour the frosting over the top of the cake and spread with a palette knife.

VARIATIONS

The same flavourings can be used as for American frosting (*see opposite*).

Makes about 175 g (6 oz)

Chocolate frosting

25 g (1 oz) plain chocolate
150 g (5 oz) icing sugar
1 egg
2.5 ml ($\frac{1}{2}$ tsp) vanilla essence
25 g (1 oz) butter

Break the chocolate into pieces and put in a bowl over a pan of hot water. Heat gently, stirring, until the chocolate has melted. Sift in the icing sugar, add the egg, vanilla essence and butter and beat until smooth.

Pour on to the cake and spread.

Makes about 225 g (8 oz)

Fondant icing

This is a soft, very sweet icing. The quantities given in this recipe make sufficient fondant to thickly coat an 18-cm (7-inch) cake.

150 ml ($\frac{1}{4}$ pint) water
450 g (1 lb) granulated sugar
25 g (1 oz) glucose or a good pinch of
cream of tartar

Choose a strong, heavy pan, large enough to avoid the syrup boiling over. Put the water into the pan, add the sugar and heat gently, without stirring, to dissolve the sugar. Bring the syrup to the boil, add the glucose or cream of tartar and boil to 116°C (240°F), then leave to cool for a few minutes until a skin forms on top. Pour slowly on to a lightly greased marble slab. Using a spatula, collect the mixture together, then work it backwards and forwards using a figure-of-eight movement. Continue until the syrup becomes opaque and firm, then knead in the hands until smooth. Colouring and/or flavouring (*eg.* lemon, coffee or chocolate) may be worked in at this stage. The icing can be used immediately, or stored.

Using fondant icing
Place the icing in a bowl over a pan of hot water and heat gently, stirring, until it is of the consistency of thick cream or until the mixture will just coat the back of a wooden spoon. Take care not to overheat the icing as this makes the texture rough and destroys the gloss. If necessary, dilute with a little sugar syrup or water.

Cakes which are to be coated with fondant icing should be glazed completely with apricot glaze (*see page 176*) and then coated with almond paste (*see page 175*), to give a really professional appearance. To ice small cakes or pastries, spear them on a fork and dip them in prepared fondant.

To ice a large cake, put it on a wire rack with a plate underneath and pour the icing quickly all over the cake. Don't touch the icing with a knife or the gloss finish will be spoilt. Decorate and leave to set.

To give a thick topping of fondant on a Victoria, Madeira or cherry cake, for example, secure a band of double greaseproof paper closely round the cake so that it comes 2.5 cm (1 inch) above the top. Prepare half the amount of fondant, *ie* make it with 225 g (8 oz) sugar and thin with syrup made with 100 g (4 oz) sugar and pour it on to the top of the cake. When the topping is set, ease off the paper collar, using a knife dipped in hot water.

Makes about 550 g (1$\frac{1}{4}$ lb)

Royal icing

See page 165 for the quantity of Royal icing required to ice various sizes of cake.

4 egg whites
900 g (2 lb) icing sugar
15 ml (1 tbsp) lemon juice
10 ml (2 tsp) glycerine

Whisk the egg whites in a bowl until slightly frothy. Sift and stir in about a quarter of the icing sugar with a wooden spoon. Continue adding more sugar gradually, beating well after each addition, until about three quarters of the sugar has been added. Beat in the lemon juice and continue beating for about 10 minutes until the icing is smooth and meringue-like. Beat in the remaining sugar until the required consistency is achieved, depending on how the icing will be used. Finally, stir in the glycerine to prevent the icing becoming hard. See notes on preparing and applying Royal icing on page 174.

Makes about 900 g (2 lb)

Note Royal icing can be made in an electric mixer but take care not to overbeat or the icing will become fluffy, resulting in a rough surface, and will break easily if piped.

Once made, turn Royal icing into a polythene container or bowl. Cover and keep for 24 hours to allow the air bubbles to rise to the surface. This is particularly important if an electric mixer has been used. Just before using, beat lightly and adjust the consistency if necessary. Royal icing dries out quickly, so keep the bowl covered with a clean damp cloth or cling film while in use.

Applying Royal icing

For flat icing and writing Test for the right consistency by standing the wooden spoon upright in the icing. It should fall slowly to one side.

For piping with star or shell nozzles The icing should be a little stiffer than for flat icing and writing so beat in a little more icing sugar.

For flooding The icing should be of a thinner consistency so beat in a little less sugar.

For peak icing ('snow') The icing should be thick enough to pull into well formed peaks with the back of the spoon.

To flat ice a cake
Place a small spoonful of icing on the cake board, place the cake on top, making sure

it is in the centre of the board. Stand the cake and board on a non-slip surface. Spoon almost half the icing on to the top of the cake and spread it evenly over the surface with a palette knife, using a paddling action to remove any air bubbles that may remain. Using an icing ruler or palette knife longer than the width of the cake, without applying any pressure, draw it steadily across the top of the cake at an angle of 30°, to smooth the surface. Neaten the edges with a palette knife, removing any surplus icing. For best results, leave to dry for about 24 hours before applying the icing to the side of the cake.

To make icing the side of a cake easier, place it on an icing turntable or up-turned plate. Spread the remaining icing on the side of the cake and smooth it roughly with a small palette knife, using a paddling action. Hold the palette knife or icing comb upright and at an angle of 45° to the cake. Draw the knife or comb towards you to smooth the surface. For a square cake, apply icing to each side separately. Neaten the edges with a palette knife, removing any surplus icing.

For a really smooth finish, apply a second thinner coat of icing, allowing the first coat to dry for 1–2 days first. Use fine sandpaper to sand down any imperfections or slight marks in the first coat. Brush the surface of the cake with a greasefree pastry brush to remove the icing dust.

Smoothing Royal icing on top of a cake

Royal icing the sides of a cake

Almond paste

See page 165 for the quantity of almond paste required to cover various sizes of cake.

225 g (8 oz) icing sugar
225 g (8 oz) caster sugar
450 g (1 lb) ground almonds
5 ml (1 tsp) vanilla essence
2 eggs, lightly beaten
10 ml (2 tsp) lemon juice

Sift the icing sugar into a bowl and mix with the caster sugar and almonds. Add essence, egg and lemon juice to make a stiff dough. Form into a ball and knead lightly.

Makes 900 g (2 lb) almond paste

Applying almond paste

Cover the cake with almond paste one week or – at the latest – two days before applying the first coat of royal icing. If the paste is not given enough time to dry out, oil from the paste may discolour the icing.

To cover a round or square cake, first measure round the cake with a piece of string. Dust your work surface liberally with icing sugar and roll out two thirds of the paste to a rectangle, half the length of the string and twice the depth of the cake. Trim the edges neatly with a knife, then cut the rectangle in half lengthways.

Brush the sides of the cake with apricot glaze. Hold a round cake on its side, between the palms of your hands, and roll it along the strips of paste. For a square cake, position one side of the cake on half of one strip of paste, and fold the other half up to cover a second side. Repeat for the other two sides. Keep the top edge of the cake square with the almond paste. Smooth the joins with a palette knife and mould any surplus paste into the bottom edge of the cake.

Brush the top of the cake with apricot glaze. Dust your working surface with icing sugar and roll out the remaining almond paste to a round or square the same size as the top of the cake. Lift on to the top of the cake with the rolling pin. Lightly roll with the rolling pin, then smooth the join and leave to dry.

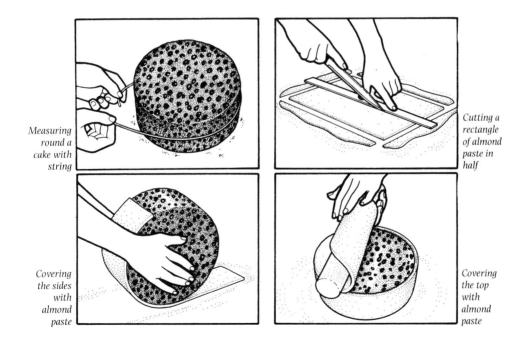

Measuring round a cake with string

Cutting a rectangle of almond paste in half

Covering the sides with almond paste

Covering the top with almond paste

Almond paste decorations
Simple but attractive decorations, particularly suitable for Christmas or Birthday cakes, can be made from almond paste. Draw the chosen shape on cardboard, or other stiff paper, and cut it out. (Stars, candles, holly leaves, Christmas trees, houses, numbers or engines all make good designs as they have bold outlines.) Colour some almond paste by kneading in food colouring, a little at a time, until the right shade is achieved. Dust a working surface with icing sugar and thinly roll out the coloured paste. Lay the cardboard pattern on the paste and cut round it with a sharp-pointed knife. Remove the pattern and leave the shapes on a plate for 2–3 days until quite dry. Stick the decorations on to the icing on the cake – which must be firm – with a blob of fresh icing.

Crushing Praline with a rolling pin

baking sheet and leave to set. Crush the praline finely with a rolling pin or in an electric blender.
Makes about 150 g (6 oz)

Crème pâtissière (Confectioner's custard)

2 eggs
50 g (2 oz) caster sugar
30 ml (2 level tbsp) plain flour
30 ml (2 level tbsp) cornflour
300 ml ($\frac{1}{2}$ pint) milk
a few drops of vanilla essence

Cream the eggs and sugar together until really thick and pale in colour. Sift and beat in the flour and cornflour and a little cold milk to make a smooth paste. Heat the rest of the milk in a saucepan until almost boiling and pour on to the egg mixture, stirring well all the time. Return the mixture to the saucepan and stir over a low heat until the mixture boils. Add vanilla essence to taste and cook for a further 2–3 minutes. Cover and allow to cool before using as required.
Makes 300 ml ($\frac{1}{2}$ pint)

Apricot glaze

100 g (4 oz) apricot jam

Place the jam in a saucepan and add 30 ml (2 tbsp) water. Heat gently, stirring, until the jam softens. Bring to the boil and simmer for 1 minute. Sieve and use as required while still warm.
Makes 150 ml ($\frac{1}{4}$ pint)

Praline

75 g (3 oz) blanched almonds
75 g (3 oz) caster sugar

Place the almonds and sugar in a small, preferably non-stick, frying pan. Heat gently until the sugar melts and cook to a rich dark brown. Pour on to an oiled

Baking Cooking in the oven by dry heat. This is the method of cooking used for most cakes, biscuits and pastries and for many other dishes.

Baking blind Baking flans, tarts and tartlets without a filling. To do this, line the flan ring or pie dish with pastry and trim the edges. Cut a round of greaseproof paper rather larger than the pastry case, place it inside the pastry and half-fill it with dried beans, rice or stale crusts of bread. Bake as directed in the recipe. Beans can be used again and again.

Beating Agitating an ingredient or a mixture by vigorously turning it over and over with an upward motion, in order to introduce air. A spoon, fork, whisk or electric mixer may be used.

Binding Adding a liquid, egg or melted fat to a dry mixture to hold it together.

Blending Mixing flour, cornflour, rice flour and similar ground cereals to a smooth cream with a cold liquid (milk or water) before a boiling liquid is added. This is done to prevent lumps forming.

Brioche A light French yeast mixture, an enriched dough usually baked in deep fluted patty tins and finished with a knob of dough placed on the top.

Caramelising Cooking white sugar (granulated or caster) with very little or no water until it turns into a nut-brown syrup. Occasionally icing sugar is sprinkled heavily on the surface of, say, a gâteau and is caramelised by means of a hot skewer; this is known as branding.

Chopping Cutting food into very small pieces. The ingredient is placed on a chopping board and a very sharp knife is used with a quick up-and-down action.

Creaming The beating together of fat and sugar to resemble whipped cream in colour and texture, *ie* pale and fluffy. This method of mixing is used for cakes and puddings containing a high proportion of fat.

Curd The solid part of soured milk or junket.

Curdling The separating of fresh milk or sauce when acid is present and excessive heat applied. Also applied to creamed mixtures when the egg is beaten in too much at a time or cold from the refrigerator.

Dariole A small, narrow mould with sloping sides, used for setting creams and jellies and for baking or steaming puddings and small cakes.

Dough A thick mixture of uncooked flour and liquid, often combined with other ingredients. The term is not confined to yeast dough, but can include mixtures such as pastry, scones and biscuits.

Dredging Coating food heavily with a dry substance or mixture, especially flour and icing sugar, but also granular sugar of any type.

Dropping consistency The term used to describe the texture of a cake or pudding mixture before cooking. To test, fill a spoon with the mixture and hold it on its side above a basin – the mixture should drop off in 5 seconds without any movement of the spoon.

Dusting Sprinkling lightly with flour, sugar, spices or seasoning.

Folding in (sometimes called cutting and folding) Combining a whisked or creamed mixture with other ingredients so that it retains its lightness. This is a method used for certain cake mixtures and for meringues. To fold in flour, sift it gently over the surface of the mixture and, with a metal spoon, incorporate it gently into the mixture using a figure of eight movement. The mixture must be worked very lightly and not agitated more than absolutely necessary, because with every movement some of the air bubbles are broken down. Folding in cannot be done with an electric mixer.

Frosting An alternative name for icing.

Genoese A sponge cake made of a whisked egg mixture enriched by the addition of melted butter. Also spelt 'Génoise'.

Girdle *see* griddle.

Glazing Applying a thin layer of syrup or jelly to the surface of a food so that the food is just coated, but the texture can still be seen. A mixture of beaten egg or milk brushed over scones or breads before baking to give a golden colour.

Griddle Flat, heavy, metal plate, usually with a hoop handle, for baking breads, scones, cakes on top of the cooker.

Grinding The process of reducing hard foodstuffs such as nuts and coffee beans to fine particles by means of a food mill or grinder.

Kneading The process used for combining a mixture (such as yeast dough or pastry) which is too stiff for stirring. Gather it into a ball and place on a surface. If it is inclined to stick, dust the surface with flour; if the dough is of a soft type, flour the hands well. Pastry and scone doughs, etc., are kneaded lightly, the outside edges being brought into the centre of the mixture with the finger-tips. Bread dough, which must be kneaded to distribute the yeast and strengthen it for a good rise, needs firmer treatment. The easiest way to deal with it is to pull out the dough with the right hand, then fold it back over itself and push it away with the ball or 'heel' of the hand; give a quarter-turn and repeat the process.

Meringue Egg white whisked until stiff, mixed with sugar and usually dried in a very cool oven until crisp.

Mocha A blend of chocolate and coffee.

Moule à manqué A shallow, sloping-sided cake tin.

Pastry blender A device for 'cutting' cooking fats and blending them into flour. It is particularly practical if the fat is a little on the soft side or the hands are warm.

Pastry wheel Small serrated wheel used for cutting pastry or biscuit mixtures.

Piping Forcing cream or butter cream out of a piping bag through a nozzle, to decorate cakes, etc. Also used for cake mixtures and meringues. The bag may be made of cotton, nylon, plastic or greaseproof paper (*see page 165*).

Praline A confection of caramelised sugar and almonds, often used to flavour and decorate cakes.

Prove To allow a yeast dough to rise a second time.

Pastry crimper Device used in a number of ways to give professional finish to a pie or flan edge and it is fine, too, for finishing a top coat of almond paste or marzipan as used on an Easter or Simnel cake.

Rice paper Edible paper made from the pitch of a Chinese tree, used when baking macaroon and other almond mixtures.

Rubbing in A method of incorporating fat into flour, used in making shortcrust pastry, plain cakes and biscuits, when a short texture is required.

Sieving Rubbing or pressing food through a sieve; a wooden spoon is used to force it through.

Sifting Shaking a dry ingredient through a sieve or flour sifter, to remove lumps and aerate dry ingredients, or to thoroughly mix two or more dry ingredients.

Straining Separating liquids from solids using a sieve, colander or muslin.

Syrup A concentrated solution of sugar in water.

Tepid Approximately blood heat, 43°C (110°F). Tepid water is obtained by adding two parts cold water to one part boiling water.

Tube pan Ring shaped tin for baking.

Turnovers Sweet or savoury filled pasties made by folding over a round or square of pastry into a semi-circle or triangle and baking on a baking sheet.

Whisk A device made of hoops of metal in a rounded shape, used to incorporate air into a mixture.

Whisking or whipping Beating a substance, *eg.* fresh cream, quickly and steadily with a whisk, in order to incorporate air, thus increasing its volume and giving a lighter consistency.

Zest The coloured part of orange and lemon peel, containing the oil that gives the characteristic flavour. To obtain zest, remove the rind very thinly, with no pith, by grating or in slivers with a potato peeler. If it is required for a sweet dish, the zest can be rubbed off with a lump of sugar and the sugar incorporated into the recipe.

INDEX